Accession no.
01144333

d

21.7.05

CHESTER CAMPUS
LIBRARY

Theatre and Consciousness

Explanatory Scope and Future Potential

Daniel Meyer-Dinkgräfe

166931x

LIBRARY

ACC. No. 01144333	DEPT.
CLASS No.	

UNIVERSITY
COLLEGE CHESTER

intell
Bristol
Portland, C

First Published in the UK in 2005 by
Intellect Books, PO Box 862, Bristol BS99 1DE, UK
First Published in the USA in 2005 by
Intellect Books, ISBS, 920 NE 58th Ave. Suite 300, Portland, Oregon 97213-3786, USA

Copyright ©2005 Intellect Ltd
All rights reserved. No part of this publication may be reproduced, stored in a retrieval system, or transmitted, in any form or by any means, electronic, mechanical, photocopying, recording, or otherwise, without written permission.

A catalogue record for this book is available from the British Library

ISBN 1-84150-130-1
Cover Design: Gabriel Solomons
Copy Editor: Holly Spradling

Printed and bound in Great Britain by Antony Rowe Ltd.

Table of Contents

Translumination (Grotowski)
Physical Presence and Neutrality (Artaud)
The Actor and the Marionette

Date and Origin of the *Natyashastra*
Scope
Rasa
Issues for Further Debate
The Perspectives of Vedic Science
    Gandharvaveda, consciousness and the primordial
    sound
    A reassessment of rasa
    Stanislavsky: general points of contact
    Artaud: The Balinese inspiration
    Grotowski's retreat from Indian material
    Barba: Theatre Anthropology
    Brook's *Mahabharata*

The Sense of Sight: Scenography
    Space
    Simultaneity of space and time
The Sense of Hearing: Sound, Meaning and the Levels of
Language
The Sense of Smell: Smell in the Indian Tradition and its
Application to Performance Practice
The Sixth Sense: New Forms of Matter
Examples of Performance Practice
    Ariadne's Thread
    Reverie II

Language of Nature (Artaud)
    Theatre of cruelty
    Language of nature
Universal Language of Theatre (Brook)
    Total and holy theatre
    The Quest for a universal language of the theatre
Theatre and Ritual
Postmodernism
Utopian Performatives

Acknowledgements

In this book I have revised material published earlier as follows: 'Hamlet at the Crossroads', Hamlet Studies 8 (1986), pp. 77-82. *Consciousness and the actor: a reassessment of western and Indian approaches to the actor's emotional involvement from the perspective of Vedic psychology*, Frankfurt am Main, Peter Lang, 1996; 'Consciousness and the Concept of *Rasa*', *Performing Arts International* 1:4 (1999), pp. 103-115; 'Suggestion in Peter Brook's *Mahabharata*', *Studies in the Literary Imagination* 34:2 (2001), pp. 117-127; 'Peter Brook and The Freedom of Intercultural Theatre', *The Paris Jigsaw*, ed. D. Bradby and M. M. Delgado, Manchester, Manchester UP, 2002, pp. 71-82; 'The Artist as Character in Contemporary British Bio-Plays', ed. D.Meyer-Dinkgräfe, *The Professions in Contemporary Drama*, Bristol, Intellect, 2003, pp. 87-100; "Hamlet's Procrastination: A Parallel to the *Bhagavad-Gita*, in *Hamlet East West*, ed. M. Gibinska and J. Limon. Gdansk: Theatrum Gedanese Foundation, 1998, pp. 187-195; 'Staging Consciousness: Updating Demastes", *Consciousness, Literature and the Arts* 4:2 (2003). http://www.aber.ac.uk/tfts/journal/archive/dmddemastes.html. Research for this book was partly funded by the Arts and Humanities Research Board (APN 10300), and by the Infinity Foundation.

Introduction

The main focus of Indian philosophy has been human consciousness and practical techniques for its development. The *Natyashastra* is the main treatise in Indian philosophy that deals with theatre aesthetics. Towards the beginning of the text we find a passage describing how theatre was created: the golden age, in which all human beings enjoyed a state of enlightenment, complete health and fulfilment, had come to an end. The silver age had begun and humans were afflicted by first symptoms of suffering. The gods, with Indra as their leader, were concerned and approached Brahma, the creator, asking him to devise a means allowing humans to regain their enlightenment, to restore the golden age. Indra specified that that means should be a fifth Vedic text, an addition to the four main texts of Indian (Vedic) philosophy (*Rig Veda*, *Sama Veda*, *Yajur Veda* and *Atharva Veda*). The fifth Veda should be both pleasing / entertaining and instructive, and should be accessible to the *shudras*, the lowest caste, because they were not allowed to read or listen to recitations of the other Vedas. Brahma listened to Indra's request, immersed himself in meditation and came up with *Natya*, *drama*, which he asked Indra and the gods to implement. Indra assured Brahma that the gods would be no good at this task, and so Brahma passed on his knowledge about *Natya* to the human sage Bharata, who in turn taught it to his 100 sons, who were thus the first actors. The knowledge imparted to Bharata by Brahma is contained in the text of the *Natyashastra* (*Shastra* is a holy text). Any performance that follows the instructions for acting contained in this text be conducive to:

> duty (*dharma*), wealth (*artha*) as well as fame, will contain good counsel and collection [of other materials for human well-being], will give guidance to people of the future as well in all their actions, will be enriched by the teaching of all scriptures (*shastra*) and will give a review of all arts and crafts (*silpa*). (Ghosh, 3-4)

Theatre in this context thus has the direct and explicit function to restore the golden age, for humankind, implying restoration of the state of perfection, liberation (*moksha*), enlightenment, higher states of consciousness for all people on earth.

In the course of this book, I want to discuss the relation of theatre to consciousness for two main reasons: to see whether we can better understand theatre as a result of such an analysis, and to think through the implications of the *Natyashastra's* claim that theatre may serve as a tool to the development of *moksha*, enlightenment, higher states of consciousness. I address those two questions within the distinct and timely context of currently thriving consciousness studies.

For the last ten years, many disciplines of learning have seen a remarkable rise of interest in human consciousness. The Centre for Consciousness Studies at the University of Arizona in Tucson has spearheaded this development with its bi-annual conferences (*Towards a Science of Consciousness*) since 1994 (www.consciousness. arizona.edu/). The peer-reviewed *Journal of Consciousness Studies* was also founded in 1994 and, by 2002, it has increased its publication to eight issues per year of 96 pages each (www.imprint.co.uk/Welcome.html). The *Association for the Scientific Study of Consciousness* (http://assc.caltech.edu/) was founded in 1996, and from it emerged the journal *Consciousness and Cognition*). The British Psychological Association has had two sections directly dealing with consciousness since 1997: *Consciousness and Experiential Psychology* (www.warwick.ac.uk/cep/), and *Transpersonal Psychology* (http://www. transpersonal-psychology.org.uk/).

Over the same number of years, interest in the relationship of consciousness to literature and theatre has equally grown. In most cases, insights from consciousness studies have been used to better understand works of literature, plays, processes of theatre and aspects of creative writing. Malekin and Yarrow's individual contributions to the field (Malekin 1981, 1983, 1992a, 1992b, 1994; Yarrow 1987, 1990, 1997a, 1997b) culminated in their joint *Consciousness, Literature and Theatre: Theory and Beyond* (1997). My own research into theatre and consciousness was published first in 1996, based on my Ph.D. research. Following several shorter papers (1996b, 1997a, b, 1998a-g), in 1999 I edited an issue of *Performing Arts International* on *Performance and Consciousness*, followed, in April 2000, by the launch of the peer-reviewed, Web-based journal *Consciousness, Literature and the Arts* (www.aber.ac.uk/tfts/journal), and in December 2001, by the publication of a issue on *Drama and Consciousness* for *Studies in the Literary Imagination*.

Many disciplines of scholarship are involved in the study of consciousness, often on an interdisciplinary basis. They include philosophy, neurosciences, psychology, physics and biology, and approaches focusing on human experience. This last aspect is of particular interest in the wide range of current consciousness research, because it cautiously heralds a shift of paradigm. Conventional science requests the subjective experience of the scientist to be excluded, in order to guarantee the objectivity of any observation. In contrast, so-called 'first-person approaches' to the study of consciousness increasingly recognise the need to critically reassess the position of the subject: they are in the process of developing scientifically sound methods of studying consciousness based on subjectivity and experience (Varela and Shear 1999).

Consciousness studies thus provides my context for addressing the two key issues at the centre of this book, to see whether we can better understand theatre as a result of such an analysis, and to think through the implications of the *Natyashastra's* claim that theatre may serve as a tool to the development of *moksha*, enlightenment, higher states of consciousness. As an appropriate structure for this context I have chosen to relate to consciousness all those aspects of theatre that are directly and indirectly implied in an apparently simple statement: 'I am going to the theatre today, to see Peter Hall's production of Peter Shaffer's play *Amadeus*'.

To start with, the statement suggests two areas of theatre: that of production (of Shaffer's *Amadeus*, by director Peter Hall, at the National Theatre in London), and of reception (by someone going to the theatre today). On the side of production, several features are directly mentioned in the statement:

1. A dramatist: *Peter Shaffer*;
2. A play: *Amadeus*;
3. A production of the play in question by a specific director, *Peter Hall*;
4. A specific venue, the *National Theatre*;

Indirectly, on the *production side,* the statement implies

5. The director works with a cast of *actors*;
6. A *design team* working on the production.

On the reception side of theatre, the statement directly implies that a specific spectator has decided to go to the theatre on a specific day to see a specific performance. From the statement, then, seven distinct aspects of theatre emerge:

1. Dramatist
2. Play
3. Director
4. Actors
5. Designers
6. Spectators
7. Venue
8. The Theatrical Experience

Our understanding of each one of those aspects, in isolation and taken together in the overall experience of theatre, can benefit from relating them to different branches of consciousness studies. Questions in that context are: What inspires the *dramatist* to write a play. This question addresses the nature of the creative process. How do different *plays* reflect human consciousness, and how does the canon of plays emerge? What systems of rehearsal and rehearsal techniques does the *director* employ in his work? What kinds of new ideas did major directors or theatre makers, such as Artaud, Grotowski, Schechner, Barba and Brook, introduce? Should *actors* be personally involved with the emotions they have to portray? Are puppets or marionettes superior to actors? What kinds of experiences do actors come across in improvisation? How to account for the designer's combination of creativity and practical skill? What part does mental imagination play in the design process? How do designers get their own spatial awareness across to their *spectators*? How does theatre affect the spectator? Why does the spectator react as he/she does? How do distance and suspension of disbelief 'work'? How does the choice of venue impact on the production process and on the audience? An improved and expanded understanding of theatre, resulting from answering the questions above in the context of consciousness studies, may, in turn, lead to new developments in theatre practice itself. In particular, I am discussing the questions raised above, among many more, in the following chapters:

1. Consciousness, Inspiration and the Creative Process

I begin the discussion of the relationship between theatre and consciousness by addressing issues of inspiration and the creative process. Following general introductory remarks, I provide a number of examples of inspiration and the creative process among dramatists, and extend that range of examples reported by representatives of other forms of art. From those examples, I extract a number of distinctive common characteristics. Having thus established the aspects that artists share in their creative process, I proceed to survey explanations of inspiration and the creative process offered across the centuries, beginning with the Greek concept of the Muses, developing towards Freudian and later psychology, and ending with very sceptical critiques of inspiration as mysterious to non-existent. The remainder of the chapter is based on the hypothesis that reports of inspiration and the creative process should be taken and studied at face value. Simply denying the existence of inspiration as non-existent, fantasy and imagination is not enough, we should be able to properly, seriously and cogently account for such processes. To do just that, I turn to one emerging field within consciousness studies, altered states of consciousness (ASC). Following a brief survey of this field, I focus on first-person approaches, i.e. attempts in science to objectively research subjective experience (which was traditionally excluded from any scientific endeavour), and within the field of first-person approaches, I explain my own choice of approach, which has at its basis the model of consciousness proposed in the Vedic Science developed by Maharishi Mahesh Yogi. I introduce this model of consciousness in some detail, as it will remain most relevant throughout the book. At the end of the first chapter, I develop a new, more comprehensive understanding of inspiration and the creative process against the background of the model of consciousness proposed by Vedic Science.

2. Consciousness Reflected in Drama

Drama reflects different states of consciousness of different characters. The chapter provides a survey of possibilities, under two major headings. I differentiate between *states of consciousness* and *development of consciousness*. In discussing *states of consciousness*, I look at sleep, dream, and waking, and altered, especially higher, states of consciousness, providing examples for each. I understand *development of the consciousness* to refer to a character's change from the beginning to the end of a play. The examples I use to illustrate this are taken from Shakespeare: Prospero in *The Tempest* and the title character in *Hamlet*.

3. Consciousness and Acting

I begin this chapter with an analysis of the seminal question whether the actor should be emotionally involved with the emotions their characters are supposed to be feeling (Meyer-Dinkgräfe, 1996). I proceed to discuss the concept of the actor's *presence*, central to Barba's theatre anthropology, and the related concepts of *state* in Ariane Mnouchkine's theatre work and Grotowski's concept of *translumination*. In relation to those concepts I subject Artaud's notion of a *physical presence and neutrality* to a reassessment from the perspective of the Vedic Science model of consciousness. I conclude the chapter with a comparison of some of the characteristics of the marionette with that of the human performer, with particular reference to Heinrich von Kleist's *Über das Marionettentheater* (1810).

4. Indian Theatre Aesthetics

In this chapter, I introduce the theatre aesthetics of the fundamental Indian text on drama and theatre, the *Natyashastra*, reassess these against the model of consciousness proposed by Vedic Science, and review the influences of Indian theatre aesthetics on Artaud, Grotowski, Barba and Brook in arriving at their concepts of theatre and their theatre practice. In the course of this argument, I also address the question if, to what extent, and how, performance that follows the guidelines of the *Natyashastra*, may serve to enhance the development of higher states of consciousness in actors and spectators.

5. Reception and Audiences

In this chapter, I want to deal predominantly with empirical spectators, not reader-response-based hypothetical constructs. My argument is grouped around the senses, dealing with scenography to represent the sense of sight, branching off into discussions of simultaneity and time in the theatre, and developments in neuroscience to explain some of the potential impact on consciousness through the sense of sight. A brief section deals with the sense of sound, going back to the model of language proposed by Vedic Science. In a section co-written with Dr Martin Mittwede, we address the potential of using smell in theatre specifically to influence the development of consciousness of actors and spectators involved. I finally write about the so-called sixth sense, referring to recent developments in physics in relation to Vedic Science in an attempt at explaining unconventional transfer of information (how do we know if someone is staring at us behind our backs?). In conclusion of the chapter, I provide two examples of unconventional productions or performances that have affected spectators very strongly in a consciousness-altering manner: Taller Investigacion de la Imagen Theatral's *Ariadne's Thread*, sometimes referred to as *The Labyrinth*, and Anna and Corrina Bonshek's *Reverie II*.

6. Concepts of Theatre Studies

In this chapter, I want to complete the picture by addressing a number of issues that have come to prominence in their own times in the course of theatre history. Since they are frequently quoted in academic contexts even today, I take for granted that they are still considered important to our understanding of theatre, and that they, therefore, merit reconsideration in the context of consciousness studies. The first two sections relate to the *language* of theatre: Artaud's conceptualisation of a language of nature, and attempts, by Peter Brook, for example, to arrive at a universal language of the theatre. In the third section I address the question of how theatre relates to ritual-in view of the fact that ritual is often quoted as a source for the development of theatre, a view recently refuted by Rozik (2000). I explain how ritual is understood in Vedic Science, and how theatre that follows the aesthetics of the *Natyashastra* can be understood in terms of Vedic ritual. The fourth section deals with the phenomenon of *postmodernism* in the context of theatre. With reference to key critics in this area, I argue that many theatre artists' search for access to pure consciousness can be understood as the search for an overarching structure so vehemently rejected by postmodernism. Finally, I discuss the concept of utopian performative, recently introduced by Jill Dolan, in the context of Vedic Science.

7. Vedic Science and Materialism: Comments on Demastes' *Staging Consciousness*

In the final chapter of the book, I discuss in depth William W. Demastes' *Staging Consciousness: Theater and the Materialization of Mind* (Ann Arbor: The University of Michigan Press, 2002). His predominant aim in discussing the relationship between theatre and consciousness is to unearth, describe and make accessible and available for further theatre practice the insight that theatre has unfathomed and to a large extent unused potential in enabling, in theatre artists and audiences, a holistic experience which is non-ordinary, non-day-to-day, what Brook calls *holy theatre*. His aim is thus very close to my own. Yet Demastes' approach is clearly and intentionally materialist, bottom-up, rather than what he would call top-down, mysterious. I summarise the main stages of Demastes' argument, and comment on them from the perspective of Vedic Science.

I conclude the book with an outlook on the scope of future research into the relationship between theatre and consciousness. Two appendices follow the bibliography: the first provides background information about Maharishi Mahesh Yogi and his Vedic Science. In the second I describe the processes of creation as proposed by Vedic Science in detail, for the reader sufficiently interested by the brief survey of that material in chapter one in relation to artists' creative processes and inspiration.

Methodology

As the preceding survey of the chapters in this book demonstrates, I raise a number of issues that I consider important for understanding theatre. I proceed to offer a brief discussion of the general debate that has existed with regard to the questions raised. The bulk of each chapter, however, is devoted to offering alternative, 'new' answers to the questions. Although I am personally convinced of my own argument, I do not lay claim to having the final answers to all questions that can be raised relating to theatre, nor the final answers to the questions I raise in the course of the book. At the end of the book I therefore provide an outlook of further issues to be discussed at a later stage. I see the book as my contribution to an ongoing debate: the new answers I offer in response to a number of specific questions are in all cases open to further theoretical modification, but also to empirical research. In the latter case, my new answers may be regarded as well-argued hypotheses, which can be further operationalised to transform them into the starting points for empirical research.

Such research can in many cases follow conventional paradigms: a hypothesis gives rise to predictions, the hypothesis and related predictions are subjected to empirical testing, which in turn either confirms the hypothesis or not. One aspect of research conducted according to this conventional paradigm is that science is expected to be value-neutral, free of non-reproducible feelings and emotions. Already the survey of the material covered in this book, however, shows clearly that a certain percentage of that material is by its very nature subjective, and based on subjective experience. Here both my argument, my new answers, and the means of subjecting those new answers to further research, are at the forefront of the paradigm shift, well under way in consciousness studies, towards first person approaches to consciousness: attempts to systematically, scientifically study experience-rather than excluding it from the scientific process. The essays in Varela and Shear's collection on *First-person Approaches to the Study of Consciousness* (1999) demonstrate clearly that their authors are aware of the pioneering nature of their approaches; they invite debate, and so do I on the argument that I present in my book. I invite a debate through the Web-journal *Consciousness, Literature and the Arts* (*CLA*), at http://www.aber.ac.uk/tfts/journal.

The reader will have noticed from the survey of chapters that in many cases, my new answers are based on concepts found in sources from India. I trust that this fact alone does not discourage the reader. Throughout, I endeavour to explain as fully as necessary the concepts from Indian philosophy which I consider relevant to my argument, and in the same way I endeavour to define the terms needed to express those concepts. When I use material from Indian philosophy, I am not proposing to import a different culture wholesale. In the first instance, I have selected only specific aspects of that culture, aspects that I argue to be relevant in answering the questions I raise. Secondly, I am not claiming that the questions I raise cannot be answered except by reference to Indian philosophy. Had my interest in theatre developed with a specialism in Japan, I might well have argued my case with reference to, say, Zeami's writings and treatises on Japanese Buddhism. Thus, readers may indeed find many parallels between the specific aspects of Indian philosophy I employ in my argument and bodies of knowledge that they know about, and those bodies of knowledge may well derive from any culture worldwide. I would be interested to hear about such parallels, and again I invite relevant comments through the *CLA* website.

1: Consciousness, Inspiration and the Creative Process

It is so well known as to be a truism that not everyone is good at everything: different people are good at different things. 'Things' can be arts, crafts, knowledge-based activities, or skills. As a result, people make use of what they are good at for various purposes: to gain enjoyment and satisfaction, and to earn their living. It is up for debate as to which of the two is more important to individuals themselves and / or to society. Some people 'are good at' writing plays. They are dramatists or playwrights. As with many other professions, occupations, or jobs, the outward measure of whether the playwright or dramatist is 'good' is the critical opinion of peers-fellow playwrights and those who read the plays and/or see them performed and comment on their reading or viewing experience. Such peer evaluation is either formal and public, or informal and private. Formal engagement with a playwright's work can take the form of critical books and essays, or comments in interviews about a playwright, on the whole produced by academics or journalists. Discussions of plays (and that implies their writers) in class at school or university levels also come under this heading. Informally, spectators may discuss the performance of a play. Evaluation, furthermore, is either contemporary to the playwright in question, or may take place after his or her death. In a number of cases, playwrights received praise, were re-evaluated as 'good' only after their deaths, lacking recognition and related financial income during their lifetimes.

What motivates a playwright to write a play? To answer this question, let us first look at motivations and processes at work in various other occupations. In the case of some occupations, the impulse of what needs doing comes clearly, and only, from outside the individual following those occupations: a car mechanic is confronted with a specific type of car and a specific kind of task in relation to the car, such as, repairing faulty brakes. Acquired knowledge and skills, based on training and experience in the job, allow the mechanic to tackle the task in hand, and the level of skill determines the speed and efficiency of the repair. In other occupations, the impulse of what needs doing comes from a combination of factors both outside and inside the individuals following those occupations. Take the example of a car manufacturer. If management requests a new model to be developed, this represents an outside impulse to the colleagues involved in the design of the new model. The designers will have to combine existing knowledge of materials and their characteristics, processes, shapes, sizes, colours, etc. to produce something new. The process and the ability involved (and required!) here are referred to as creativity. Creativity is also an essential asset in many aspects of (business) administration and management.

Creativity research is a vast field, as documented, for example, by the *Encyclopedia of Creativity* (1999) and at least two specialist refereed journals, *Creativity*

Research Journal and *Journal of Creative Behavior*, and there is an equally strong market in creativity enhancement programmes[1]. The playwright may function within the parameters set by those two scenarios (outer motivation and creativity): several fairly uncomplicated possibilities come to mind. A playwright who has already written several plays with more than one character may want to experiment with form and thus decide to try his/her hand at a one-person show. Thus British dramatist David Pownall said: 'As a writing exercise it's very very exciting and good for me. You have to entertain with just one person on the stage' (Meyer-Dinkgräfe, 1985a). Some playwrights confirm that particularly writing one-person shows is motivated by commercial reasons: plays that require only one performer, together with a minimum requirement for design, are more flexible and easier to sell than a play with a large cast (Meyer-Dinkgräfe, 1985a, MacDonald, 1985, Gems, 1985, Drucker, 1985). One might be tempted to cite commercial reasons for a playwright's interest in a type of play that appears to be commercially successful. Since the late seventies, for example, plays about artists have thrived in Britain, a trend triggered by the success of Peter Shaffer's *Amadeus* and *Piaf* by Pam Gems. Some plays in the wake of those two trendsetters were clearly poor attempts of jumping the bandwagon. For instance, *Cafe Puccini* premiered in the West End in 1986, and failed mainly because the production expected actors to sing Puccini arias, accompanied by four strings, piano, flute and accordion. Trained opera tenors have their problems with Calaf's aria *Nessun Dorma* from Puccini's *Turandot*. If an actor with some voice training attempts to sing this aria live on stage, it is, according to one critic, a laudable act of bravery, 'but no one should have done this to him or to us!' (Colvin, 1986: 21). The show closed after only forty-three performances. *After Aida* is another example of a commercially intended but unsuccessful play, dealing with the last phase of Giuseppe Verdi's career. It played for twenty-eight performances. *Times* critic Wardle wrote:

> There is no dramatic situation. The setting [the stalls of a theatre] is merely a play-ground where speakers can address us with memoirs, team up for brief scenes and rehearsals (...) members retreat to the stalls to read newspapers or sit looking bored; a sight that leaves you wondering why you should be interested in a spectacle they cannot be bothered to look at (1986).

Superficial 'outside', commercial reasons, however, are not sufficient to explain all dramatic output. In the majority of cases, the processes involved in playwrighting (as with many other artistic activities) go beyond 'outside' motivation and even the kind of creativity described above as relevant to car design or management: playwrights claim an inner need to write a particular play. In those cases, creativity is closely linked with inspiration, defined by the *Oxford English Reference Dictionary* as 'a supposed force or influence on poets, artists, musicians, etc., stimulating creative activity, exalted thought, etc.' (1996)

Interviews with playwrights provide rich source material for a study of inspiration. On the basis of a several descriptions of inspiration by playwrights themselves, taken from a range of interviews, I will derive a number of general points of information about inspiration. I will place them in the context of attempts, over the centuries and in the Western tradition, at explaining inspiration. The chapter concludes with an alternative explanation developed within the context of Indian philosophy.

Examples of Inspiration among Playwrights

I want to begin this section with three almost randomly selected quotations.

Playright	Quotation
Alan Ayckbourn	Most of what I do, I believe I do instinctively. In my *Absurd Persons Singular* there are three kitchens at Christmas. You need three there. I don't know why; you just do. Two kitchens would not be interesting. And in that play you also get this Christmas, last Christmas and next Christmas. Everything seems to link to three. I am sure that somewhere in the middle of the universe there is a unit of three. (DiGaetani, 1991: 19)
Christopher Hampton	I never really know what I'm writing a play about; I only know that I'm interested in something, and I don't know the reason why. I'm sort of at the mercy of my... (DiGaetani) Muse? (Hampton) Instinct, I was going to say - a better word, I think. I trust my instinct too because my experience is that whenever I try to write on a particular thesis, the result is not interesting. There is an element - which you can call either mystery or poetry - which is absolutely essential in the theatre. Otherwise the play lacks resonance. It just sits there and tells you what it wants to tell you, as if you're watching the news on television. The best moments in theatre are those moments when you are irrationally moved. Art is always more complicated than the terms by which you can define it. (DiGaetani, 1991: 132)

David Mamet	There's a curious phenomenon that happens when you compose a play or a movie. The creation very quickly takes on a life of its own. I have no idea why; it's just words on paper. But the art I can compare it to in my experience is carving wood. You start to carve wood, and very quickly the thing takes on a life of its own. Part of the wisdom of wood carving is to realize when the wood is telling you where it wants to go. Obviously it's going to be a duck if you start out to make a duck, but the kind of duck it's going to be is largely dictated by the kind of wood. And there is similar phenomenon in writing drama. You start out with an idea, it becomes something else, and part of the wisdom is learning to listen to the material itself. Much of the material, of course, is subconscious. (Kolin and Kullman, 1996: 183)

These three statements share a few common characteristics: the dramatists in question *don't know why*, *don't understand why*, *have no idea why* they write as they do, they talk about *instinct, inspiration, mystery and poety*, and *miracle*. Let's keep those shared characteristics of dramatic writing in mind and look more precisely at some dramatists who share writing about fellow artists.

David Pownall had read the minutes of the composers' conference held by the communist party in 1948 in Moscow: 'Those minutes froze your blood on the one hand, but they also made you laugh. There was a kind of mixture of horror and mockery (...) and I immediately knew that I wanted to write a play about this' (Meyer-Dinkgräfe, 1985a). The result is *Master Class*, which shows a fictional meeting between Stalin, Shostakovich and Prokofiev in the Kremlin. Pownall's intention in writing the play was to convey, if possible, the same feelings to the audience he had experienced while reading the minutes. While Tom Kempinski was working on *Duet for One*, he was suffering the first stages of agoraphobia. For him, the psychiatrist character in the play, Dr. Feldman, and the artist, Stephanie, represented the life-supporting and life-threatening forces within himself, in his struggle between survival and suicide (Glaap, 1984).

The examples of Pownall and Kempinski show that inspiration is again central to their creative acts, and it is very personal events in the lives of the dramatists that serve as inspirations to write a play about a fellow artist. Generally speaking, dramatists have to depend on their intuition, as Peter Shaffer puts it: 'One is not finally aware of why one idea insisted or the others dropped away (...) The playwright hopes that one will say: 'Write me! Write me!'' (Buckley, 1975: 20). Many dramatists confirm that they had reached a stage in their artistic development at which they wanted to reflect about the nature of art and the implications of being an artist.

Having established some common patterns relating to the creative process characteristic of dramatists, I now want to compare those findings with reports by artists in other genres about their creative process.

Examples of Inspiration among other Artists

Not only playwrights have described what inspired them to write their plays. We have similar accounts also from representatives of other forms of art. All the cited artists are famous ones, those who have achieved greatness in their fields. This could at first sight be due to the fact that only because they are famous have their experiences been recorded and published. Moreover, however, current research suggests that high achievers in any field or occupation are likely to have more frequent instances of experiences such as inspiration, than less high achievers (Harung et al., 1996). Composer Johannes Brahms (1833-1897) described the creative process of his composing on the condition that the material be published only fifty years after his death. Inspiration for Brahms originates in a level of reality that is both real and apparently unmanifest:

> It happens not only through the power of will, through conscious thinking, which is a product of development of the physical level and dies with the body. It can only happen through the inner forces of the soul, through the real I, which physically survives death. Those forces are dormant for conscious thought, unless they are illumined by spirit. (Volkamer, 1996: 26)

Later, Brahms adds:

> Initially I know (...) that it is a real, lively force, the source of our knowledge. You cannot experience through conscious thought, which is the product of the realm of matter; it can be perceived only with the true, eternal Ego, the inner force of the soul (...) I always think about all this, before I start composing (...) Immediately afterwards I sense vibrations that permeate me through and through. They are the spirit that illumines the inner forces of the soul, and in this state of rapture I see clearly what is dark in my usual state of mind; then I feel able to allow myself to be inspired from above, like Beethoven. (...) These vibrations take the shape of specific mental images, after I have inwardly uttered my wish and decision of what I want, namely to be inspired to compose something that uplifts and supports humankind-something of lasting value. Immediately ideas come streaming towards me (...) Not only do I see specific themes in front of my mind's eye, but also the appropriate form in which they are shaped, the harmonies and orchestration. Bar by bar the fin-ished work is revealed to me. (Volkamer, 1996: 26-7)

Fellow composer Richard Wagner (1813-1883) reports:

While working (...) I had many wonderful and enlivening experiences in the invisible realm, which I can describe, at least to some extent. First of all I believe that this universal, vibrating force connects the human soul with that omnipotent central force, from which our life principle derives, to whom we all owe our existence. For us this force represents the link to the highest power in the cosmos, of which we are all a part. If it were not like that, we would not be able to connect with it. Those who are able to connect will get inspiration. (...) I sense that I am one with this vibrating force, that it is omniscient, and that I can create out of it to an extent that is limited only by my own ability. (Volkamer, 1996: 29)

Poet William Wordsworth (1770-1850) coined the now famous phrase 'emotion recollected in tranquillity' in the context of describing the creative process:

I have said that poetry is the spontaneous overflow of powerful feelings: it takes its origin from emotion recollected in tranquillity: the emotion is contemplated till, by a species of reaction, the tranquillity gradually disappears, and an emotion, kindred to that which was before the subject of contemplation, is gradually produced, and does itself actually exist in the mind. In this mood successful composition generally begins, and in a mood similar to this it is carried on; but the emotion, of whatever kind, and in whatever degree, from various causes, is qualified by various pleasures, so that in describing any passions whatsoever, which are voluntarily described, the mind will, upon the whole, be in a state of enjoyment. (1969: 740)

Finally, Franz Kafka (1883-1924) wrote:

It is not necessary that you venture out of doors. Stay at your table and listen. Don't even listen, just wait. Don't even wait, be completely still and alone. The world will offer itself to you to be discovered, it cannot do otherwise. Enchanted it will writhe in front of you. (1988)

For further collections of such accounts, see Ghiselin (1952) or Shrady (1972).

Common Characteristics of Reported Inspiration
Looking across those, and many more reports of inspiration provided by artists across the genres, it is possible to extract a number of characteristics they all share.

- Many artists do not clearly know how they get their important creative ideas, and refer to inspiration or instinct if asked to explain;
- Inspiration is considered a blessing;
- Artists blessed with inspiration attribute the creation of their best work to inspiration;
- Specific procedures help Brahms to gain intentional access to a state of inspiration. Most artists, however, have to rely on coincidence;
- Inspiration is associated with a specific mental state that is different from the ordinary state of waking. It is within this state of being that the creative process takes its origin, the source from where it develops;

- This state is often located between waking and sleeping;
- Inspiration is very powerful and creates awe-hence its attribution to the divine.

Explanations of Creative Inspiration

Having established common characteristics reported by artists about their inspiration and about the processes involved in their creative activities, I now want to analyse attempts in Western history of ideas to explain, or make sense of, creative inspiration. From the beginnings of recorded histories of art in any form, inspiration, as described in the material above, has been part of the arts and the creative process. In Greek times, artistic inspiration was attributed to the *Muses*. They are goddesses, daughters of Zeus and Mnemosyne (memory). Initially there were three Muses, later expanding to nine:

1. Calliope (Fair Voiced), epic poetry
2. Clio (Proclaimer), history
3. Erato (Lovely), love poetry and mimicry
4. Euterpe (Giver of Pleasure), music
5. Melpomene (Songstress), tragedy
6. Polyhymnia (She of Many Hymns), sacred poetry (sometimes also related to geometry, mime, meditation and agriculture)
7. Terpsichore (Whirler), dance
8. Thalia (Flourishing), comedy and playful and idyllic poetry
9. Urania (Heavenly), astronomy

The Muses preside over the art they are associated with, and, most important in our context, they provide the inspiration to the artists excelling in their art. The Greeks conceptualised the mind as having two chambers; one in which new thoughts occur, controlled by the gods. The gods, through the Muses, project their ideas by inspiring (literally: breathing into) one of those two chambers in human minds (Dacey, 1999: 310). From there, the material provided by the gods proceeds into the second chamber, where the inspired individual expresses it through speech and writing. The model of the two chambers of the mind has been termed *bicameral* mind by Jaynes (1977). While inspired, artists are thus as if possessed, divinely mad. Plato's dialogue *Ion* deals with inspiration by the Muses. Here, Plato argues that 'all good poets, epic as well as lyric, compose their beautiful poems not by art, but because they are inspired and possessed'. He described the poet as 'a light and winged and holy thing', concluding that 'there is no invention in him until he has been inspired and is out of his senses, and the mind is no longer in him: when he has not attained to this state, he is powerless and is unable to utter his oracles (...) [T]he poets are only the interpreters of the Gods by whom they are severally possessed.'. Aristotle at one point raised doubts about the bicameral model of the mind, but did not pursue those doubts. As a result, this model prevailed until the end of the Middle Ages. Humanistic views, characteristic of the Renaissance and later periods, saw the belief that 'humans have the ability to solve problems through their own mental efforts, without having to rely on inspiration from the gods or from God' (Dacey, 1999: 309).

In 1767, Duff wrote what is thought to be the first major inquiry into the creative process. Dacey calls him a precursor of the biopsychosocial theory of creativity, which holds that 'all human acts are born of a complex interaction of biological, psychological and social forces (1999: 309). Duff related creativity to genius, which he saw as emerging from a combination of imagination, judgment and taste. Genius, according to Duff, has nothing to do with anything supernatural; it is exceptional, but nevertheless within the potential of every human being; genius is different from talent.

In the Romantic period, the outward focus of inspiration, as initiated by an influence from the Muses, was gradually replaced by an inwards focus: artists create from within themselves, gaining access to realms of their consciousness that prove, to them, to be sources of inspiration. For Shelley, in his *A Defence of Poetry*, the mind in the process of creation is 'as a fading coal which some invisible influence, like an inconstant wind, awakens to transitory brightness'. We are unable to predict its 'approach or its departure'. The influence that causes the mind to create is invisible, unpredictable, and short-lived: inspiration is already declining when the process of composition begins. The influence itself, inspiration, however, is considered very strong indeed: 'Could this influence be durable in its original purity and force, it is impossible to predict the greatness of the results' (quoted in Clark, 1997: 143-4).

In the wake of discoveries in relation to genes and inheritance, two camps developed in describing and explaining creative genius: associationism and gestalt views. Associationism implies the 'proposition that the mind consists entirely of ideas (words, images, formulas, etc.), each of which is associated with other ideas' (Dacey, 1999: 309). Creativity means the development of new ideas through such processes of association. The gestalt approach, on the other hand, implies that the creative genius does not work from the parts or elements towards the whole, as in associationism, but the other way round: holistically, from the wholeness (of gestalt) to the parts. Gestalt is the German term for mental patterns and forms. In the creative process, such mental patterns and forms are formed and altered.

With developments in anatomy and related physiology, different mental functions began to be associated with specific areas of the brain, a development of major importance in twenty-first-century consciousness research. William James (1842-1910) argued strongly for the nurture side of the growing nature (genes) versus nurture (environment) debate, and was supported in this by Freud's (1856-1939) view that creativity was the 'result of overcoming some traumatic experience, usually one that happened in early childhood' (Dacey, 1999: 320). Freud's view clearly relates to the popular assumption that the development of creative genius is related to suffering.

Creative activity, according to Freud, is a way in which the mind is able to cope with conflict between the three elements that constitute it; creative processes are a form of sublimation, transforming unacceptable impulses of the *id* (which remains responsible for the drive, the energy of highly creative people), and helps the release of conflict arising from any repression of the *id* impulses by *ego* and *superego*. Humanist psychologists (Abraham Maslow (1908-1970) and Carl Rogers (1902-1987) were early important representatives) argue that creativity is one characteristic of self-actualising people. Csikszentmihalyi has developed the concept of *flow*, a state of consciousness experienced and enjoyed as full absorption with the work one is doing at the moment. Non-humanistic psychologists have difficulties, though, with matching the statistical fact of a high correlation between mental illness and creativity to the claim that creativity is in fact a feature of people who are mentally healthy, above-average, as humanist psychologists would claim. (Conti and Amabile, 1999: 255-6). The clue to solving this argument could be that transpersonal psychology may tend to regard as normal, or even very good in relation to human spiritual development, states of consciousness conventionally regarded as symptoms of mental illness.

C. G. Jung (1875-1961) had a detailed view on artistic creation. The process of artistic creation is a 'feminine' quality; it can be conscious and intentional. Artists creating in that mode are in control, they know at every stage what they are doing, and for what purpose. They are 'expressing a symptom of their experience' (Jones, 1999: 116), and creating a piece of psychological art. Artists creating from the unconscious create visionary art. They are amazed and overwhelmed by what they create; they create symbols out of the collective (rather than the personal) unconscious. Works of art created from the collective unconscious are more likely to be great works of art, due to their immense impact on the viewer (or reader, or spectator): their own collective unconscious is stirred, thus providing one of the most important functions of art in society: revitalising 'our connection to the past in a way that is understood by today's culture' (116).

To some extent, the spark that sets creative writing, or artistic creation processes going, can be related to the concept of insight. Insight is the ability of suddenly seeing and understanding clearly 'the inner nature of things, esp. by intuition' (Sternberg and Davidson, 1999: 57). According to Sternberg and Davidson, insight is an important human characteristic because it is universal and interesting to everyone. Insights have led to many of the great discoveries throughout history. As with inspiration, insight has been explained in three ways:

1. as a gift to humans from higher powers, such as the Muses (the mystical view);
2. as involving processes that are in place for any kind of problem-solving situation, and therefore nothing special (even though having an insight might *feel* special when it occurs);
3. as involving special processes. They include
   a. Gestalt psychology, maintaining that the whole is more than the sum of its parts;
   b. the three-process view: insight combines varying degrees of sifting relevant information from among the many stimuli people encounter, combining appropriate aspects of information, and comparing 'newly acquired information with information acquired in the past' (Sternberg and Davidson, 1999: 65).

c. a view that makes use of one of the first psychological attempts to understand creativity, Graham Wallas' four-stages model of mental preparation, incubation, illumination and verification. People unable to solve a problem will go into the phase of incubation; the unsolved problem will be, as it were, at the back of their minds, and they will process information from the environment in such as way as to filter out anything that might help to solve the problem.

The creative process has also been linked to intuition, which is a very controversial concept in psychology. Some researchers dismiss it as non-existent, or an esoteric phenomenon beyond the realm of science. Popular assumptions imply that intuition is the power of 'knowing something without reasoning or learned skill' (Policastro, 1999: 93). Other scientists have made some progress in describing phenomena that come under the heading of intuition, and conclude from their studies that intuition, contrary to popular belief, 'arises from knowledge and experience'. Further concepts are introduced in the attempt to explain und understand intuition. However, such concepts (for example, cognitive style, or domain-specific expertise), are in themselves constructs developed to make sense of other characteristics of human behaviour, and each comes with its own range of divergent theories and approaches.

Not only psychologists research creative inspiration. Models from a wide range of disciplines or fields of research are used in attempts to explain the phenomenon of the creative act, or inspiration, for example chaos theory, the theory of non-linear dynamical systems (Schuldberg, 1999: 259). The creative act, inspiration, anecdotally assumed to be 1%, precedes, and gives rise to, the creative process, the remaining 99%. Pribram proposes that in the brain, sensory input is relayed to two distinct areas, the hippocampus, and the 'sensory-specific "association" systems of the neocortical isocortex'. In both hippocampus and in the neocortex, such sensory input causes specific patterns of neuronal activity. If the patterns elicited in hippocampus and in neocortex match, the sensory input is considered familiar, and 'the matching activity ceases. When, on the other hand, a mismatch exists, the input is considered "novel" and the matching operation continues interactively until the neocortical pattern has been modified sufficiently to produce a match' (Pribram, 1999: 216).

Nobody denies that many artists experience inspiration. Some of those ascribe their inspiration to the Muse, which they can hear speaking to them. One scientific attempt at explaining the voice within relates to brain physiology. The two hemispheres of the brain develop independent of each other. The linking element, *corpus callosum*, forms only by the age of three. The right hemisphere, usually the non-dominant one, is responsible for language. Possibly, language develops before the *corpus callosum* connects both hemispheres. 'Thus, the non-dominant hemisphere would learn its own language and develop its own dialogue. If this separate language center could persist even after the two sides are joined, we could then see a source for the voice within'. (Durrenberger, 1999: 176)

Some creative artists and creativity researchers report and study a dark side to the creative process, which, they argue, needs to be addressed to do justice to the full range of creativity. The dark side of creativity is predominantly associated with gruesome and unethical innovations or practices, across the arts and sciences, technology, business and politics, such as 'the bloody spectacles of the Coliseum of Rome' (McLaren, 1999: 484). Perhaps related to the so-called dark is the alleged, popularised and scientifically researched relation between (artistic) creativity and madness. Some psychologists argue that the daily behaviour of many artists shows aspects of mental illness. Some art is explained by the trauma of their creators: for example, Hitchcock was falsely accused of theft as a boy and imprisoned for a few days without knowing why. This childhood experience makes for tense moments and plots in many of his films. Arnold Ludwig's studies showed statistical evidence of the following: there was indeed a correlation of mental illness and people who were creative artists. In particular: musicians and substance abuse, poets and mania and psychosis. Suicide was highest among poets, musicians and fiction writers. People in architecture and non-fiction writing had much less mental illness. (Durrenberger 1999: 176).

Critique of Inspiration

Timothy Clark has charted the history of inspiration from the Greeks to the present (1997). He points out repeatedly that many critics, some of them creative writers themselves, dismiss accounts of inspiration as 'trite, mystifying and even embarrassing'. In this section I want to discuss some of those critiques. Critics at times balk at the idea that all work allegedly resulting from inspiration is supposed to be automatically 'great'. The problem Clark refers to here is one of dubious causality: 'inspiration is said to *cause* enhanced creativity' (31). He also points out the often ignored downside to inspiration: the frustration if the insight gained while it lasts is lost as soon as the duration of insight is over, as well as the 'recurrent complaint of writers that composition makes them ill' (32). Clark quotes Tchaikovsky: 'If that condition of the mind which we call inspiration lasted long enough without intermission, no artist could survive it' (Harding, 1940: 12; quoted in Clark, 1997: 39). He counters the recorded experience, claimed as inspiration, that poets hear a voice speaking to them, with reference to the phenomenology of reading: Stewart argues that '[e]ven the internal "voice" of silent reading is not really silent, the reader of these very words, for example, is hearing them in a sense, or imagining hearing them (...)' (Stewart, 1990: 24, quoted in Clark, 1997: 38). Others complain that referring to the creation of a work of art through inspiration leaves the creative process in a historical vacuum: writing, painting, or composing appear to take place independent of the historical circumstances relevant to the inspired artists. Clark does not mention two further possible reasons for denying or at least seriously doubting the existence of inspiration: such critics may never have experienced inspiration for themselves, and are thus certain that it cannot exist. Or, devoid of inspiration themselves, they might be envious or jealous of those who get inspiration. Thus, inspiration as described by artists can be, and has been, explained away as an exaggeration, in line with Romantic thought about genius. The elements of inspiration that are too embarrassing, to use Clark's term, to stomach in today's post-Romantic, science-dominated society are then explained in terms of historical conditioning or contemporary neuroscience. Finally, artistic creativity lays claim to originality. This approach is of course not acceptable to postmodern thinkers, who maintain that 'every text indicates another text, behind every image lies another image' (Brown, 1999: 425).

Altered States of Consciousness

Taking the accounts of artists about inspiration at face value, and as accurate fact rather than mood-making, self-justification or self-aggrandizement, it is obvious that the artists' experiences related to inspiration represent states of consciousness that are certainly not common, or everyday. Within the field of consciousness studies, they fall under the category of altered states of consciousness (ASC). Historically, the study of ASC initially focused on undesirable states of consciousness that were considered in need of treatment. In 1969, Ludwig, for example, lists as maladaptive functions of ASC:

> attempts at resolution of emotional conflict, defensive functions in certain threaten-ing situations, a breakthrough of forbidden impulses, escape from responsibilities and inner tensions, symbolic acting-out of unconscious conflicts, the manifestation of organic lesions or neurophysiological disturbances, an inadvertent and potentially, dangerous response to certain stimuli. (18-19)

This emphasis on negative attributes of ASC is in line with Tart's claim that orthodox psychology regarded ASC as 'a temporary reorganisation of brain functioning', and held that 'our ordinary state of consciousness is generally the most adaptive and rational way the mind can be organised, and virtually all ASC are inferior or pathological', going into ASC spontaneously is a sign of mental illness, and 'deliberately cultivating ASC is also a sign of psychopathology' (Tart, 1975: 79-81).

Over the years, the attitude in psychology towards ASC has gradually changed. Thus, one of the earliest attempts at providing a clear survey of mental states which includes ASC was provided by Fischer (1971). Taking the 'normal' state between daily routine and relaxation, he conceptualised states characterised by relatively more or less arousal than the normal state. Ergotropic states, characterised by an increase of arousal, and corresponding increase of hallucination, were charted on a scale ranging from aroused (sensitivity, creativity, anxiety) to hyperaroused (acute schizophrenic states and catatonia) to ecstatic (mystical rapture). Trophotropic states, characterised by a decrease of arousal, also show three gradual stages: tranquil, hypoaroused (with Zazen as one of the specific states), and finally *yoga samadhi*. It is meditative practice that brings the latter two about. Fischer, indicating that both paths may lead to the same ultimate experience, refers to the climax of both ends of the spectrum as Self. This relation of ergotropic and trophotropic states is further emphasised by the indication that the high arousal of mystical rapture may within seconds give way to full hypoarousal characteristic of *samadhi*.

Inspiration, as described by artists, is on the one hand 'located' somewhere between waking and sleeping, and thus closer to the trophotropic state on Fischer's scale (decrease of arousal). On the other hand, there is certainly an increase in creativity, characteristic, on Fischer's scale, of an increase of arousal. Fischer's model does not quite manage to explain inspiration satisfactorily.

John H. Clark (1983) constructs a map of mental states, similar to a map in geography. It 'represents a large amount of information crowded into a very small space' (1). He defines as 'mind' 'the whole range of mental states, i.e. of conscious states, sleeping and waking, which a person can experience' (2). A 'mental state' is defined as 'the values taken by a person's set of "main" mental variables at any particular time' (2). The main variables are 'mind work, general mood: pleasant or unpleasant; intensity of general mood and aspects of mind; on-line and off-line functions; sleeping or waking; concentration and diffusion of attention; and attention and things' (13). Clark's incorporation of states of mental illness necessitates the inclusion of some extra variables such as 'Anxiety; Obsessions; Compulsions; Phobias; Irritability; Hallucinations; Delusions; Pain; Disorientation; Anger; Fear; Guilt; Repugnance; Boredom; Depersonalisation; Derealization' (13-14). However, as opposed to other researchers writing about states of consciousness, Clark also incorporates desirable, 'higher' mental states in his map. For this purpose, he discusses mysticism, which 'concerns an unusual kind of experience obtained other than by the senses' (16). Clark identifies seven main ideas in the content of mystical states, and relates those to some faculties of the mind (20):

Seven main ideas (aspects of mind)	Faculty
K Knowledge, significance	
U Unity, belongingness	
E Eternity, eternal now, being	Cognition
L Light, exteroception	
B Body sense, interoception	Perception
J Joy	Emotion
F Freedom	Volition

Clark also extracts certain recurrent comments on mystical states in the writings by the mystics. They are intensity; certainty; clarity; ineffability; sudden onset; and change of personality (22-24). Finally, he differentiates between an average state, a state of peak experience (expressly borrowing the term from Maslow), and the mystical state proper (which is more intensive than the peak experience, but still within the range of being describable in words) (25). The climax of a transition from average state to peak experience to mystical experience proper is referred to as the 'Void'. Clark describes it as ineffable, and 'a place of sudden transition' (25), and associates it with the Buddhist concept of Nirvana.

Locating inspiration on Clark's map is not too difficult: many of the common features of inspiration bear a striking similarity to the recurrent comments on mystical states listed above. However, categorising the artists' experience does not provide a full explanation, although it may represent its first stage.

First-Person Approaches and Vedic Science

So far in this chapter, I have charted the existing debate, across a range of disciplines, relating to artistic inspiration and artistic creativity. I now begin the process of introducing, as promised in the introduction, new, alternative views. Consciousness studies, initially dominated by hard sciences, are currently experiencing a shift in paradigm. By definition, the Western, science- and objectivity-oriented mindset had to cancel out subjectivity. It is striking that in 1998, one of the first major projects run under the auspices of the Center for Consciousness Studies specifically addressed the issue of dealing with human subjectivity in a scientific context. *First-person approaches* have attracted much attention (Varela and Shear, 1999). They vindicate and develop further the early attempts by Fischer or John H. Clark at making sense of the experiences of ASC in a solid context. At the same time, they integrate writings on mysticism, such as Stace (1960). Not surprisingly, the strongest arguments in that debate came from scholars whose thought has been influenced by non-Western philosophy, in which a more holistic, all-encompassing view of consciousness is not only theorised, but where numerous physical and mental techniques are provided which may well serve as the scientific tools of the future. Thus, ASC are not merely considered in comparison with ordinary functioning of consciousness, but in the wider context of higher states of consciousness as described in the literature of predominantly Indian philosophy (Shear and Jevning, 1999).

In the following sections, I will provide a brief survey of the model of consciousness in Indian philosophy, and discuss the value this model has for the explanation of artistic inspiration. Indian philosophy is a vast field, with many different approaches to consciousness. From within this field, I have selected the conceptualisation of consciousness in the tradition of Vedanta, as developed over the last 40 years by Maharishi Mahesh Yogi in terms of Vedic Science. In Appendix (1) I provide background information about this contemporary sage and philosopher, and define the term Vedic Science further.

The model of the mind as proposed by Vedic Science, and as such based on Vedanta philosophy distinguishes, initially, between three basic *states* of consciousness: waking, dreaming and sleeping. During the waking state of consciousness, several *functions* of consciousness can be differentiated, including decision-making, thinking, emotions, and intuition. Vedanta postulates a fourth state of consciousness which serves as the basis of the states of waking, dreaming and sleeping, and their related functions. The fourth state is without contents, but fully awake. It is referred to as *pure consciousness* (Forman, 1990), or *samadhi* in Sanskrit. It has been described, albeit in different terms, across cultures. W. T. Stace, for example, writes about *pure unitary consciousness* in the context of Christian mystic experiences (1960). If pure consciousness is not experienced only briefly, and 'just' on its own, but together with waking or dreaming or sleeping, according to Vedic Science, higher states of consciousness have been achieved. Tables 1 and 2 show the levels of the mind and states of consciousness as proposed by Vedic Science.

Table 1: Levels of the mind according to Vedic Science

Number	Every subtler level encompasses the less subtle levels	Level of the mind	Hierarchy of expression,concreteness and manifestation
1		Senses	Most expressed, most concrete, most manifest
2	Encompasses 1	Desire	Less expressed, less concrete, less manifest
3	Encompasses 1,2	Mind	Less expressed, less concrete, less manifest
4	Encompasses 1,2,3	Intellect	Less expressed, less concrete, less manifest
5	Encompasses 1,2,3,4	Feeling, emotions, intuition	Less expressed, less concrete, less manifest
6	Encompasses 1,2,3,4,5	Ego	Least expressed, least concrete, least manifest
7	Encompasses 1,2,3,4,5,6	Pure consciousness	Not expressed, not concrete, unmanifest

Table 2: States of consciousness according to Vedic Science

	State of consciousness	Experience of pure consciousness	Mode of perception
1	Waking	Absent	Conventional
2	Dreaming	Absent	Absent (interior)
3	Sleep	Absent	Absent
4	Pure consciousness	Present	Absent
5	Cosmic consciousness	Present	Witnessing
6	Refined cosmic consciousness	Present	Refined
7	Unity consciousness	Present	Unified

Let me explain what higher states of consciousness are, first in the context of psychology, and then by way of a number of experience reports. In a developmental psychology context, the phrase *higher stages of human development* would be used synonymously to *higher states of consciousness*. Thus, in a collection of views on *higher stages of human development*, Alexander and Langer take Piaget's theory of cognitive development as a starting point. Piaget assumed that all development comes to an endpoint in *formal operations*, which, under normal conditions, is reached between 15 and 20 years of age. Some contemporary developmental psychologists hold that development is possible in adulthood beyond formal operations. They either reject or adopt Piaget's concept of hierarchies, which implies that abilities develop hierarchically, i.e. 'later stages encompass and in some way reorganize their predecessors' (1990: 11). To give just one example for each category: Levinson argues that in adult life, specific eras, or 'seasons' have their own, distinct characteristics, but they are not higher than preceding ones. As Alexander and Langer put it, 'the endpoint of the life course involves interests and endeavours that typify the last season, but it does not necessarily reflect a logical culmination of capacities or fruition of potential' (11). Similarly, Dittmann-Kohl and Baltes propose *wisdom* as 'one of the fullest expressions of synthesized intelligence', involving 'the integration of cognitive, affective, and reflective components and that it transcends mere factual and procedural knowledge to encompass means-end evaluation' (12). Focusing on hypothetico-deductive thinking, Richard and Commons argue in favour of four hierarchical postformal stages:

In the first (systematic), systems supplant propositions as the object of cognitive operations; in the second (metasystematic), the thinker constructs relations between systems; in the third (paradigmatic), the relations between systems come to be recognized as a unified paradigm; in the last (cross-paradigmatic), different paradigms come to be comprehended and related. (13)

Hierarchical stages of moral reasoning are the centre of Kohlberg's research. He proposes a level that is beyond 'formal operations and beyond linear extrapolation of the progression of prior stages', and 'the development of this final, postformal stage involves a level of experience transcendental to operational thought' (16). Finally, Alexander and Langer argue that consciousness does not only involve the process of knowing (cognitive and moral reasoning, at the centre of most of developmental theory), and the objects known ('the physical world and social relations'), but also 'the knower or self', not restricted to reasoner and information processor (epistemic self), but also as 'locus or source of human consciousness and identity (i.e. the ontological self')' (18).

In answer to the question 'What are the highest possible forms of human development?' (Alexander, and Langer, 1990: 3), Vedic Science proposes that it is possible not only to have occasional experiences of higher states of consciousness as described by the mystics, or called 'peak experiences' by Maslow, but to systematically develop such more advanced states of consciousness as phenomena of permanent daily experience.

Alexander holds that assessing the possibilities of adult development beyond Piaget's stage of formal operations, involves three related issues:

Does development towards the endpoint proceed through qualitatively distinct stages? What mechanisms underlie this development? What major areas get developed (e.g., cognition and affect), and how do they interrelate? (3)

Based on the proposition to regard pure consciousness as a fourth state of consciousness next to the commonly known and experienced ones-waking, dreaming, and sleeping-Vedic Science describes three further stages of consciousness development. Termed 'cosmic consciousness', a fifth state of consciousness is characterised by the coexistence of waking, or dreaming, or sleeping, and pure consciousness. In cosmic consciousness, the level of pure consciousness, which is never overshadowed in daily experience by the activities and experiences of the individual psyche, becomes a 'stable internal frame of reference from which changing phases of sleep, dreaming, and waking life are silently *witnessed* or observed' (Alexander and Boyer, 1989: 342). Just as the states of waking, dreaming, sleeping, and of pure consciousness can be researched with reference to different, and state-specific subjective experiences as well as equally different and state-specific patterns of bodily functions such as EEG activity, eye movement, metabolic rate, breathing patterns, Galvanic skin response, and concentrations of various hormones in the blood, which are open to psychophysiological empirical studies, cosmic consciousness, too, has its state-specific patterns of subjective experience and psychophysiological variables.

In the course of introducing the Vedic Science model of consciousness, I have so far established the relationship between waking, dreaming and sleeping as the three conventional states of consciousness, and pure consciousness as the fourth state. In addition, I have begun to explain in terms of developmental psychology, the meaning if *higher states of consciousness* and *higher stages of human development* with reference to the fifth state of consciousness, called cosmic consciousness. Now I want to provide a number of experience reports of cosmic consciousness. The following is a description of witnessing dreaming:

> Often during dreaming I am awake inside, in a very peaceful, blissful state. Dreams come and go, thoughts about the dreams come and go, but I remain in a deeply peaceful state, completely separate from the dreams and the thoughts. My body is asleep and inert, breathing goes on regularly and mechanically, and inside I am just aware that I am. (Alexander et al., 1986: 295)

This double nature of experience, pure consciousness witnessing the activities of waking, dreaming, and sleeping, is not equivalent to an uncomfortable dissociation or split personality, as evident, for example, in Thoreau's description in *Walden* of occasionally *witnessing* his own thoughts and feelings:

> I only know myself as a human entity; the scene, so to speak, of thoughts and affec-tions; and am sensible of a certain doubleness by which I can stand as remote from myself as from another. However intense my experience, I am conscious of the pres-ence and criticism of part of me, which, as it were, is not a part of me, but spectator, sharing no experience, but taking note of it: and that is no more I than is you. When the play (...) of life is over, the spectator goes his way. It was a kind of fiction, a work of imagination only, as far as he was concerned. (Thoreau, 1960: 94-5)

The following lines of the modern Hispanic poet Juan Ramon Jimenez demonstrate his recognition of the 'witnessing' pure consciousness to be his essential nature:

I am not I

   I am this one

Who goes by my side unseen by me;

Whom I, at times, go to visit,

And whom I, at times, forget.

He who keeps silent, serene, when I speak,

He who forgives, sweet, when I hate,

He who takes a walk where I am not,

He who will remain standing when I die. (quoted in Bly, 1982: 32)

Referring to a contemporary woman athlete, Billie Jean King, Alexander points out that 'witnessing' as an experience characteristic of cosmic consciousness is not limited to quiet moments. King experienced 'witnessing' during a tennis match and describes it in relation to 'its value for spontaneous right action and personal fulfilment':

> I can almost feel it coming. It usually happens on one of those days when everything is just right. (...) It almost seems as though I'm able to transport myself beyond the turmoil of the court to some place of total peace and calm. Perfect shots extend into perfect matches. (...) I appreciate what my opponent is doing in a detached abstract way. Like an observer in the next room. (...) It is a perfect combination of [intense] action taking place in an atmosphere of total tranquillity. When it happens I want to stop the match and grab the microphone and shout that's what it's all about, because it is. It's not the big prize I'm going to win at the end of the match or anything else. It's just having done something that's totally pure and having experienced the perfect emotion. (King and Chapin, 1974: 199)

A number of psychophysiological studies have shown a significant correlation between the enhanced frequency of reported experiences of higher stages of consciousness and physiological variables. The variables studied include, among others, periods of virtual respiratory suspension, increased alpha and theta EEG coherence; increased capacity for absorption; self-actualisation; internal locus of control; decreased symptoms of stress; and improved ability on measures of fluid intelligence, creativity, perceptual and motor skills (Alexander and Boyer, 1989: 348).

The next stage of development, according to Vedic Science, is called 'refined cosmic consciousness'. In cosmic consciousness, the field of pure consciousness is permanently experienced together with waking, or dreaming, or sleeping. This level of functioning is maintained in refined cosmic consciousness and 'combined with the maximum value of perception of the environment. Perception and feeling reach their most sublime level' (355).

British poet Kathleen Raine (1908-2003) reports her experience of seeing a hyacinth, suggestive of an experience of refined cosmic consciousness as predicted by Vedic Science:

> I dared scarcely to breathe, held in a kind of fine attention in which I could sense the very flow of life in the cells. I was not perceiving the flower but living it. I was aware of the life of the plant as a slow flow or circulation or a vital current of liquid light of the utmost purity. I could apprehend as a simple essence formal structure and

dynamic process. This dynamic form was, as it seemed, of a spiritual not a material order; or of a finer matter, or of matter itself perceived as spirit. There was nothing emotional about this experience which was, on the contrary, an almost mathematical apprehension of a complex and organised whole, apprehended as whole, this whole was living; and as such inspired by a sense of immaculate holiness. (. ..) By 'living' I do not mean that which distinguishes animal from plant or plant from mineral, but rather a quality possessed by all these in their different degrees (Raine, 1975: 119)

The philosopher Fichte (1762-1814) describes the experience of refined perception like this:

(...) and the universe appears before my eyes clothed in a more glorious form. The dead inert mass which only filled up space, has vanished: and in its place there flows onward, with the rushing music of mighty waves, an endless stream of life and power and action, which issues from the original Source of all life. (Alexander et al., 1990: 322-323)

The final level of human development, according to Vedic Science, is called 'unity consciousness'. In this state of consciousness, 'the highest value of self-referral is experienced' (Alexander and Boyer, 1989: 359). The field of pure consciousness is directly perceived as located at every point in creation, and thus 'every point in creation is raised to the (...) status' of pure consciousness. 'The gap between the relative and absolute aspects of life (...) is fully eliminated' (360). The experiencer experiences himself and his entire environment in terms of his own nature, which he experiences to be pure consciousness. The *Bhagavad-Gita* describes unity consciousness thus: 'The yogi who is united in identity with the all-pervading, infinite Consciousness, and sees unity everywhere, beholds the Self present in all beings, and all beings as assumed in the Self' (Goyandka, 1984: 106). Maharishi Mahesh Yogi translates:

He whose self is established in

Yoga, whose vision everywhere is

even, sees the Self in all beings,

and all beings in the Self. (1969: 441)

The *Yoga-Vasishta* describes unity consciousness similarly:

I salute the self! Salutations to myself-the undivided consciousness, the jewel of all the seen and unseen worlds (...) you have been gained. (...) What ever there is in the universe is the one self. In the past, the present and in the future, here, there and everywhere (...). The self is the eternal existence. I, the self, alone am. (Venkatesananda, 1984: 393-4)

Descriptions of unity consciousness are also found in the Upanishads: 'I am that [Brahman]. Thou art that. All this [universe] is nothing but that.' or 'All this is Brahman alone. There is none other than Brahman and that is I' (Aiyar, 1914: 23, 86).

Gustave Flaubert (1821-1880) describes a transient experience that suggests this state in the 1849-1858 version of his novel *The Temptation of St. Anthony*'

> It is true, often I have felt that something bigger than myself was fusing with my being: bit by bit I went off into the greenery of the pastures and into the current of the rivers that I watched go by; and I no longer knew where my soul was, it was so diffuse, universal, spread out. (...) Your mind itself finally lost the notion of particularity which kept it on the alert. It was like an immense harmony engulfing your soul with marvellous palpitations, and you felt in its plenitude an inexpressible comprehension of the unrevealed wholeness of things; the interval between you and the object, like an abyss closing, grew narrower and narrower, until the difference vanished, because you both were bathed in infinity; you penetrated each other equally, and a subtle current passed from you into matter while the life of the elements slowly pervaded you, rising like a sap: one degree more, and you would have become nature, or nature become you (...) immortality, boundlessness, infinity. I have all that, I am that! I feel myself to be Substance, I am Thought! (...) I understand, I see, I breathe, in the midst of plenitude (...) how calm I am! (Orme-Johnson, 1987: 339)

Inspiration and Vedic Science

Reviewing the experience of inspiration reported by artists in all genres in the light of the model of consciousness proposed by Vedic Science allows a significant advance in understanding and explanation of inspiration compared with previous attempts.

The qualities of the experience

The descriptions of artistic inspiration suggest that those artists have temporarily experienced pure consciousness, sharing some or all of the following qualities:

* loss of self while consciousness is nevertheless maintained. The loss of self is commonly experienced as an absorption into something greater than the mere empirical ego;
* experience of the multiplicity of objects of perception as nevertheless united. Everything is in fact perceived as 'One';
* perception of an inner subjectivity to all things, even those usually experienced in purely material forms;
* the temporal spatial parameters of the experience. Essentially both time and space are modified. The extreme is an experience that is both 'timeless' and 'spaceless';
* the experience is one of valid knowledge. Emphasis is on a nonrational, intu-

itive, insightful experience that is nevertheless recognised as not merely subjective;
- the impossibility of expressing the experience in conventional language. The experience simply cannot be put into words due to the nature of the experience itself and not to the linguistic capacity of the subject;
- positive affect quality of the experience. Typically the experience is of joy or blissful happiness;
- the intrinsic sacredness of the experience. This includes feelings of mystery, awe, and reverence that may nevertheless be experienced independently of traditional religious language. (adapted from Gelderloos and Beto, 1989: 93)

Apparent adverse implications of inspiration and the creative process

According to Tchaikovsky, an artist would not be able to survive too long an exposure to inspiration, and Timothy Clark mentions those artists who complain about creation making them ill. This seems to be a contradiction: how can an experience be related both to highest creativity and suffering? Of course, this contradiction is at the centre of the romantic idea that great art can only be created by suffering artists. However, Vedic Science provides an explanation of Tchaikovsky's notion without insisting on the causal link of suffering and creativity as inevitable. It is the human nervous system, predominantly the brain, which allows individual experience of pure consciousness and higher states of consciousness that Vedic Science identifies at the basis of inspiration. To sustain the power of pure consciousness, the nervous system has to be trained and ready. If the surge of pure consciousness, resulting from coincidental contact with it, hits an unprepared nervous system, suffering in various forms may result. Thus, Tchaikovsky suggests it is a blessing that exposure to inspiration (i.e. exposure to pure consciousness) does not last too long.

The relation of inspiration and quality of inspired work of art

According to Vedic Science, pure consciousness is at the basis of all creation, and it is in itself the field from which all laws of nature operate. Human physiology allows the experience of this level of nature. Nature at the level of pure consciousness is conceptualised as free from fault or error. Thus, the experience of pure consciousness in humans can give rise only to thoughts and action that are in accordance with the laws of nature characteristic of pure consciousness. The closer the artist gets to pure consciousness, and the more he or she can take out of that contact (i.e. the better the artist is able to put the inspiration into its appropriate form), the better the work of art that results. This is of course a big claim to make, at least potentially controversial in the context of political correctness. Future research is needed on the relationship between consciousness and the canon, to discuss this issue in appropriate detail.

The artist's inspiration and the creative process

Since the artist creates from the level of pure consciousness, and thus from the level of nature, the processes of inspiration and creative activity mirror the processes of creation overall. Vedic Science describes the process of creation as follows: the first word of the *Rig-Veda* is *Agnim*. The sound of *A* represents the fullness of the absolute, *Brahman*, of unmanifest wholeness. The next sound, *G*, represents the collapse of fullness in a point value. There is a gap between *A* and *G*, and between this first syllable and the next one, etc. The mechanics of the gap is as follows:

1. The sound value collapses into the point value of the gap. This process is called *Pradhvamsa Abhava*.
2. The silent point of all possibilities within the gap, called *Atyanta Abhava*.
3. The structuring dynamics of what happens in the gap, called *Anyonya Abhava*.
4. The mechanics by which a sound emerges from the point value of the gap, i.e. the emergence of the following syllable. This is called *Prag Abhava*. (adapted from Nader, 1995: 34)

Appendix (2) provides a more detailed description of the process and how it sequentially unfolds, giving rise to the entire universe. As Bonshek points out, 'In terms of the artist's creative process, the artist's own unbounded consciousness collapses onto a point value-an idea, inspiration or inner vision-and in a sequential unfoldment, this thought or picture is transferred into form' (2001: 260).

Everyone an artist?

Vedic Science suggests everyone can gain access to pure consciousness within their own minds, either coincidentally, or through the practice of appropriate meditation techniques. Does that mean that everyone has the potential of being a great artist? Yes and no. Not every human being is born to be an artist, but people who are will be able to fulfil their potential by tapping the source of pure consciousness for their creations. The concept of *dharma* helps to understand this. On a general level, *dharma* is 'that invincible power of nature which upholds existence. It maintains evolution and forms the very basis of cosmic life. It supports all that is helpful for evolution and discourages all that is opposed to it' (Maharishi Mahesh Yogi, 1969: 26).

On the personal level, one meaning of *dharma* is 'allotted duty', 'that which it is natural for one to do, that for which one was born' (191). *Dharma* can also be associated with law, justice, customary morality, reflective morality, duty and conscience (Kuppuswami, 1977: 24). According to Kakar, *dharma* refers to the ground plan of any person's life, as the individual's life cycle, *ashramadharma*, and, most important, the individual's 'own particular life-task, his *svadharma*' (1981: 37). According to the *Bhagavad-Gita*, each individual has 'his own inborn nature, *svabhava*, and to make it effective in his life is his duty, *svadharma*' (Kuppuswami, 1977: 129). This individual life-task is not absolute, but embedded in the individual's historical condition:

> Hindu philosophy and ethics teach that 'right action' for an individual depends on *desa*, the culture in which he is born; and *kala*, the period of historical time in

which he lives; on *srama*, the efforts required of him at different stages of life; and on *gunas*, the innate psycho-biological traits which are the heritage of an individual's previous lives. (Kakar, 1981: 37)

In the course of time, Kakar argues, *svadharma* came to mean 'traditional action (...) in the sense that an individual's occupational activity and social acts are right or 'good' if they conform to the traditional pattern prevalent in his kinship and caste group' (37).

It is important to note that the concept of *dharma* functions on two levels, originally, *dharma* describes how nature functions. This applies to the level of *moksha*, liberation, enlightenment, the highest state of consciousness, where such functioning in accordance with the laws of nature, of the cosmos, is automatic, spontaneous, fully life-supporting for all concerned, and not subject to manipulation or misuse. *Dharma* also functions as a means to gain higher states of consciousness in the first place, laying down rules intended to serve as guidance for non-enlightened people on their path to enlightenment. Such rules originate from enlightenment. However, applied rules of *dharma* vary according to the historical and cultural circumstances of the times in which they were written down. For example, in Vedic times (2500 BCE to 500 BCE), women enjoyed equal status to men, participating fully in religious and social activities (Kuppuswami, 1977: 183). At a later stage, documented in the *Manusmritis*, a major text in the canon of *dharmashastra*, holy texts on *dharma*, the role of women in society had changed considerably (Doninger, 1991). Thus, as soon as *dharma* becomes open to individual, culture-bound interpretation, it becomes open to manipulation and misuse. Someone might, for example, wish to maintain his status of power by convincingly suggesting to others that their *dharma* is to be in a position of comparatively less power. Once open to ignorance, *dharma* as a concept may be misused. As a cosmic, universally applicable force or pattern of nature's functioning, however, *dharma* is not changed by such misuse. On a relative level, open to misuse, there may well be clashes between what someone is told to be his duty, and that same person's 'real' *dharma*, vocation in life. If *dharma* has its own way, in an enlightened society, duty and vocation will be the same.

On the basis of this concept of *dharma*, we can say that not everyone will be an artist, but only those whose *dharma* it is to be one. Whether someone's *dharma* is to be an artist will be known to the person in question, intuitively, by way of enjoyment of the chosen path, and success, both inward and outward. Those who are artists by way of *dharma* will not all create the same art, of course: according to Kuppuswami, 'the ruling idea in ancient Indian thought is unity in diversity, not uniformity' (183). Although the basis of creation, pure consciousness, is the same and links all individuals, and thus all artists, the infinite dynamism, the potential for infinite possibilities that characterise this field cause the infinite variety of manifest creation, including the variety among human beings. Thus people will not become more alike on their path to enlightenment. On the contrary, each person will develop the full potential of his or her individuality. This applies to every person in every profession.

Summary

In this chapter, I have discussed the nature of artistic inspiration, focusing on the dramatist, but placing dramatists' reports about their creative process and inspiration in the context of reports by artists in other genres. I surveyed past and current Western attempts at explaining creative inspiration, and the concomitant critique of the concept of creative inspiration. I introduced the model of consciousness proposed by Vedic Science, and reassessed creative inspiration against that model, arguing that the artist's creative inspiration is a process that mirrors cosmic creation on the level of the individual, representing an experience of pure consciousness. Regarding the creative inspiration in this way allows us to explain and better understand a range of experiences reported in conjunction with the moment of inspiration and the ensuing creative process.

Notes

1. See, for example, the website http://www.creax.com/creaxnet/creax_net.php.

2: Human Consciousness Reflected in Drama

In this chapter, I refer to drama, written text that serves as the basis for performance in the theatre, and I discuss the ways consciousness is reflected in drama. Two fundamental areas can be differentiated: states of consciousness, such as sleep, dream, all kinds of waking states, and altered states of consciousness; and development of consciousness, also more commonly referred to as development of character: a character is not the same at the end of the play compared with the beginning, he / she has overcome obstacles (or not), and has changed, for better or worse. Throughout this chapter, I illustrate my argument with reference to examples from a range of plays. The choice of such examples was driven by the relevance they have to the argument I am proposing.

States of Consciousness

In drama, characters are either shown in a specific state of consciousness, or they talk about their own or other characters' observed state of consciousness. In my discussion of consciousness in the first chapter, I introduced sleep, dream and waking as conventional states of consciousness, and altered states of consciousness. I want to address those four areas one by one. The sections on sleep, dream and waking are brief, because the discussion remains within the confines of more conventional observations. In the section on altered states of consciousness I refer again to the Vedic Science model of consciousness.

Sleep

Common sense suggests that at least five distinct modes of consciousness are related to sleep: falling asleep, sleep itself, waking up, insomnia, and sleepwalking. A sixth sleep-related state, during which the sleeper talks aloud, probably combines sleep with dream. Here is a funny example for waking up: in German playwright Curth Flatow's 1973 comedy *Der Mann, der sich nicht traut...* (*Happy Wedding*), the main character, divorced registry officer Leonard Hunter, wakes up one morning with some difficulties realising where he is. Waking up here makes for much comic business. The stage directions read like this:

> *One can hear the noise of an approaching plane. Hunter gets restless. The plane thunders over the roof. Hunter opens his eyes, startled, and sits up. For a moment he doesn't know where he is.* (1)

Then he does remember his whereabouts: he is in Julia's flat, in her bed, after having spent the night with her. He only met her the day before-she is the aunt of Susan, the girl his son wants to marry against his wishes, and Julia had come to his office to plead for him to give his permission to his son and her niece. Through a series of funny events, he ended up at her place sleeping with her.

Then he remembers, and the thought of what has happened makes him visibly happy-he is beaming! He reaches out next to him, hesitates...

Julia! *he looks under the cover. Julia's tousled head appears at the foot end of the bed. It was hidden under the pillow.*

Waking up, then, is shown from various perspectives: Hunter doesn't remember where he is, and beams once he does remember. Julia emerges from sleep in an unexpected way (and therefore funny), with her head at the foot end of the bed. The explanation follows immediately:

JULIA

(*dozy*) Are you looking for something in particular? (*takes cotton wool out of her ears*)

HUNTER

(*surprised*) What are you doing down there?

JULIA

(*while she changes her position*) Because there was no more space up there. First you pulled the cover away from me, then you lay transverse.

Having thus discussed an example of waking up in the context of comedy, insomnia and sleep walking, although potentially powerful states of consciousness for comedy, have more immediate potential for tragedy. Disturbances of sleep might be in need of treatment, and thus a topic for psychological or medical practice and research. In Shakespeare's *Macbeth*, for example, the witches bring sleeplessness; after Macbeth has killed Duncan, Macbeth starts suffering from insomnia and towards the end of the play, Lady Macbeth is observed sleepwalking by both her gentlewoman and the doctor. We see and hear her, and the doctor comments on her behaviour. Such depictions of sleep disturbances-insomnia and sleepwalking, can be interpreted within at least two distinct contexts. Research can provide information about general assumptions about insomnia and sleepwalking prevailing at the time the play featuring those states of consciousness was written. In contrast to such a historical approach, it is equally possible to apply later theories of medicine and psychology, in an attempt to show archetypal patterns in dramatic literature.

The borderline area between sleep and dream is best depicted by characters in drama who are asleep but talk out loud, either to themselves, but to even more theatrical effect, to others who are clearly awake. A good example is *Das Käthchen von Heilbronn* by Heinrich von Kleist (1777-1811). The play, written in 1808, is in the Romantic tradition and deals with fifteen-year-old *Käthchen*, who falls head over heels in love with Graf Wetter vom Strahl, a knight, when he happens to ride past her father's house. She follows him everywhere, although he is rather irritated by her advances, certainly not returning her feelings. One day, a servant tells Strahl that Käthchen is around again, asleep. Strahl decides to exploit his knowledge that her sleep is very sound, that she dreams all the time, and that she is prone to talking in her sleep. He approaches her with the intention of finding out the root cause of her infatuation with him. He talks to her, and she answers back, although her eyes are shut and she does not move. It is clear, too, that she dreams a completely different environment than they are in. In her dream state, Käthchen reveals that on New Year's Eve two years ago, a friend had cast some lead and predicted for Käthchen that a wonderful knight would marry her. That same evening Käthchen had prayed to God to show her that knight in her dream. Later that night a cherub had brought Strahl into her room. She had called for her friends to join her, but their light had dispersed what she thought was a dream. Strahl is stunned: he had been seriously ill at that time two years ago. In what he thought was a delirious state of consciousness, he has seen himself be guided by a cherub to a small bed chamber in a house he did not know, where the cherub had introduced him to a young girl. The girl was Käthchen. When the servants had come in with light, he had found himself back in his own bed, recovered.

Dreams

Unlike sleep, dreams have contents, which we may or may not remember on waking up. Dreams may be experienced as pleasant, neutral, or unpleasant (nightmares). In drama, nightmares would range among forms of disturbances of sleep, discussed above. For example, in Aeschylus' *The Persians* (written 472 BCE), queen Atossa, widow of Dareius and mother of Xerxes, the Persian king who is taking the Persian army in a war against Greece, talks about her nightmares. In many cases, dreams, related by characters from memory after they occurred serve the function, within the play, of revealing something about the dreaming character to him or herself, to the other characters, or the reader/spectator. Future events in a play's plot may be shaped by a dream and its interpretation. In *Die Braut von Messina* (1803) by Friedrich Schiller (1759-1805), the Queen of Sicily, Isabella, is already mother of two small sons, who are forever fighting, when she falls pregnant again. During her pregnancy, her husband has a frightening dream, which Isabella, many years later, relates to her sons. At the King's request, an Arab astrologer, trusted by the King but regarded with suspicion by the Queen, interprets this dream: if the newborn baby were a daughter, she would lead to the deaths of the two sons, and bring ruin to the royal house. As a result of this interpretation, the King orders his newborn daughter to be thrown into the ocean. The mother, however, rescues the child and has her brought up, in secret, in a monastery. In the end, however, the prediction comes true: both sons, Cesar and Manuel, fall in love with Beatrice who, unknown to them, is their sister. When Cesar finds Beatrice in Manuel's arms, he kills his brother. When Isabella reveals Beatrice's true identity, Cesar kills himself. Isabella had a dream herself, and again it is its interpretation that causes her to save her daughter. As in the case of her husband, Isabella seeks advice from someone versed in such matters. With hindsight, Isabella realises the ambiguity of the monk's interpretation of her dream. Generally speaking, as with sleep, the interpretation of the dreams can take place on the basis of a reconstruction of what the author could have known about dreams and the way they function at the time of writing, or on contemporary knowledge about the meanings of dreams. Krasner thus comments on the symbolic function of sleep and awaking in Chekhov's *Uncle Vanya* (1994), while Klein thus focuses on the dreams in Shaffer's plays (1989).

Some entire plays aspire to adopt the form of a dream, such as Strindberg's *A Dream Play*, characterised by a constant, apparently arbitrary flow and shift of characters and spaces. Other plays contain dream sequences, or dream-like scenes, such as Shakespeare's *A Midsummer Night's Dream*.

Waking

Among the states of consciousness depicted in theatre, waking is clearly the dominant one: in at least 99% of scenes, characters are awake. Wakefulness is characterised by any number of possible combinations of a character's intuition, emotion, thought, decision-making, desire and sensory experience, and many other factors. Future research should look in depth at the relation between findings in consciousness studies and aspects of the waking state of consciousness as depicted in plays. The table below is intended to provide an idea of the range of possibilities. In the first column, I have selected some headings and related disciplines from the classification used by the *Centre for Consciousness Studies*, Tucson, Arizona, USA. In the second column, I give examples how a specific branch of consciousness studies may be relevant for better understanding aspects of the waking state of consciousness as depicted in plays:

Consciousness Studies	Plays: The depiction and impact of
Personal identity and the self (philosophy)	characters' search for, or problems with, their identity.
Free will and agency (philosophy)	the question of free will versus (divine) determination
Vision (neuroscience / cognitivescience and psychology)	blindness / visual impairment
Motor control (neuroscience)	physical disabilities
Pharmacology (neuroscience)	drug use and abuse
Emotion (neuroscience)	various states of emotion
Memory (cognitive science and psychology)	memory on character, character development, events and motivation
Learning (cognitive science and psychology)	aspects of education
Language (cognitive science and psychology)	the use of language
Unconscious / conscious processes (cognitive science and psychology)	whether character's action is conscious or unconscious
Intelligence (cognitive science and psychology)	characters' intelligence
Creativity (cognitive science and psychology)	characters' creativity
Psychoanalysis and Psychotherapy (experiential approaches)	psychoanalysis / psychoanalysts

Altered States of Consciousness (ASC)

Apart from sleep, dream and waking states of consciousness, whose representation in drama I have discussed so far, several kinds of ASC are depicted in drama. As in real life, they range from undesirable to desirable, and can have comic or tragic effect. A few examples should demonstrate that range.

- Intoxication is a favourite ingredient of comedy. Famous drunks in comedy include Sir Toby and Sir Andrew in *Twelfth Night*, or Trinculo and Stephano in *The Tempest*. There is also Elwood P. Dowd, the main character in Mary Chase's *Harvey*, memorably played by James Stewart in the 1950 film based on the 1944 Pulitzer Prize-winning play. This frequently tipsy character's best friend is Harvey, a six foot, three inch tall white rabbit, whom no one else can see.

- Intoxication is used to more serious effect in Albee's *Who's Afraid of Virginia Woolf*, and in Williams's *Cat on a Hot Tin Roof*.
- Accidents sometimes cause non-ordinary states of mind. A fall from a horse, while dressed as Henry IV, causes the main character in Pirandello's *Henry IV* to go mad, at least for a while, and believe that he really is Henry IV.
- In *Woman in Mind*, Alan Ayckbourn shows the gradual decline of the main character, Susan, into madness. Her real family, boring clergyman Gerald, introvert son Rick, and interfering sister-in-law Muriel, are increasingly replaced by a fantasy family, lively husband Andy, flamboyant brother Toby, and charming daughter Lucy. Susan can conjure them up initially at will, but in the end they take over.
- The cashier in Georg Kaiser's *Von Morgens bis Mitternachts* (*From Morn to Midnight*) is a creature stuck in boring daily routine, until, that is, an elegant lady comes to the bank to cash a cheque for a large sum. The manager refuses to give her the money. The cashier steals a large amount of money from the bank, to start a new life with the elegant lady. She is not, however, a criminal, as he had assumed, and rejects him. The cashier flees into the woods, where he expresses an extraordinary state of consciousness in a long monologue.
- Thornton Wilder's play *Our Town* shows some of the characters after death, and Emily returning to relive a special day in her life.

ASC include higher states of consciousness as proposed by Vedic Science. Instances of higher states of consciousness in drama often create a very impressive and moving impact on the audience and possibly also for the actor relating such experiences. A few further examples should serve to illustrate this. In *The Dresser*, Harwood manages to give us a moving impression of a great artist, who rises to a climactic, epiphanic experience during the performance of *King Lear* which forms the frame of the play, and which will be his last performance (he dies at the end of the play):

> Speaking 'Reason not the need', I was suddenly detached from myself. My thoughts flew. And I was observing from a great height. Go on, you bastard, I seemed to be saying or hearing. Go on, you've more to give, don't hold back, more, more, more. And I was watching Lear. Each word he spoke was fresh invented. I had no knowledge of what came next, what fate awaited him. The agony was in the moment of acting created. I saw an old man, and the old man was me. And I knew there was more to come. But what? Bliss, partial recovery, more pain and death. All this I knew I had yet to see. Outside myself, do you understand? Outside myself. (Harwood, 1980: 70).

According to Vedic Science, in cosmic consciousness, the level of pure consciousness, which is never overshadowed in daily experience by the activities and experiences of the individual psyche, becomes a 'stable internal frame of reference from which changing phases of sleep, dreaming, and waking life are silently *witnessed* or observed' (Alexander and Boyer, 1989: 342). This fictional account of *witnessing* activity, characteristic of cosmic consciousness, has its parallels in real-life experiences. The actor Ray Reinhardt reports:

> There are two stages of having the audience in your hand. The first one is the one in which you bring them along, you make them laugh through sheer skill-they laughed at that, now watch me top it with this one. But, there's a step beyond that which I experienced, but only two or three times. It is the most-how can you use words like satisfying? It's more ultimate than ultimate: I seemed to be part of a presence that stood behind myself and was able to observe, not with my eyes, but with my total being, myself and the audience. It was a wonderful thing of leaving not only the character, but also this person who calls himself Ray Reinhardt. In a way, I was no longer acting actively, although things were happening: my arms moved independently, there was no effort required; my body was loose and very light. It was the closest I've ever come in a waking state to a mystical experience (Richards, 1977: 43).

An equally striking example of a desirable ASC experienced by a character in drama occurs in Athol Fugard's *The Road to Mecca*. The main character of this play, Miss Helen, is an elderly lady who has started creating strange sculptures in her garden not long after her husband's death. Inside her house she has created a highly exotic combination of mirrors, candles, and blue and golden walls to allow a remarkable display of light when the sun shines, or when the candles are lit. In the course of the play it turns out that all this creativity had been inspired by an ASC experience on the evening of her husband's funeral. She had been alone in her room, staring at a candle, when suddenly the vision had started. Miss Helen recounts her experience in the play to the play's two other characters, Elsa, a young teacher, and the village priest Marius:

> [*She looks around the room and speaks with authority*]
>
> Light the candles, Elsa. That one first.
>
> [*She indicates a candelabra that has been set up very prominently on a little table. ELSA lights it.*]
>
> And you know why, Marius? That is the East. Go out there into the yard and you'll see that all my Wise Men and their camels are travelling in that direction. Follow the candle on and one day you'll come to Mecca. Oh yes, Marius, it's true! I've done it. That is where I went that night and it was the candle you lit that led me there.
>
> [*She is radiantly alive with her vision*]
>
> A city, Marius! A city of light and colour more splendid than anything I had ever imagined. There were palaces and beautiful buildings everywhere, with dazzling white walls and glittering minarets. Strange statues filled the courtyards. The streets were crowded with camels and turbaned men speaking a language I didn't understand, but that didn't matter because I knew, it was Mecca. And I was on my

way to the grand temple. In the centre of Mecca there is a temple, and in the centre of the temple is a vast room with hundreds of mirrors on the walls and hanging lamps. And that is where the Wise Men of the East study the celestial geometry of light and colour. I became an apprentice that night. Light them all, Elsa, so that I can show Marius what I've learned.

[*ELSA moves around the room lighting the candles, and as she does so its full magic and splendour is revealed.* (1985: 71-72)

Although the concept of *peak experience* (Maslow, 1962) allows the comparison of experiences of desirable ASC, and allows classification of specific experiences as *peak experiences*, it does not have explanatory value to account for the existence of such experiences. In terms of Vedic Science's model of consciousness, Miss Helen's vision in Fugard's play could be described as a temporary experience of refined cosmic consciousness. Just as Raine's vision (see pages 27-28), Miss Helen's happens unexpectedly. Raine emphasises the non-emotional nature of the experience, and also Miss Helen's account of her experience comes across as genuine, devoid of sentimentality or mood-making. Miss Helen's experience in Fugard's *The Road to Mecca* shares many other characteristics of peak experiences: Miss Helen was inspired to artistic creativity by her vision. The experience began unexpectedly. Both the experience itself, and even her report of it several years later are full of joy and liveliness. The experience is mainly visual. After her husband's death, the experience gave her self-justification and affirmation; now, in the dramatised scene of the play the vivid recollection of the experience serves the same purpose: cornered by the village priest Marius to sign the documents needed to put her into an old people's home, the recollection gives her strength to refuse her signature. She also becomes able to accept that she is too old to manage on her own altogether, and will accept more help in the future.

This brings us to the end of the discussion of the first major heading in this chapter: states of consciousness as expressed or described in drama. My discussion of sleep, dream, waking remained within conventional terms of reference, whereas I conducted my analysis of altered, especially higher, states of consciousness in drama in terms of the model of consciousness proposed by Vedic Science.

Development of Consciousness

Two examples from Shakespeare serve to illustrate the second fundamental mode of consciousness reflected in drama: development of consciousness. First, I refer to *The Tempest*, arguing that Prospero's development of consciousness is closely related to his use of magic, and, most important in that context, the fact that he abandons magic at the end of the play. The second example relates to the title character in *Hamlet*. Here, I argue that Hamlet's procrastination is closely related to development of consciousness: Hamlet is able to commit the act of revenge only once he has achieved equanimity, in obedience to the Ghost's command, 'taint not thy mind' (I.v.85).

Prospero's enlightenment

Prospero performs magic, has power over spirits, has a magic garment, a book of spells, and a staff (or magic wand). At the end of the play he abjures what he himself calls *rough magic*, asking for the audience's approval and applause with 'what strength's mine own'. Since Prospero uses the term *magic* himself, it is no wonder that critics to date have discussed Prospero's *magic*, often within the historical contexts of what was known of magic in Shakespeare's time. Within that context, views differ as to whether Prospero's magic was white or black, or a strange mixture of both. Prospero's abjuration of his art has been regarded as either due to the fact that the project, for which he learnt his art of magic, is complete, or a realization that his powers are limited and at an end. Dongchoon Lee provides a useful survey of the literature in 'Prospero's Magic Power and Its Limitations in *The Tempest*'. The material in Michael Srigley's *Images of Regeneration* (1985) would provide a very useful matrix against which my own arguments could be developed further. I do not wish to take up the historical dimension of the debate surrounding Prospero's magic. Instead, I want to offer a different perspective: that of regarding what has been described as Prospero's magic as his supernatural abilities, and to relate Prospero's supernatural abilities to the supernatural abilities described in the *Yoga Sutras* of Patanjali. I do not claim that Shakespeare knew the Vedic text dating from around 350-250 BCE (Karambelkar xii). Rather, I suggest that the comparison I want to develop provides a striking example of a literary universal, as defined by Hogan:

> For any given domain (e.g., narrative), universals are features (properties, relations, structures) of works in that domain that recur across genetically and areally unrelated traditions with greater frequency than would be predicted by chance (2003)

The model of consciousness proposed by Vedic Science provides the conceptual framework for the *Yoga Sutras*. The third chapter of Patanjali's *Yoga Sutras* describes that by setting specific intentional impulses at the level of pure consciousness, so-called supernatural abilities are developed, also referred to as *siddhi*. It is important to note that within the context of the *Yoga Sutras*, the *siddhis* are within the potential range of every human being: all it takes is the practice of a few meditative techniques. They appear supernatural only if the mindset at a given time and in a given culture regards them as such. In our days, the *siddhis* are not within the range of everyday experience, and we thus regard them as supernatural. The *siddhis* listed in the *Yoga Sutras* include the following, (adapted from Karambelkar, 1986)

Sutra	Siddhi
16	Knowledge of past and future
17	Comprehension of the languages of all creatures
18	Knowledge of previous lives
19	Knowledge of others' minds
21	Invisibility
24	Great physical strength
25	Knowledge of hidden or far-distant things
27	Knowledge of stellar constellations
28	Knowledge of the stars and their movements
29	Knowledge of the systems of the body
30	Disappearance of hunger and thirst
32	Ability to perceive siddhas (higher-order beings)
33	Omniscience
36	Heightened sensory perception
38	Entering someone else's body
42	Moving through space – flying
44	Mastery over the elements
48	Ability to physically move at the speed of the mind

Prospero has devoted much time to his study of 'liberal arts', and has withdrawn from worldly pursuits in the course, foremost among them the ruling of his Dukedom. He has become an ascetic, devoted to spiritual practice, for the bettering of his mind, which include practises leading to supernatural abilities, to which he refers as magic. His knowledge, symbolised by his books, is of more worth to him than his Dukedom. Is this a sign of naivety? Does Prospero immorally abandon his duty? Or is letting go of worldly attachment an aspect, a phase, or a stage of Prospero's life journey towards enlightenment (in the sense of *moksha*, liberation, the highest state of consciousness)?

Prospero's state as an ascetic, a seeker of truth, has not much changed on the island he now lives, with only Miranda as a fellow human, half-human Caliban, and the section of the spirit world he as access to (and which he commands), Ariel and some minor spirits. Prospero commands the elements (Sutra 44), he causes the storm, and it is carried out precisely as he wants it, so that, despite appearances and likelihood, all involved survive without any damage at all. He uses Ariel as the tool of much (though not all) of his 'magic'; his ability to communicate with Ariel suggests his ability to 'comprehend the language of all creatures (Sutra 17), a view confirmed by his further ability to communicate with, and even teach human language, to half-human Caliban.

Prospero knows what goes on in other characters' minds (Sutra 19): he realises Gonzalo's nobility and goodness, the evil nature of his brother and Sebastian, Miranda's innocence, her genuine love for Ferdinand as well as Ferdinand's love for Miranda. This knowledge is touching in the case of Gonzalo, moving and heartening in the cases of Miranda and Ferdinand, and quite a challenge in the cases of Antonio and Sebastian, because Prospero's anger at his brother's past behaviour towards him threatens his equanimity, mercy, and thus further progress towards enlightenment. Prospero's ability to know what goes on in other characters' minds also allows a new reading of his words to Miranda:

Here cease more questions:

Thou art inclined to sleep; 'tis a good dullness

And give it way: I know thou can'st not choose

And later: 'Awake, dear heart, awake! Thou hast slept well; Awake'

Either Prospero causes Miranda to fall asleep, because he wants to talk to Ariel without her noticing it, or he 'merely' knows that she is about to sleep, and later, that she has slept well, and 'merely' expresses his knowledge of her state of mind. A similar influence on another character's behaviour is also evident when Prospero prevents Ferdinand from attacking him (Sutra 44: mastery over the elements). When a little later on in that scene Prospero says to Ferdinand,

Come on; obey:

Thy nerves are in their infancy again

And have no vigour in them

and Ferdinand confirms: 'So they are...', it is again possible that Prospero exerts his influence over Ferdinand, or that he observes Ferdinand's state of mind, which Ferdinand had not been aware of himself.

Ariel suggests that Prospero's art includes the knowledge of past and future (Sutra 16)

My master through his art foresees the danger

That thou, his friend, are in...

Prospero watches the encounter of Alonso and his party with the banquet he conjures up for them, and the other characters on stage do not see him. One plausible explanation may be that he is hiding behind some object on stage, invisible to the other characters but visible to the audience. However, the effect on the spectators would certainly be more impressive if the blocking made clear that Prospero is invisible to the other characters on stage through his art. (Sutra 21, invisibility)

Prospero calls spirits 'from their confines' to put on a pageant before Miranda and Ferdinand. It comes to an abrupt halt when Prospero remembers Caliban's

LIBRARY, UNIVERSITY COLLEGE CHESTER

conspiracy against him, aided by the two clowns from Alonso's party. The ephemeral nature of the spirits, over whom Prospero has control, reminds him of death. Knowledge of death is described as a *siddhi* in Sutra 22. That Prospero has not yet achieved full enlightenment (*moksha,* liberation) is evident from his anger at the planned assault. Anger itself need not be a sign of lacking development: it may be an appropriate reaction, in the sense of righteous anger in one enlightened, but in one on the path towards enlightenment, anger is a sign of continuing weakness. Hence, Prospero admits to Ferdinand that he is vexed, and asks him to forgive this sign of weakness.

Repeatedly, precision of timing is important for Prospero's plans. That precision of timing is related to the stars.

> and by my prescience

> I find my zenith doth depend upon

> A mostx auspicious star, whose influence

> If now I court not but omit, my fortunes

> Will ever after droop.

The ability of knowing about the stars, their constellation and their influence on humans, contained in the Vedic system of Jyotish (Vedic astrology), is covered by Sutras 27 and 28.

The attainment of *siddhis* is a phase, and at the same time a tool, in attainment of the highest goal, *moksha*. Both functions, as tool and as phase, are limited in time. Thus the *Yoga Sutras* clearly state that only once the powers of the *siddhis* have been renunciated, abandoned, will even the seed of defects be eliminated, and thus enlightenment will be gained. At the end of *The Tempest*, Prospero abjures what he comes to regard as rough magic, in an achievement of virtue. Prospero does not master all the *siddhis* listed in the *Yoga Sutras*. We may thus conclude that he has not reached *moksha* at the end of *The Tempest*, a view that would support interpretations of the play's end as gloomy and dark. We may also decide to assume that the *siddhis* that Prospero *does* attain stand for all *siddhis*, and that he thus *does* gain *moksha* at the end of the play, through the very act of abandoning them. The decision of how to interpret this aspect of the play will of course have a strong impact on directing choices in any theatre production. The *moksha* version, for example, might show Prospero in a different kind of permanent light effect from the abjuring speech onwards, a light effect used markedly, so as to be noted by the spectators, but briefly, in each instance of a *siddhi* being referred to or shown on stage.

Hamlet's Procrastination

In the preceding section I demonstrated how Prospero's development of consciousness is closely related to his use of magic, and, most important in that context, the fact that he abandons magic at the end of the play. I presented my argument in terms of the model of consciousness proposed by Vedic Science, and under recourse to the *Yoga Sutras* of Patanjali. In this section I provide the second example of the *development* of a character's *consciousness* in drama: *Hamlet*. Again, my terms of reference are the model of consciousness proposed by Vedic Science, and another aspect of Vedic literature, the *Bhagavad-Gita*.

Hamlet's procrastination has fascinated literary critics of all ages. In more recent times, Lawlor wrote:

> Hamlet delays his revenge on Claudius because of an aversion from the deed of vengeance, an aversion whose true nature remains hidden from him, but is apprehended by the Elizabethan audience as the deep-seated scruple about the justice of revenge (1950: 110)

Phillips, on the other hand, found it more convincing to believe that Hamlet procrastinates only on a gross, physical level: 'The delay is suspense, and suspense is the most subtle form of revenge to which, consciously or unconsciously, Hamlet could subject the King' (1980: 48). Wagenknecht gives four reasons for Hamlet's procrastination: an earlier death of Claudius would mean the end of the play; Hamlet has to take revenge without 'tainting his mind'; Hamlet is fully aware of the size of his task; Hamlet cares about his reputation (1949: 188-95).

I propose that a parallel between *Hamlet* and the *Bhagavad-Gita* can further elucidate the reason for Hamlet's procrastination. The *Bhagavad-Gita* is the major part of the *Mahabharata*, one of the two great epics of Indian literature (the other one is the *Ramayana*). The *Bhagavad-Gita* is set on a battlefield. Two armies are about to fight each other, one representing good, the other one evil. The two opposing groups are led by different members of the same family. The hero of the *Bhagavad-Gita* is called Arjuna, he fights on the side of the good.

At the beginning of both the *Bhagavad-Gita* and *Hamlet*, we find a state of disorder, a battlefield and murder, usurpation and incest, respectively. In both works of literature it is the task of the heroes, Arjuna and Hamlet, to restore cosmic order. Arjuna is aware of this, and so is Hamlet:

> The time is out of joint. O cursed spite

> That ever I was born to set it right. (I.v.196-7)

At the beginning of the *Bhagavad-Gita*, Arjuna raises his bow. In his commentary on the first six chapters of the *Bhagavad-Gita*, Maharishi Mahesh Yogi explains this as a sign that Arjuna is ready for action (1969: 41). When Hamlet is told by the Ghost of his father that someone has killed his father, he reacts thus:

Haste me to know't, that I, with wings as swift

As meditation or the thought of love

May sweep to my revenge. (I. v. 29-31)

This passage shows that Hamlet, too, is ready to act. It also indicates Hamlet's most recent preoccupations: 'meditation' alludes to his studies at Wittenberg, and 'thoughts of love' points at Hamlet's love for Ophelia. After the Ghost has left, Hamlet again shows his readiness to act in his swearing revenge:

[...] Remember thee?

Alas, poor Ghost, whiles memory holds a seat

In this distracted globe. Remember thee?

Yea, from the table of my memory

I'll wipe away all trivial fond records,

All saws of books, all forms, all pressures past

That youth and observation copied there.

And thy commandment all alone shall live

Within the book and volume of my brain,

Unmixed with baser matter. Yes, by heaven! (I. v. 95-104)

Despite this initial readiness to act, both heroes do not immediately carry out what their duty would be-they hesitate. Arjuna shows anger at the evil army. Maharishi Mahesh Yogi comments:

Lord Krishna had seen that Arjuna was outraged, Anger is a great enemy; it reduces one's strength. (...) Lord Krishna is required to do something to restore Arjuna to his normal stature. But this alone will not suffice, something more is necessary to make Arjuna strong. Anger in him indicated that he is not really strong, for anger is a sign for weakness. (1969: 46-7)

Hamlet shows anger and hatred towards Claudius throughout the play, even before knowing about the murder. The scene in Gertrude's room (III. iv) provides a very striking example of this. Polonius has hidden behind an arras to eavesdrop on Hamlet's conversation with his mother. Early on in the scene Hamlet hears Polonius and cries: 'How now? A rat? Dead for a ducat, dead!' (III. iv. 22) It becomes obvious a few lines later that Hamlet had been addressing the King: To

Gertrude's question 'O me, what hast thou done?' (III. iv. 25) Hamlet answers: 'Nay I know not. Is it the King?' (III. iv. 25-6). Hamlet knows that his major fault is to be passion's slave (Cf. III. ii. 72). This is his 'stamp of one defect' (I. iv. 31) that overshadows his entire character.

Chaos is at the beginning of both the *Bhagavad-Gita* and *Hamlet*, there are two heroes whose task it is to restore cosmic order, both heroes are ready to act, yet in both cases anger, showing weakness, prevents them from action. Lord Krishna is Arjuna's spiritual leader. To overcome Arjuna's anger, Lord Krishna asks him:

> Partha (Arjuna)! Behold these
>
> Kuru gathered together. (Maharishi Mahesh Yogi, 1969: 46)

'Partha' reminds Arjuna of his mother, thus creating a wave of love in his heart. Maharishi Mahesh Yogi comments:

> Having created this wave of love in Arjuna's heart, Lord Krishna desires to strengthen it; and for this he says: 'Behold these Kuru gathered together.' This quickens all the ways of the heart, where different relationships are held in different degrees of love. Seeing all his dear ones 'together' in one glance, his whole heart swells with love. (1969: 47)

Intellectually, Arjuna knows that some of his relatives fight in the good army, and some fight in the evil one. This creates within him a conflict between heart (love for all his relatives) and intellect (realization that he will have to kill some of his relatives). This becomes evident in the first twenty-two verses of the first chapter of the *Bhagavad-Gita*.

Arjuna's heart and mind, thus established on a high level of alertness, gain a state of such self-sufficiency that communication between them is almost lost, and with it is lost the spur to acting (...). This situation, where consciousness is in a state of suspension, where both the heart and the mind are on the highest level of alertness, provides the ideal occasion for the divine intelligence to overtake and shape the destiny of man (1969: 26-7)

This is how Lord Krishna sets the hero of the *Bhagavad-Gita* on the path of development of consciousness to overcome his weakness. I propose that parallel to Lord Krishna in the *Bhagavad-Gita*, in *Hamlet* it is the Ghost who serves as Hamlet's spiritual leader. In order to be able to go into detail, the nature of the Ghost will have to be established first. Is it an evil being or a good one? Back in 1963, Warhaft wrote that nobody could seriously doubt the identity or veracity of the Ghost (200). Elinor Prosser's Hamlet and Revenge brought new life to the discussion (1967). In the Ghost's passages we find a pattern of three that is repeated six times altogether:

List, list, O, list (I. v. 22)

But this most foul, strange and unnatural. (I.v.28)

Of life, of crown, of queen at once dispatched (I.v.75)

Unhouseled, disappointed, unaneled. (I. v. 77)

O horrible! O horrible! Most horrible! (I. v. 80)

Adieu, adieu, adieu. Remember me. (I. v. 91)

Number symbolism describes the number three as follows:

> Number three represents complete harmony and balance. It also means divine Trinity and the three aspects of God, creative, maintaining and destructive. All creative forces have three aspects: The three dimensions of space; three aspects of time: past, present and future; the three aspects of life on earth, birth, life and death; and the three worlds, heaven, earth and hell. (Haich, 1971: 45)

Thus not only the allusion to the Holy Trinity points to the idea of the Ghost as a representative of the divine, but also the other aspects mentioned in the description: To those who can see him, the Ghost appears in the dimension of space. The three aspects of time can be found in the dramatized present, in which the Ghost talks about the past (his murder) and about the future (revenge). He was born as a human being, lived and died, thus representing the three aspects of life on earth. Finally, in addition to his life on earth, he will go to heaven after he has spent his time in purgatory (hell).

If we thus accept the Ghost as a representative of the divine, how does he go about changing Hamlet? The important line is 'Taint not thy mind' (I. v. 85). In this, the Ghost does not allude to Gertrude, but to Hamlet's 'stamp of one defect', his temper. Hamlet is not to carry out revenge in a state of frenzy, of 'tainted mind', but in a state of balance, which Hamlet himself appreciates as ideal in Horatio (Cf. III.ii.63-4). It is this command of the Ghost that creates in Hamlet a similar state of alertness of heart and intellect as Lord Krishna had created in Arjuna's mind. Hamlet is still unbalanced and cannot act until he has reached a state of evenness.

Lord Krishna accompanies Arjuna on his entire way to that state of balance where Arjuna can finally act. Guided throughout, Arjuna moves on a direct path to his goal. Hamlet, however, meets the Ghost only twice in the play. Moreover, Lord Krishna is regarded as an incarnation of the divine, the Ghost is 'only' a representative of God. Therefore, Hamlet's path is not free from mistakes, even if it leads to a similar goal in the end. As described elsewhere (Meyer-Dinkgräfe, 1986: 77-82), Hamlet is faced with a crucial decision twice. He has to choose between the difficult task of the Ghost and Claudius' offer of an easy life at court. Hamlet makes the right choice in following the Ghost. Hamlet's second choice is the mode of revenge. Here his initial decision to follow the Senecan tradition of the revenger who takes to ranting in order to get into the mood for revenge turns out to be wrong. It is opposed to the Ghost's command 'Taint not thy mind'. The result is inner chaos, as best demonstrated by Hamlet's 'To be or not to be' soliloquy (Cf. III.1. 59-89). Hamlet has the intellectual insight that ranting as well as the entire traditional role of the revenger are not going to get him anywhere (Cf. II.ii. 578-583). But, as the events in Gertrude's room show, intellectual insight is not enough. Change has to take place on a more subtle level than the intellect.

It should be kept in mind that for Arjuna, similar distractions from the direct path to a state of balance are not necessary because he is in constant contact with his spiritual leader, Lord Krishna. Hamlet has to make mistakes in order to learn.

Hamlet's change in Act V has been widely discussed in Hamlet-scholarship. One can generalize the opinions: most authors tend to agree that Hamlet does indeed change between Acts IV and V, and most of these regard it as a change for the good, in that Hamlet becomes able to accept divine providence as a guiding principle of life[1]. However, they claim that this change is not foreshadowed anywhere in the play before Act V. I suggest that a specific principle of characterization, which Shakespeare employs throughout the play to characterize Hamlet, does indeed provide a hint at Hamlet's change in Act V. In abstract terms, the principle is the following: At a given point in time (A), Hamlet has a certain thought. He seems to drop that thought, but at point in time (B) he takes up that thought again, sometimes modified. Two examples should substantiate this suggestion:

> At point in time (A), Hamlet thinks about suicide for the first time in the play:' Or that the Everlasting had not fixed / His canon 'gainst self-slaughter' (I.ii.131-2). In his 'To be or not to be' soliloquy, Hamlet comes back to the question of suicide. At this point in time (B), however, his thoughts about the same subject are modified. He rules out suicide as a way of action for himself because of the fears of 'The undiscovered country, from whose bourn / No traveller returns (...)' (III.i.79-80)

At the end of his first soliloquy, Hamlet says: 'But break my heart, for I must hold my tongue.' (I.ii.159) In many stage productions of Hamlet, Horatio and Marcellus appear a second before this line so that it works as Hamlet's reaction to seeing the two men. I suggest a different interpretation: Hamlet has a strong foreboding about his father's death, but he does not dare to think further about it, even less to speak it out aloud. Therefore, at point in time (A), he must be silent. However, in Act one scene five the Ghost tells him: 'The serpent that did sting thy father's life / Now wears his crown.' (I.v.39-40), and at this point in time, (B), the foreboding has been confirmed, as shown by Hamlet's exclamation: 'O my prophetic soul! / My uncle' (I.v.41).

This same principle of characterization can be found as an indication of Hamlet's change in Act V. Following the shock Hamlet gets on accidentally murdering Polonius, a shock even more increased by the second appearance of the Ghost, Hamlet comments:

(...) For this same lord,

I do repent; but heaven hath pleased it so,

To punish me with this and this with me,

That I must be their scourge and minister. (III.iv.174- 177)

The terms 'scourge' and 'minister' are very important for a thorough interpretation of this passage. According to Bowers, a minister is God's servant, he can carry out even an act of blood revenge without accumulating guilt. A scourge, on the other hand, is already doomed (1955). In the passage quoted above, Hamlet for the first time in the play talks about divine providence and its influence on him: 'Heaven hath pleased it so'. At the same time, he realizes that his position in the world is to be God's minister, and that by killing Polonius in a rash way, his mind most certainly 'tainted', he has become a scourge. Hamlet knows that he will have to pay for this death: 'I will bestow him and will answer well / The death I gave him. '(III.iv.178-9).

Soon after this, Hamlet seems to be giving up thoughts of divine providence: 'My thoughts be bloody, or be nothing worth. '(IV.iv.66). Yet at point in time (B), throughout Act V, and especially when confronted with the foreboding of death, it is obvious that Hamlet has now accepted divine providence as the guiding principle of (his) life.

In the end, Hamlet kills Claudius and is himself killed by Laertes. Thus he restores cosmic order as God's minister. With his own death he atones for the deaths he had caused as God's scourge. In the *Bhagavad-Gita*, Arjuna reaches a state of balance, as Hamlet does in Shakespeare's play. As Arjuna was guided by Lord Krishna throughout his spiritual development, however, he does not have to make mistakes, and thus he does not have to die in the end.

Summary

In this chapter, I outlined the ways in which consciousness is represented in drama, either as a state, or in terms of character development. I differentiated the distinct states of sleep, dream and waking and their representation in drama in conventional terms, and applied the model of consciousness proposed by Vedic Science in my discussion of altered, in particular higher states of consciousness represented in drama. The Vedic Science model of consciousness also provided the basis for my interpretation of character development (Prospero in Shakespeare's *The Tempest*, and the title character in Shakespeare's *Hamlet*). In addition, in those sections I took recourse to two further aspects of Vedic literature: Patanjali's *Yoga Sutras*, and the *Bhagavad-Gita*, respectively. I drew attention to the finding that drama covers the representation of the entire possible range of consciousness, its states and its development, and claimed that recourse to Vedic Science and Vedic literature helps us to make better sense of that range. I shall come back to this finding when I address the question of how drama and theatre may affect the consciousness of reader/spectator and the production team, in chapter five on *reception and audiences*.

Notes

1. S. F. Johnson published a survey of articles on that question: 'The Regeneration of Hamlet', Shakespeare Quarterly 3 (1952), 190-6. After that, see Elias Schwartz, 'The possibilities of a Christian Tragedy', College English 21 (1960), pp 208-13; Fredson Bowers, 'Hamlet's Fifth Soliloquy, III. 2. 406-417', in: Essays on Shakespeare and Elizabethan Drama', ed. Richard Hosley (Columbia, 1962), 213-22; Peter Ure, 'Character and Rhole from Richard III to Hamlet', Stratford-upon-Avon Studies 5(1964), 9-28; Fredson Bowers, 'Dramatic Structure and Criticism: Plot in Hamlet', Shakespeare Quarterly 15 (1964), 207-218; Myren Taylor, 'Tragic Justice and the House of Polonius', Studies in English Literature 8 (1968), 273-81; Harold Skulsky, 'Revenge, Honour and Conscience in Hamlet', PMLA 85 (1970), 78-87; Geoffrey Hughes, 'The tragedy of a revenger's loss of conscience: a study of Hamlet', English Studies 57 (1976), 395-409; Alan Sinfield, 'Hamlet's special Providence', Shakespeare Survey 33 (1980), 89-97. John W. Mahon, 'Providential Visitations in Hamlet', Hamlet Studies 8 (1986), 40-51; Daniel Meyer-Dinkgräfe, 'Hamlet at the Crossroads', Hamlet Studies 8 (1986), 77-82.

3: Consciousness and Acting

Whenever we go to see a 'show' at a conventional theatre or any other performance venue, what we see in the first place are actors or performers on some shape of stage. Numerous other people are involved in the production: the playwright, perhaps a dramaturg, a director, designers, administrators, front-of-house staff and many more. However, the audience does not see them directly. What we see, and hear, are the actors. It is, therefore, not surprising that the bulk of writing in the context of theatre is about acting, and it is here that we are likely to find much material by way of relating theatre to consciousness. I begin this chapter with an analysis of the seminal question whether the actor should be emotionally involved with the emotions their characters are supposed to be feeling (Meyer-Dinkgräfe, 1996). I proceed to discuss the concept of the actor's *presence*, central to Barba's theatre anthropology, and the related concepts of *state* in Ariane Mnouchkine's theatre work and Grotowski's concept of *translumination*. In relation to those concepts I reassess Artaud's notions of *physical presence and neutrality*. I conclude the chapter with a comparison of some of the characteristics of the marionette with that of the human performer, with particular reference to Heinrich von Kleist's *Über das Marionettentheater* (1810).

The Actor's Emotional Involvement

Among the issues discussed in theories of the theatre in relation to the actor, the extent of the actor's emotional involvement in the emotions of the character he is playing has gained a prominent position, even before Diderot (1713-1784) formulated his famous paradox of acting in 1773. The Spanish theorist Alonso Lopez Pinciano (fl. 1597-1627) argued that although the actor

> must transform himself into the character he is imitating so that it appears to every-
> one else as no imitation, (...) it seems more likely that the best actor would concen-
> trate on technique and move to tears without weeping himself. (Carlson, 1984:
> 59-61)

Jusepe Antonio Gonzalez de Salas, in a text published in 1663, on the other hand, held that the actor 'must truly experience the passions of the play as interior feeling rather than guileful appearance' (Carlson, 1984: 65-66). Pinciano, then, champions technique, Salas emotional involvement. This dichotomy of technique versus emotional involvement is taken up by the subsequent major theorists of the theatre up to Diderot: Luigi Riccoboni (1676-1753, involvement); Antonio Francesco Riccoboni (1707-72, technique); St. Albine (1699-1778, involvement) (Carlson, 1984: 159). Following Diderot's *Paradox of Acting*-which consists in the claim that the actor should stimulate the spectator's emotions without being emotionally involved himself-the issue of the actor's emotional involvement has gained further momentum with growing interest in psychology in general since the last half of the nineteenth century. The key figure in this development is Stanislavsky, who in turn directly influenced Meyerhold, Strasberg and Brecht.

Diderot

One of the earlier major Western theorists to tackle the question of the actor's emotional involvement in acting is Diderot. He differentiates between two types of actors. The one plays from the heart, from 'sensibility', immersing himself, while acting, in the feelings of the character he plays. According to Diderot, this way of acting yields poor results: 'their playing is alternately strong and feeble, fury and cold, dull and sublime (...)' (1955: 15). Moreover, the actor loses his self-control and the acting varies from performance to performance because it depends on the actor's daily ups and downs. The actor is unable to pull together his 'individual actions into a coherent whole' (Gossman & MacArthur, 1984: 113-4). Such acting will have much less effect on the spectators than acting based on the actor's self-control.

Rather than playing from the heart, rather than feeling the emotions of the character while acting the part, the actor 'must have in himself an unmoved and disinterested onlooker. He must have, consequently, penetration and no sensibility' (Diderot, 1955: 14). Such an actor, Diderot's ideal, is guided by the intellect. He will have a highly developed ability to observe nature, to imitate it, and to accurately repeat a pattern of acting that has developed during the rehearsal period. He is thus able to create a coherent and unified role. He does not feel while acting, but makes his impression on the audience by 'rendering so exactly the outward signs of feeling' (19). Diderot describes the English actor David Garrick as an example for such acting:

> Garrick will put his head between two folding doors, and in the course of five or six seconds his expression will change successively from wild delight to temperate pleasure, from this to tranquillity, from tranquillity to surprise, from surprise to bland astonishment, from that to sorrow, from sorrow to the air of one over-whelmed, from that to fright, from fright to horror, from horror to despair, and thence he will go up again to the point from which he started. Can the soul have experienced all these feelings and played this kind of scale in concert with his face? (32-33)

The paradox is that emotions in the spectators are stimulated by an unemotional imitation of emotions by the actor.

Diderot's paradox is rooted in the history of theatre, science, and philosophy of his time. According to Grear, seventeenth-century France saw a 'revival of interest in *pronunciatio*', the 'theory of oratorial delivery' (1985: 225). Diderot's central concern, 'the extent to which an actor should identify (...) with the emotions of the character he portrays' (225), is also the major issue discussed in the *pronunciatio* part of classical rhetorics. Grear refers to Cicero and Quintilian: Cicero advised the orator to use the rules of the art to portray those emotions he wanted to create in the spectators (226). Quintilian also emphasised the rules of the art, but added to the 'rationally prepared pathos (...) an element of imaginative identification (...)' (226). The mechanism was this:

> The same devices of style and delivery worked out by the orator to move his audience would, during the performance itself, work upon the orator himself, enabling him to imagine the scene and further assist his ability to portray passions realistically. (226)

Grear shows that French seventeenth-century theatre theory initially followed Quintilian as just summarised. However, from 1670 onwards, this 'formalist' position was challenged, as part of 'a larger movement against hypocrisy and insincerity' (226-7). The emphasis shifted from rational principles of acting to an emotional approach (229). It is against the latter that Diderot's *Paradox* argues.

To evaluate the implications of Diderot's theory, its central term, 'sensibility', has to be understood within the context of the theories of psychology and physiology that influenced Diderot. Roach takes up this key term, pointing out that in Diderot's time the word 'sensibility'

> resonated through complex layers of meaning in science, literature, and moral philosophy, ascending from the most rudimentary responsiveness of nervous fibres to the highest expressions of humane sympathy and imagination. (1981: 52)

In his discussion of the physiological background of the *Paradox*, Roach refers to Diderot's own work in the fields of psychology and physiology (52). Diderot is influenced by the empiricist philosophers Locke and Hume, in putting forward 'a theory of mind which based everything on discrete sensations provided by the senses' (Hamlyn, 1990: 211). In this context, Diderot regards the body as a 'virtually soulless machine' which has 'biological drives but not will' (Roach, 1981: 58). The functioning of the human machine depends on the control of the mind over the nerves. When the mind is in control of the nerve activities, the machine functions properly. When the nerves dominate, the functioning of the machine is disturbed: 'Rationality and self-possession inevitably yield before the inexorable pressure of strong feelings' (54). The feelings, in turn, have specific corresponding involuntary effects on the physiology. For example, the feeling of fury 'inflames the eyes, clenches the fists and the teeth, furrows the brows' (54). Diderot believed most feelings to be directly related to what he regarded as the physical centre-the diaphragm. Just as the brain 'propels the mechanism of thought' (55), the diaphragm propels the mechanism of feeling. Negative emotions lead to a contraction of the diaphragm, positive, such as happiness, to an expansion. As any feeling has an involuntary effect on the body in general, also the specific reaction of the diaphragm is involuntary and cannot be intentionally suppressed (55). Once the diaphragm starts reacting, i.e. once feelings dominate, the mental faculties such as reason and judgment are rendered ineffective.

In this context, the term 'imagination' is to be separated from the term 'sensibility' as discussed above. In the rehearsal process, not during the actual performance, imagination has an important function for the actor. In creating the pattern for a role that is to be repeated performance after performance without emotional involvement, the actor draws on two important functions: memory and imagination. 'Memory retains the image, imagination revives it, vivifies it, and combines it with other images to form the living mosaic of the inner model' (57). Roach explains that this theory again is grounded in Diderot's understanding of physiology: if patterns enlivened in the memory of the actor are increased in their intensity by the actor's imagination, the revived sensations 'can duplicate actual experiences' (Diderot, 1955: 61). Thus, during the rehearsal period the actor can feel and physically experience the emotions of the character he is playing, observe those, and develop the pattern of the automatised performance on that basis. This process is intellectually controlled and leads to performance equally controlled by the intellect. By contrast, acting from the heart, dominated by emotions, by the diaphragm, is never controlled, because the cause-effect chains of feeling and physiological reaction are involuntary.

Diderot's basic assumption about the relationship of mind and body, their functioning as one entity in the process of combining memory and imagination, leads to an apparent contradiction:

> If the actor's mind and body constitute a single entity, then how can his mind coldly direct his body through sequences of passions without mentally experiencing the same emotions? (62)

According to Roach, Diderot followed the notion common in his time that mind/body can simultaneously be engaged in two separate activities because 'its components resemble those of a stringed instrument' (Diderot, 1955: 26). The more the actor's discriminating qualities of the mind are developed, the more will he be able consciously to detach himself from the emotions of the character, the closer will he reach towards Diderot's ideal. Such a level of acting presupposes, according to Diderot, a nature-given talent and a long process of learning and experience (53).

Diderot's theory of the emotional stimulation of the spectators through an emotionally uninvolved actor is paradoxical on the level of an ordinary waking state of consciousness as described by Vedic Science. On this level of consciousness, pure consciousness as the basis of the mind is not open to direct experience. It is overshadowed by the (sensory) objects of experience. In such a state, detachment from one's own experiences and actions is difficult, and ordinarily considered as undesirable, a symptom of mental disturbance. Roach refers to the actor's ability to detach himself from his body as a 'highly unusual, even freakish capacity' (Roach, 1981: 61). Related 'out-of-body-experiences' are delegated to the domain of 'popular psychology' (62).

According to Vedic Science, in the state of cosmic consciousness pure consciousness is by definition experienced as separate from the manifest levels of the mind (ego, feelings, mind, intellect, senses). This experience of pure consciousness could be associated with Diderot's 'disinterested onlooker' whom the actor must have in himself (Diderot, 1955: 14). Pure consciousness is fully developed in cosmic consciousness, and the actor's development towards that stage is characterised by his increasing ability to perform with growing realisation of the pure consciousness. This growth will be experienced both in time quantity, as well as in quality, i.e. depth. Initially, the experience of 'witnessing', characteristic of cosmic consciousness, will be experienced for short periods during a performance, the length of experience will increase, and ultimately the experience of the pure consciousness will be maintained throughout activity, no longer limited to acting on stage. Simultaneously, the functioning of the expressed levels of the mind will be improved, so that the actor can meet Diderot's demand for penetration, an intellectual quality. Moreover, the actor's ability to observe nature as source for imitation will be enhanced by heightened sensory functioning.

In chapter two, I quoted a passage from Ronald Harwood's play *The Dresser* to illustrate the idea of *witnessing* one's activities from the perspective of pure consciousness in a theatrical context. This fictional account of *witnessing* activity, characteristic of cosmic consciousness, has its parallels in real-life experiences, as demonstrated by the account provided by actor Ray Reinhardt.

Dual consciousness also appears to be important to representatives of contemporary Indian dancers who stand in the most direct tradition of the *Natyashastra*. Thus, Padmanathan Nair, a renowned Kathakali dancer told Richard Schechner: 'A good actor is one who understands the character very well, thus becoming the character itself. [...But] we should not forget ourselves while acting. While acting, half of the actor is the role he does and half will be himself' (Schechner and Appel, 1990: 36). It is not clear either from Nair's formulation or from the context whether Nair has a glimpse of cosmic consciousness in mind here, or just an intellectual type of dual consciousness.

Diderot claims that the actor should not feel while acting. Understanding this claim from the perspective of Vedic Science leads to a modification of Diderot's assumptions. The 'disinterested onlooker', identified as pure consciousness, does indeed not feel in the sense that once a person has risen to cosmic consciousness, pure consciousness is no longer overshadowed by any experience. Because pure consciousness, the essence of the actor's consciousness, is not involved, the actor can afford to be involved on the manifest level of the emotions and feelings. In permanent cosmic consciousness, the emotions are developed to the fullest possible degree, thus allowing the actor deep penetration of the character's emotions as set out by the dramatist, and the actor's fully developed intellect will allow a 'rendering of the outward signs of feeling' (Diderot, 1955: 17) that, together with the emotions actually felt, will provide maximum effect on the audience. Approximations of that ideal mark performances on the path to the state of cosmic consciousness.

The actor's development of consciousness entails the development of pure consciousness as a 'disinterested onlooker', witnessing, and not overshadowed by any experience of the senses, the mind, the intellect, the emotions or the ego. Proposing the 'disinterested onlooker' to be pure consciousness implies that the actor need not be emotionally uninvolved on the expressed level of the mind relating to the emotions. On the contrary, the actor in cosmic consciousness, always witnessing the actions of the expressed levels of the mind including the emotions, is fully able to feel and portray the emotions the character is believed to be feeling.

Stanislavsky

Stanislavsky's systems of actor training and acting have had a major influence in Western theatre history of the late nineteenth and twentieth centuries. If it is not directly practised, the differences most frequently represent conscious developments of Stanislavsky's theories (e.g. Strasberg and his 'Method'), or outspoken opposition to them (e.g. the early Brecht). On the issue of the actor's emotional involvement while acting, Stanislavsky appears to take the opposite view from Diderot: 'an actor is under the obligation to live his part inwardly, and then to give to his experience an external embodiment' (Stanislavsky, 1986: 15). This obligation of the actor is in line with Stanislavsky's view of the fundamental aim of the art of acting, 'the creation of this inner life of a human spirit, and its expression in an artistic form' (14). The inner life has to be created and lived in every performance, not just in rehearsal as Diderot argued. The important force that has to be tapped to allow such an 'inspired' acting, is the subconscious. Thus, the more the actor can use his subconscious forces, the more will he be able to 'fit his own human qualities to the life of this other person, and pour into it all of his own soul' (14). Stanislavsky describes the ideal of acting in the following words:

> The very best that can happen is to have the actor completely carried away by the play. Then regardless of his own will he lives the part, not noticing how he feels, not thinking about what he does, and it all moves of its own accord, subconsciously and intuitively. (13)

This ideal appears to imply that the actor has lost self-control, a state that Diderot had warned against (Diderot, 1955: 17). Stanislavsky recognised that the subconscious and whatever arises from that realm, is not only inaccessible to consciousness (Stanislavsky, 1986: 13) but also beyond the control of the will. For that reason Stanislavsky sought to develop procedures allowing the actor to use the subconscious forces through conscious techniques.

In preparing for a part, the actor begins by dividing the play into units 'which, like signals, mark his channel and keep him [the actor] in the right line' (114). Understanding the structure of the play constitutes the outward purpose of the division into units. This outward purpose is complemented by an inner purpose, which, according to Stanislavsky, is far more important. The inner purpose is the 'creative objective' which lies 'at the heart of every unit' (116). Stanislavsky provides a detailed definition of right objectives. To be able to 'live his part inwardly' (15), the actor's objectives must be 'directed toward the other actors, and not toward the spectators' (118). The actor's orientation towards fellow actors results in the actor's concentration on the fictional reality of the play. This fictional world, through the actor's objectives, is to be 'real, live, and human, not dead, conventional, or theatrical' (119). The objectives must be precise, clear-cut, they should attract and move the actor, and they should be personal to the actor, but still analogous to those of the character the actor is portraying (118-9).

Establishing the units and objectives of play and character allows the actor to arrive at a comprehensive understanding-both intellectual-outward (units) and emotional-inward (objectives)-of the play and the character he has to portray. The emotional, intuitive grasp of the role is not completed, however, with the association of the objectives resulting from the units of the play. Stanislavsky recognised that 'direct, powerful and vivid emotions do not (...) last over long periods or even for a single act. They flash out in short episodes, individual moments' (175). Moreover, Stanislavsky asserts that we cannot control such 'spontaneous eruptions of feeling' (175): 'They control us. Therefore we have no choice but to leave it to nature (...) we will only hope that they will work with the part and not at cross-purpose to it' (176). No matter how irresistible and moving a force those direct, powerful and vivid emotions may be, they are not sufficient for the actor's daily task of performance.

Stanislavsky does not argue, then, in favour of a loss of self-control, in favour of leaving it to nature and hoping for the best. He recognises the creative potential of a spontaneous eruption of emotions, but at the same time he realises the dangers inherent in this eruption: dangers arise because the eruption is beyond the actor's control. It is in this context that Stanislavsky explicitly warns the actor: 'Never lose yourself on the stage. Always act in your own person, as an artist' (177).

Once the actor has established the emotion-dominated objectives of his part, he can use the technique of emotion-memory to gain controlled and repeatable access to his unconscious. Stanislavsky explains that

> just as your visual memory can reconstruct an inner image of some forgotten thing, place, or person, your emotion-memory can bring back feelings you have already experienced. They may seem to be beyond recall, when suddenly suggestion, a thought, a familiar object will bring them back in full force. Sometimes the emotions are as strong as ever, sometimes weaker, sometimes the same strong feelings will come back but in a somewhat different guise. (168)

Thus, the actor uses his own past emotions as creative material, assisted by 'feelings that we have had in sympathising with the emotions of others' (190). Stanislavsky all along emphasises that the emotions should be spontaneous: 'The work of the actor is not to create feelings but only to produce the given circumstances in which true feelings will spontaneously be engendered' (Stanislavsky, 1949: 266).

While the emotion memory is a technique, allowing the actor to suffuse his acting with genuine emotions of his own which are analogous to the emotions the character portrayed is supposed to experience, several techniques in turn are used by the actor to stimulate the emotion memory: initially, the actor has to believe in the validity of the objectives for the play and the character. Such belief, a sense of truth, is spontaneously followed by desire, in turn, leading to action (269). The action takes the form of physical motor-adjustments, which are in line with the emotions felt. A further technique to stimulate the emotion memory is an awareness of tempo-rhythm, both of movement and regarding speech. Stanislavsky explains that both our actions and our speech

> proceed in terms of time. In the process of action we must fill in the passing time with a great variety of movements, alternating with pauses of inactivity, and in the process of speech the passing time is filled with moments of pronunciation of sounds of varying lengths with pauses between them. (181)

Indeed, there is 'some kind of tempo-rhythm inherent in every minute of our inward and outward existence' (192).

Each actor will have to find his own tempo-rhythm for both movement and speech, in line with the requirements of the part. Tempo-rhythm is closely interrelated with feelings, the 'inward existence': as Stanislavsky points out, 'every human passion, every state of being, every experience has its tempo-rhythms' (192). The actor can either intuitively apply the tempo-rhythm appropriate to a character and a situation on the stage. If the actor, however, lacks such intuition, he can work 'from the outside in' (193), beating out the rhythm. By intentionally adopting a tempo-rhythm appropriate to specific emotions, those emotions can be triggered, stimulated in the form of emotion-memory. Through an awareness of tempo-rhythm the actor can 'be put into a state of genuine excitement and get from it an emotional impact' (185).

The emotions certainly have an important function in acting, but they are not isolated. Feeling unites with mind and will to form a 'triumvirate' of motive forces (Stanislavsky, 1986: 249). They can be stimulated independently and in their interaction. Again, Stanislavsky argues that the motive forces sometimes function spontaneously, subconsciously. However, if they do not, the actor can turn to any of the three components of the 'triumvirate', either mind, or feelings, or will: if he turns to the mind, the mechanism will be as follows:

> The actor takes the thoughts in the lines of his part and arrives at a conception of their meaning. In turn, this conception will lead to an opinion about them, which will correspondingly affect his feeling and will. (249)

Using the interaction between the three inner motive forces is at the basis of Stanislavsky's psycho-technique. It encompasses emotion-memory to stimulate feelings (and, in turn, tempo-rhythm of movement and speech to stimulate emotion-memory). The mind is directly affected by thought. However, Stanislavsky argues that 'there is no direct stimulus by which you can influence the will' (250). There appears to be a contradiction in this point: when arguing for *will* as the third inner motive force, Stanislavsky points out that units and objectives are techniques of 'arousing inner living desires and aspirations' (247). Stanislavsky clarifies the point by proposing that will and feeling are inseparable, and some objectives 'influence the will more than the feeling and others enhance the emotions at the expense of the desire.' (250-1)

All elements of the psycho-technique assist the actor's energies to converge towards a holistic and organic expression of a character on the stage. Stanislavsky regards the holistic value of acting on two levels: on the level of action, he coined the phrase 'through line of action' (274). On the level of speech, the equivalent to 'through line of action' is the called 'subtext' (1949: 108). Stanislavsky defines the subtext as

> a web of innumerable, varied inner patterns inside a play and a part, woven from 'magic ifs,' given circumstances, all sorts of figments of the imagination, inner movements, objects of attention, smaller and greater truths and a belief in them, adaptations, adjustments and other similar elements. (108)

All the elements that compose the subtext lead to the ultimate super-objective of the play (108), which gives the play and the characters their holistic and organic shape.

The actor approaches a part both intellectually and intuitively, to stir his motive forces-feelings, mind and will-to reach into the unconscious, the subtext of the play in order to develop a grasp of the play and the character to be portrayed that leads to genuinely felt and experienced performances. The technique of emotion-memory appears most important because it most efficiently enables the actor to gain access to the subconscious: the subconscious creative objective is the best, because it takes possession of an actor's feelings, and carries him intuitively along to the basic goal of the play' (1961: 52), the super-objective. Such unconscious objectives are consciously 'engendered by the emotion and will of the actors themselves' (52). The unconscious is set to work by a conscious stimulus. The unconscious objectives 'come into being intuitively' (52). If the actor left the unconscious objectives to themselves once they have been consciously stimulated, the actor might well lose his self-control. Stanislavsky however points out clearly that once the unconscious objectives have come into being, 'they are then weighed and determined consciously' (52).

Diderot saw an actor who fully involves himself in the emotions of the character he has to portray as being in danger of losing his self-control. He therefore advised actors to act without emotional involvement, but by perfection of the art of imitating real-life emotions. Stanislavsky no less realised the same risk of an actor's loss of self-control. On the other hand, Stanislavsky holds that acting in which the emotions are not genuinely felt, but merely mechanical, does not do justice to the demands of the art of acting. He thus provides the actor with techniques intended to stimulate as much unconscious, intuitive, emotional material as possible, while at the same time ensuring that such techniques did not lead to an undesirable state of lost self-control. Stanislavsky quotes the actor Salvini as saying: 'An actor lives, weeps and laughs on the stage, and all the while he is watching his own tears and smiles. It is this double function, this balance between life and acting that makes his art' (1986: 267). Stanislavsky's reference to this double function, the witnessing of the process of acting by the actor himself, might resemble Diderot's call for the 'unmoved and disinterested onlooker' (Diderot, 1955: 14).

Thus, the paradox takes a decisive shift from Diderot to Stanislavsky. Diderot's paradox is the emotional stimulation of the audience through an emotionally uninvolved actor. In the case of Stanislavsky, the paradox exists not in the interaction between actor and spectator, but within the actor, the actor's art of being both deeply emotionally involved-down to the level of the unconscious-and yet still in conscious control of the acting through this ability to watch.

The discussion of Diderot's theory of acting has revealed the importance the influence of the state of the art in physiology and psychology studies had for the development of the theory. Placing his theory of acting into a wider framework of philosophical arguments about the relationship of mind and body has also proved useful. The same is true for an assessment of Stanislavsky's concepts.

The importance that Stanislavsky placed on the subconscious for inspired acting reflects the increasing interest in the psyche, pioneered by Freud. The foundation of Stanislavsky's system, gaining access to the subconscious through conscious procedures, has led scholars to draw parallels between Stanislavsky and basic principles of Freudian psychoanalysis (Kesting, 1989: 123). Kesting proposes further parallels between Stanislavsky's theory of acting and Freud's seminal discoveries in psychology: one of Freud's techniques of assessment was the *free association procedure*, in which the patients reported on whatever 'thoughts and memories occurred to them' (Ryckman, 1985: 46). Likewise, Stanislavsky sought to use the emotion memory of the subconscious as a vehicle to free the actor's inspiration (Kesting, 1989: 123). Stanislavsky's concept of 'subtext', those elements implied in the play and the part, but not directly expressed, mirror, according to Kesting, Freud's construct of the *Id*, and the super-objective of the play, in turn, resembles Freud's concept of the *Super-Ego* (Kesting, 1989: 123). Such parallelisms are in danger of being mechanical, however: the subtext, though invisible in itself, can be made visible through the actor, whereas by definition the unconscious cannot be made visible. The super-objective is defined as giving the play and the characters their holistic shape, whereas the super-ego is defined as 'the individual's internalisation of societal moral values (...) preventing the individual from expressing primitive urges publicly, and (...) encouraging the individual to set goals that would establish him or her in a career as a productive citizen' (Ryckman, 1985: 33).

It is perhaps more appropriate to draw parallels, between Stanislavsky's system and Freud's first topography, where he differentiates the unconscious, the preconscious, and the conscious. The area of the mind Stanislavsky wishes to access, which he calls the subconscious, could resemble the preconscious in Freud's first topography of the mind: whereas unconscious contents are in principle not accessible to consciousness, preconscious contents are not yet available to consciousness but can be made available (Bice and Kennedy, 1986: 48). In any case, if at all, Freudian psychoanalysis provides parallels, points of contact, with Stanislavsky's theory of acting, and not historical sources of influence.

Roach regards the unconscious, to which Stanislavsky attributed 'major powers of artistic creativity' as 'a subconscious repository in a pre-Freudian physiological sense' (1985: 205). The physiological sense of the subconscious is further explained by taking up Strasberg's statement about the concept of emotion-memory central to the American *Method*: 'The emotional thing is not Freud, as people commonly think. Theoretically and actually, it is Pavlov' (Strasberg, 1966: 198). Roach convincingly argues the influence of Pavlov's theories of reflex on Stanislavsky's system. For example, Pavlov saw the relationship between inner and outer world as a continuous process, a chain of interdependent learned or conditioned reflexes: learned mental reflexes are substitutes for innate physical ones. In parallel, Stanislavsky's system

> defines individual units and objectives as 'bits' in what will eventually, after sufficient rehearsal, become the 'unbroken line of action' or 'the score of the role.' This line is a chain of mutually inter dependent reflex desires and reflex actions. (Roach, 1985: 205)

Regarding the affective memory, it has been shown that Stanislavsky directly derived this concept from Theodule Ribot's *The Psychology of the Emotions*, translated into Russian in the 1890s, and one of the books in Stanislavsky's library (Strasberg, 1966: 111).

A comparison of Diderot and Stanislavsky leads to the conclusion that apart from the shift of emphasis in the paradox from the actor - spectator relationship in Diderot to the actor - actor dimension in Stanislavsky, there are, as Roach points out, many parallels between the evolution of Diderot's and Stanislavsky's theories:

a) Emotion is beyond the direct reach of the will.
b) Major powers of artistic creativity are attributed to the unconscious mind.
c) The unconscious mind is interpreted as a subconscious repository in a pre-Freudian physiological sense.
d) The actor's creativity is regarded highly, but an inner model of charact brought forth collectively with the playwright is conceived of.
e) Belief in long rehearsal periods to prepare a role meticulously.
f) Emphasis on the need for absorption in the stage task.

The role is regarded as a score or inner model of physical actions overseen by the dispassionate half of a divided consciousness. (Roach, 1985: 204-5)

Not only the scientific theories influencing Diderot and Stanislavsky have to be considered, but also the individual ways in which the authors arrived at their theories of acting. Originally a follower of the emotional approach to acting, Diderot arrived at his views as documented in *The Paradox* after his acquaintance with the sensibility debate in science and after having seen Garrick perform. He was further influenced by his contacts with actors, and by frequently attending performances. Thus, Diderot was well informed, but still an outsider. Stanislavsky, on the other hand, arrived at his system through direct experience in acting and directing. His own experiences led him to abandon the mechanical, uninspired and ultimately frustrating way of acting he had been accustomed to for a long time and to develop his system. This inside approach with experiences unique to it placed Stanislavsky in a position to take the same concern that guided Diderot-the risk of the actor losing self-control through (over-) indulging in an involvement with the emotions of the character-to a different end. Stanislavsky was primarily concerned with providing practical assistance to actors and directors, leading to an emphasis on practical techniques that can be applied in the day-to-day routine of rehearsal and performance in the theatre. As a result of this priority to practical matters, Stanislavsky refers to the paradoxical nature of the conscious control over simultaneously occurring phenomena of emotional involvement only in passing.

The proposed solution to Diderot's paradox from the perspective of Vedic Science also applies to Stanislavsky. Whereas Diderot proposed unemotional acting stimulating emotions in the spectator, Stanislavsky described the actor's art of being both deeply emotionally involved while acting and yet in conscious control of acting through watching himself. Vedic Science would argue that the actor's deep emotional involvement is facilitated through the actor's development of consciousness. This development goes along with the growing ability to experience pure consciousness as a witnessing agency of consciousness together with the witnessed objects of (sensory) perception, together, that is, with any activity.

Reactions to Stanislavsky: Meyerhold, Brecht, and Strasberg

Diderot changed his views on acting from an endorsement of the actor's emotional involvement to the position documented in the *Paradox*. Stanislavsky changed his views from mechanical acting and dictatorial directing to the system outlined above. At the same time, he supported the experiments of Meyerhold, who maintained that the 'truth of human relationships and behavior was best expressed not by words, but by gestures, steps, attitudes and poses' (Roose-Evans, 1989: 29). Meyerhold believed that a 'theatre built on psychological foundations is as certain to collapse as a house built on sand' because psychology was incapable of providing answers to many questions. Instead, 'a theatre which relies on *physical elements* is at very least assured of clarity' (Braun, 1969: 199). Consequently, Meyerhold placed much emphasis on the actor's physical training and discipline: he wanted an actor so 'thoroughly trained that he could respond immediately, as if by reflex action, to the needs dictated by his part or by the director' (Leiter, 1991: 56). To achieve this aim, Meyerhold developed an acting method called *biomechanics*. It was 'a gymnastic based upon: preparation for action-pause-the action itself-pause-and its corresponding reaction' (Roose-Evans, 1989: 28). Once the actor had mastered biomechanics, 'he could go beyond the needs of psychological character depiction and 'grip' his audience emotionally through physiological process' (Leiter, 1991: 56). As Meyerhold put it:

> All psychological states are determined by specific physiological processes. By correctly resolving the nature of his state physically, the actor reaches the point where he experiences the *excitation* which communicates itself to the spectator and induces him to share in the actor's performance: what we used to call 'gripping' the spectator. It is this excitation that is the very essence of the actor's art. From a sequence of physical positions and situations arise those *'points of excitation'*, which are informed with some particular emotion. (Braun, 1969: 199)

According to Meyerhold, the actors were not to identify emotionally with the characters they had to portray, as in Stanislavsky's approach to acting, 'but to consciously comment on the character by remaining clearly distinct from it' (Leiter, 1991: 57). This concept foreshadows Brecht's views. Meyerhold's insistence on non-involvement mirrors Diderot, and is in contrast to Stanislavsky. The paradox in Meyerhold's argument, however, differs from Diderot's: Meyerhold asserted that the 'correct postures and moves' which the actor achieves through mastery of biomechanics, will 'lead naturally to an emotional state in the actor and, by extension, affect the audience' (Leiter, 1991: 56). The paradox lies in the assumption that physical movements are not the result of emotion but their stimuli.

In developing his theory of acting, Meyerhold was influenced by his materialistic worldview. The general 'Zeitgeist' of the nineteenth century with the industrial revolution, colonialist international politics, and hunger for money had suggested materialism. It was consciously theorised by left Hegelians and some scientists (Hirschberger, 1981: 468). In pre- and post-revolutionary Russia, Marxism, in its variety of Leninism, had strong influences on Meyerhold, claiming that all phenomena of reality are of a material nature, and all cognition like a copy or photocopy of that material reality (482). The machine was regarded as 'the representative symbol of modern life' (Leiter, 1991: 56), and biomechanics was devised as an acting system 'as technically precise as the miracles of technology' (56). Meyerhold's ideas are also in line with the James/Lange theory that physical action precedes emotion. From the perspective of Vedic Science, the body is an expression of consciousness, but the relation of mind and body is not, therefore, unilateral. The mind can influence the body and vice versa. It is, therefore, possible to create specific emotions by manipulating the body accordingly. An important, and genuine, not rhetorical, issue in this context remains: spontaneity. The arousal of emotions through the body might be conceptualised as a purely intentional, intellect-dominated activity. In contrast, it could be a spontaneous (in Barba's terms, accultured) event, which Meyerhold aims for when he demands from the actor, in line with Pavlov's studies of conditioned response behaviour, the origin of behaviourism, a reflex-like realisation of an impulse.

Brecht's theory of acting has frequently been referred to as constituting the direct opposite of Stanislavsky's approach. Indeed, early in his theatre career Brecht wrote: 'I don't let my feelings intrude in my dramatic work. It'd give a false view of the world. I aim at an extremely classical, cold, highly intellectual style of performance' (Willett, 1978: 14). Neither the actor nor the spectator should identify with the character's emotions.

To achieve such a distance of both actor and spectator from the character, Brecht developed the concept and practice of the *alienation effect*. According to Knopf, Brecht first used the German term *Entfremdung* in 1930; from 1936 to 1940 he used both *Verfremdung* and *Entfremdung*, and eventually settled for *Verfremdung* (1980: 383). The German term *Verfremdungseffekt*, is commonly translated as *alienation effect*. Alienation properly translates as *Entfremdung*, synonymous, in English, with estrangement. The German *fremd* means unfamiliar, strange. *Verfremdung* thus implies defamiliarisation, and in that sense distancing, but not estrangement. Applied to acting, the alienation effect means that the actor 'does not allow himself to become completely transformed on the stage into the character' (Willett, 1978: 137). Instead, the actor *shows* the character, he 'reproduces their remarks as authentically as he can; he puts forward their way of behaving to the best of his abilities and knowledge of men' (137). Consequently, the character's emotions have to be externalised,

> developed into a gesture. The actor has to find a sensible perceptible outward expression for his character's emotions, preferably some action that gives away what is going on inside him. (139)

'Showing' thus becomes multi-perspectival, avoiding dogmatism. Because the actor is not emotionally involved with the character, because the actor does not identify with him, he can include a running commentary in his authentic showing of the character. The actor can 'pick a definite attitude to adopt towards the character whom he portrays, [and] can show what he thinks of him (...)' (139). Thus the spectator, not asked to identify himself with the actor/character either, can intellectually observe and criticise the character portrayed. The spectator thus reaches the ideal of a 'smoking-observing' status of an 'expert' (Innes, 1981: 11).

While emphasising the actor's and spectator's distance to the character, Brecht wanted to avoid mechanical, stylised, or abstract acting: 'he aimed for truth to life, naturalness, and close observation of actual behaviour' (Leiter, 1991: 170). Actual behaviour, natural life, are characterised to a large extent by emotions. Therefore, Brecht could not do without emotions on the stage; indeed, his epic theatre did employ emotional effects. Their function, however, is not to stimulate the spectator's identification with the particular emotion, but to serve as a 'technique of positive reinforcement for the intellectual message' (Innes, 1981: 11-12).

The clue to understanding the difference in the way Brecht treated emotions in the theatre lies in his views on empathy. In psychology, empathy is defined as an individual's ability to 'partially and temporarily suspend the functions that maintain one's separateness from others (usually called ego-boundaries)' (Stern, 1980: 81), leading to an immediate, precognitive experience of the emotional state of another individual as one's own. According to Brecht, the aesthetic assumption that emotion can only be stimulated through empathy is crude and inaccurate. Brecht rejects empathy, because it is identification, which he wishes to avoid. Brecht maintains, however, that the 'rejection of empathy is not the result of the rejection of emotions, nor does it lead to such' (Willett, 1978: 145). What Brecht aims at, then, is that the actor presents emotions without having to take recourse to empathy while performing on the stage. This, to Brecht, means doing more than just getting into the character. Yet the distanced attitude of the actor does not mean that 'if he is playing passionate parts he must himself remain cold' (193). The actor is allowed feelings, with an important qualification: 'It is only that his feelings must not, at bottom, be those of the character (...)' (193). In other words, the actor must not allow empathy, the unity of his and the character's feelings, to arise while showing those feelings, nor may the actor's 'exhibiting of outer signs of emotions' lead him to become infected himself by those emotions (94).

As a result of such a way of acting, the spectator's empathy is expected not to be stimulated either, allowing the spectator's intellect to critically judge the character, including the character's distanced and empathy-free emotions. In different terms, Brecht's stance resembles Diderot's aims for an actor who is not 'carried away'- subjected to empathy, in Brecht's terms. It also mirrors Stanislavsky's ideal of the actor: he inwardly lives the character, and yet there is the paradoxical second aspect of the actor's consciousness that serves as an uninvolved witness to all emotional involvement, thus safeguarding that the actor is not carried away by his emotions.

There are two or three sources for Brecht's concept of the alienation effect: one originates in Brecht's interest in Chinese theatre. The Western sources are Russian Formalism and Hegel and Marx. In 1917 Victor Sklovskij defined the term *alienation* in the field of the arts. In a broader sense, alienation motivates the artistic process and stands behind all acts of theoretical and practical curiosity, not merely as a procedure, but as a noetic principle. As a result, the individual is enabled to recognise voluntary and forced modes of perception and experience, norms and modes of behaviour as 'a pair of glasses' that has placed itself in between unmediated 'seeing' and 'real reality'. Once those glasses have been recognised as such, one can take them off and turn them into an object (no longer only medium) of perception and reflection (Hansen-Löve, 1978: 19). The object of perception is perceived in a non-expected, different context and environment.

Whereas there are opinions that the formalists were not much interested in developing an explicit theory of drama or dramaturgy, Hansen-Löve argues that the formalists considered techniques of dramatic alienation as constitutive for modern theatre to such a large extent that they preferred to concentrate on less manifest techniques of literary alienation, taking theatrical alienation as already tolerated and canonised. Hansen-Löve refers to the alienation effects in Meyerhold's stage practice: mechanisation of movements in biomechanics, and the actor distancing himself from his role (361-2). The view that Russian Formalism influenced Brecht is refuted by Knopf because Brecht used the concept first in 1930, five years before his visit to Moscow-although the term he used then is *Entfremdung*, not *Verfremdung* (Knopf, 1980: 379).

Hilton regards Marx-Hegelian views of history as the source of Brecht's concept:

> Underlying the dynamic of history is the fact that man is alienated, either from God (Hegel) or from the fruits of his labours and from power (Marx). Alienation in the theatre is an aesthetic correlative to economic alienation, a means of showing the historical process at work behind any human action. (1987: 61)

Knopf denies that Marx's use of the word *Entfremdung* matches Brecht's concept, but points to some parallels between Hegel's theory of cognition and Brecht's concept of alienation. Hegel argued that the known is not cognised only because it is known: only such things that are not accepted by feeling or faith in an unmediated fashion can be understood. Similarly, Brecht saw the function of the alienation effect in making events and actors on the stage unfamiliar to the spectator so that the spectator might notice them (Knopf, 1980: 379).

The alienation effect is the major technique of Brecht's *epic theatre*, which Brecht regarded as 'the only dramatic means adequate for the elucidation of the complex workings of capitalist society' (Braun, 1982: 168). Alienation increases the spectator's distance from the events on the stage. As Chaim explains, an increase of distance leads to an increase of the spectator's awareness of the fictionality of the work. This produces a 'dislocation of associations' (Chaim, 1984: 32). The spectator is led to view the events on the stage in a larger perspective, from the outside. The spectator applies critical judgement. Increased distance thus encourages the development of a historical perspective towards one's own time, demonstrating to the audience that events must be viewed within a particular 'historical field' (Chaim, 1984: 32).

Here Brecht clearly shows influence from Marx. Theatre serves a function in capitalist society: it can help to make the workers aware of 'historical fields', ultimately aware of their own misery in capitalism, an awareness that will lead to the formation of class-conscious proletariat, as antithesis to the dominating, ruling class of capitalists.

The assessment of Brecht's theory of acting has shown that Brecht, too, places emphasis on the actor's dual consciousness of emotionally involved and non-involved, witnessing aspects of consciousness. Brecht, however, shifts the emphasis from emotion to empathy. The question of how to define empathy and how to place this human function within the framework of consciousness has to be added to the catalogue of open issues drawn up at the end of the preceding chapters.

Brecht required the actor to feel the emotions of the character without empathy, i.e. without being involved with the emotions. Brecht hoped to achieve this aim by emphasising the intellect through which the actor should work, and the spectator's intellect which should be stimulated. According to Vedic Science, complete noninvolvement is possible only when pure consciousness is experienced as independent of, and witnessing all activities of the mind. In such a state, cosmic consciousness, neither emotional involvement nor empathy will overshadow the actor's experience of pure consciousness. As a result, the actor's performance will affect the spectator on all levels of the mind. This does not imply that all levels of the spectator's mind are necessarily influenced equally. Different dramatists will have different aims for their plays, intending to affect primarily the spectator's emotions, or his/her intellect, or leading to the experience of pure consciousness. The actor in cosmic consciousness, having by definition developed the full capacity of the intellect and the emotions, will be able, if he/she and/or the director should choose, to do full justice to the dramatist's intentions as to which level of the mind to influence most.

Stanislavsky's system was further developed, modified, and made popular in America mainly by Lee Strasberg. The major point of departure for Strasberg was the 'magic if'. For Strasberg, this concept meant a series of questions which the actor has to ask himself: 'Given the particular circumstances of the play, how would you behave, what would you do, how would you feel, how would you react?' (Strasberg, 1988: 85). Strasberg agrees that this understanding of the 'magic if' helps the actor in plays 'close to the contemporary and psychological experience of the actor' (85) but fails in plays that do not fulfil that requirement, e.g. classical plays. In the recognition of the principal value of the 'magic if', and in an attempt to escape its drawback, Strasberg developed the principles of motivation and substitution; regarding motivation, he credited Stanislavsky-student Vakhtangov with the initial reformulation of Stanislavsky's proposition: 'The circumstances of the scene indicate that the character must behave in a particular way; what would motivate you, the actor, to behave in that particular way?' (85). The actor should not try to imagine to be the character and derive his emotions from such an imagination. Instead of imagining to be the character, the actor should apply the substitution technique. Strasberg comments as follows:

> The actor is not limited to the way in which he would behave within the particular circumstances set for the character; rather, he seeks a substitute reality different from that set forth in the play that will help him to behave truthfully according to the demands of the role. It is not necessarily the way he himself would behave under the same circumstances, and thus does not limit him to his own natural behavior. (60)

To achieve this substitute emotion, the actor uses several techniques, with an emphasis on the emotion memory.

A question arises about the degree of truthfulness in acting to which such a substitution technique leads. If the actor follows Stanislavsky's line, he will, with all the training of body, voice, and mind at his disposal, attempt to 'inwardly live the character' (Stanislavsky, 1986: 14). To the extent that his training and his gift allow, he will become the character, and the degree to which he is able to emotionally affect the audience will be directly dependent on his ability to live the character. The Stanislavsky actor thus is guided in his attempts to internalise the character's emotions by the causal conditions set forth in the play as leading to the emotions of the character. The actor following Strasberg, it appears, initially understands the emotions that the character is believed to be feeling. Instead of trying to inwardly live the character, he substitutes the causal conditions leading to the character's emotions as set forth in the play, by causal conditions of his own making, which are supposed to lead to the same emotions as if the causal conditions were taken from the play. The spectator is confronted with an emotion that outwardly might fit the situation of a specific scene in the play. However, what the spectator is not aware of is that the emotions do not have their origin in the sequence of causal conditions in the play, but in potentially 'arbitrary', unsequenced, unrelated, individual substitutes: substitute A for emotion A, substitute B for emotion A', with A' following causally from emotion A, whereas substitute B is not necessarily related to substitute A.

Two questions result: will the spectators feel the difference between genuine and substitute emotions, and does the use of substitutes make acting easier for the actor, does it require less technique, less skill, less art, than a 'through-line' of emotion?

Bloch's Alba Emoting

Meyerhold had argued that the actor who has mastered biomechanics will be able to generate body postures which in turn will arouse emotions in the actor. By extension, these emotions will then affect the audience. Ekman's research showed that voluntary facial expression can arouse emotions normally associated with those facial expressions.

Susanna Bloch has developed an acting technique which proposes to unite the 'method' school of acting 'which asserts that the main project in acting is the creation of emotion *in the actor*' and Diderot, who asserts that 'it is unnecessary, counterproductive even, for actors to worry about *feeling* emotions' (Bloch, 1993: 121). For the purpose of her studies, Bloch defined emotions as 'distinct and dynamic functional states of the entire organism comprising particular groups of effector systems (visceral, endocrine, muscular) *and* particular corresponding subjective states (feelings)' (123).

Laboratory research led to the conclusion that 'specific emotional feelings were linked to specific patterns of breathing, facial expression, degree of muscular tension, and postural attitudes' (124). Of the complex neuromuscular, visceral, and neuroendocrine reactions 'which are activated during a natural spontaneous emotion', only those two that can be voluntarily controlled and therefore reproduced were selected for further study: breathing rhythm and a 'particular expressive attitude', both facial and postural (125). Whereas Ekman studied only the emotional impact of re-creating facial expressions corresponding to specific emotions, Bloch adds breathing pattern and posture; in her view, this addition reduces the possibility that the expressions resulting from facial mimicry 'may appear to the observer as artificial masks rather than re-created emotions' (125).

After establishing these three 'emotional effector patterns', further experiments with 'naive subjects' were carried out, showing that 'if instructions for reproducing an emotional effector pattern are correctly followed, the appropriate actions will trigger the corresponding subjective experience in the performer' (127). The effectiveness of this technique is reported to be so powerful that a specific 'step-out' technique had to be developed, allowing the actor to 'switch off' the emotion intentionally activated by using the ALBA EMOTING technique. The technique comprises six basic emotions: joy, anger, sadness, fear, eroticism, and tenderness. Once actors achieve 'mastery' in reproducing these six, they can combine them in an infinite number of degrees of intensity (130). Testing some of Bloch's techniques, Rix was impressed by the results and emphasised especially the strong potential of 'the breathing patterns as a tool for emotional work' (Rix, 1993: 14). Rix, however, also raises some important questions:

> How to avoid leading students into intense emotional territory for which they are unprepared; what to do when and if that happens; how to teach the technique so that students feel empowered rather than manipulated; how to work with students who can't reproduce breathing patterns; how (or whether) to integrate the technique into existing approaches to emotion, including memory-based ones. (144)

Vedic Science argues that mind and body are mutually interrelated, they influence each other. Thus it is perfectly within the framework of the model of the mind proposed by Vedic Science that a process like Alba Emoting should work. However, the question arises as to the level of consciousness achieved through such a technique. It is likely that the mind remains quite strictly bound to the level of the intellect, at which the decision is made which kinds patterns to produce, and to which degree, in order to produce a specific kind of emotion, then to decide when to use the 'turn off' technique and to start the new pattern for a new emotion. It is difficult to conceive of such a complicated process becoming second nature, 'accultured, extra-daily behaviour' to use Barba's terms. Even though emotions are said to be generated through the intellectual technique, the intellect remains in control. I have indicated earlier that the intellect is less comprehensive than the emotions. As a result, it is likely that the emotions generated by an intellectual technique such as Alba Emoting will ultimately remain on the level of mood-making, lacking the depth of 'true' emotions. Scientific physiological data appear to contradict this interpretation, because, according to Bloch and colleagues, the physiological parameters of the emotions are clearly present, as if the emotions were really felt without the stimulus of technique to induce them. Further research into physiological correlates of emotions would be needed to establish whether there is a difference between original emotion and technique-induced emotion. Such research will then also be able to establish whether Alba Emoting might be adapted to facilitate the development of higher states of consciousness. For an actor in at least cosmic consciousness, an intellectual technique such as Alba

Emoting will become unnecessary: emotions will arise spontaneously from the specific need of any given dramatic situation.

Presence (Barba)

What makes an actor a great actor? Certainly, great actors have the ability to convey strong emotions, no matter which of the schools discussed in the first section of this chapter they may follow, if any. Great actors have charisma on stage, they have an aura, they manage to create an atmosphere around them, in a word: they have *presence*. What, though, is *presence* precisely? What are its constituents, elements, aspects and characteristics? Can it be trained, and if so, how? In this section I want to address those and related questions, again concluding with a reassessment of views against the Vedic Science model of consciousness.

Since *presence* is recognised as an essential aspect of acting, much has been written about it. The actor's *presence* is a central concept in the theatre anthropology developed by Eugenio Barba. He was inspired to set this priority of his practical work, and his research based on it, by one fundamental question: 'Why, when I see two actors doing the same thing, I get fascinated by one and not by the other' (1985: 12).

Barba spent some years at Grotowski's Laboratory Theatre in Poland, and continued his teacher's research into the psycho-physiological basis of acting (Innes, 1981: 11). Barba founded the Odin Teatret in Norway in 1964, moving to its permanent home in Holstebro, Denmark, in 1966. In the early 1970s, non-Scandinavians joined the group, and it has by now included members from Italy, the USA, Britain, Canada, Germany, Spain, and Argentina. The Odin Teatret became the centre for the government-funded Nordisk Teaterlaboratorium (Watson, 1993: 101), inspired by Grotowski's Laboratory Theatre. Its activities reach beyond Barba's direct theatrical activities at the Odin Teatret:

> It is a major teaching center, it arranges performances for international companies in various parts of Scandinavia, it publishes and sells theatre books, it makes and rents films on the theatre, and it is the umbrella organization for several groups associated with the Odin. (3-4)

In 1979, the activities of the Nordisk Teaterlaboratorium culminated in the foundation *International School of Theatre Anthropology* (ISTA), which

> is a most unusual school that has no classrooms or students, meets only periodically, has no curriculum, and has no graduates. Nevertheless, it is one of Europe's most important theatre research institutions. (149)

Holstebro functions as the administrative centre of ISTA; its primary work takes place, as Watson describes, at public sessions 'held from time to time at the request of particular funding bodies' (149). At these sessions, Eastern and Western master performers share their expertise with 'relatively young, inexperienced' Western actors and directors. These practitioners are joined by 'intellectuals including theatre scholars, anthropologists, psychologists, biologists, and critics' (149).

Theatre anthropology is the key concept in Barba's theatre theory and practice, and it subsumes a variety of concepts. One of those is most relevant to the discussion of the relationship between theatre and consciousness: the actor's *presence*. Barba uses a number of terms synonymously with *presence*, to highlight different characteristics. Thus, he talks about *body-in-life*, *scenic bios*, *life*, *power*, and *energy*.

Barba enumerates three levels of the *body of theatre*, each with its sub-categories, which together make up *presence*. The three levels are

a. extra-daily behaviour

b. the organ of u-topia

c. the elusive third organ

I want to briefly describe each one of those.

Extra-daily behaviour

Barba distinguishes between daily behaviour, i.e. mainly unconscious 'processes through which our bodies and voices absorb and reflect the culture in which we live' (1985: 32), and extra-daily behaviour, i.e. the specific codes of movement pertaining to specific performance forms, which, in their aesthetic function, differ from daily behaviour (1985: 32).

Extra-daily behaviour has to become second nature to the actor in performance: Barba appropriately warns against getting stuck on the level of the intellect, of conscious observation, during performance, which is detrimental to the flow of energy. Extra-daily behaviour follows five distinct principles.

1. alterations in balance

2. the law of opposition

3. coherent incoherence (also referred to as consistent inconsitency)

4. equivalence

5. a decided body

(Watson, 1993: 33, and Barba, 1995: 13-35).

Whereas in daily behaviour, all movements of the body tend to follow the principle of least action, leading to a 'minimum expenditure of energy for standing, sitting, and walking' (Barba, 1985: 33), extra-daily behaviour of performance requires shifts in balance, which in turn lead to more energy being required for movement, for remaining still, or for retaining balance. The second principle, the law of opposition, is closely related to the alterations of balance. In both cases, daily behaviour patterns have to be distorted. In Western classical ballet the dancer maximises the opposition between body weight and gravity in 'soaring feats of lightness and grace' (Barba, 1985: 34). The dancer spends much energy in the attempt to free himself from the force of gravity. The surplus of energy needed in performance is incoherent, or inconsistent with daily life, because it 'makes no sense from a practical, daily life, point of view'. However, it is also understandable, and in that sense coherent or consistent that the actor spends this much more energy in extra-daily, performative activity, because the excessive energy expenditure is a major source of the dynamic in each of the performance genres (Barba, 1985: 35). In the process of developing skills in extra-daily behaviour, actors will need to abandon modes of behaviour that have become unconsciousness and thus automatic. Such modes have to be replaced by extra-daily, artificial equivalents. True achievement in performance comes when such artificial equivalents become the performer's second nature. Finally, the performer's body has to be in a state of being decided. As Grotowski explained,

> If an actor *wants* to express, then he is divided. One part of him is doing the willing, another the expressing; one part is commanding and another is carrying out the commands. (Barba, 1995: 33).

The decided body is related to Barba's concept of *sats*, a term taken from the Norwegian language, which means impulse, preparation, to be ready to..., and which Barba defines as

> the moment in which one is ready to act, the instant which precedes the action, when all energy is already there, ready to intervene, but as if suspended, still held in the fist, a tiger-butterfly about to take flight. (1995: 40)

Three levels of the body

Extra-daily behaviour is the first of three levels of the theatre's body that combine to give rise to *presence*. Its five components can be trained. Barba suggests a sequence of development of proper (extra-daily) technique for the actor: the actor first has to distance himself from 'incultured' spontaneity. He has to understand the difference between himself in daily mode of behaviour and the techniques which characterise the extra-daily mode of performance (Barba, 1989: 312). It is as if the actor has to learn all movements on the stage anew: he undergoes a process of physical acculturation (312). However, the more conscious the actor is of his extra-daily movements, the more he becomes blocked. The actor has to aim for accultured spontaneity rather than incultured spontaneity.

In the process, Barba pinpoints a paradox at the centre of the actor's art and methodology: it is located in the actor's interaction with his role and with the audience. Barba argues that an actor does not merely present the fictional world of the play, nor does his activity end in his own experience of portraying a fictional character. For Barba, performance is a 'dialectic between the two', what he calls 'the anatomical theatre' (Watson, 1993: 39). In the performance, the actor portrays the fictional score, i.e. the 'physical actions and vocal delivery decided upon in rehearsal and repeated in each performance' (39), and his meeting with it. This meeting will vary from performance to performance, depending on several factors:

> the audience's reaction to the piece, the actor's psycho-emotional responses to events on stage as well as in the theatre, and the actor's personal associations with particular actions and/or situations in a work s/he has developed with his/her colleagues over a period of some eighteen months to two years. (39)

The relationship between (rehearsed) score and (unrehearsed, spontaneous) meeting with the score is characterised by tension. Barba maintains that it is through the convergence of these opposing forces, that our personal experiences can reach others, and be transformed into a social experience: through theatre (Barba, 1979: 134).

Here Barba's theatre aesthetics differ substantially from Grotowski's: for Grotowski, the convergence of opposing forces of score and the actor's experience was 'the means by which the actor instigated a process of self-revelation that affected the spectator' (Watson, 1993: 40). This implies that the performer's catharsis leads to catharsis in the audience. For Barba, the convergence of score and the actor's experience enriches the 'relationship between the performer and his/her audience directly' (40).

It is in this relationship between actor and spectator that Barba's paradox is located: the actor's 'articulate actions' on the stage are perceived by the spectator as objective signs. These objective signs, however, result from subjective processes within the actor. Barba raises the question: 'How can the actor be this matrix and be able, at the same time, to shape them into objective signs whose origin is in his own subjectivity?' (1979: 35).

The externalisation of subjectivity, i.e. emotions, has to be disciplined. In Barba's theatre anthropology, discipline is closely related to training: 'Training is a process of self-definition, a process of self-discipline (...)' (73). The emphasis on training is an emphasis on the body, which in turn is in line with the general tendency among contemporary theatre theorists and artists to stress the importance of the actor's body. Training thus appears outwardly physical, but, as Barba points out,

> it is not the exercise in itself that counts-for example, bending or somersaults-but the individual's justification for his own work, a justification which although perhaps banal or difficult to explain through words, is physiologically perceptible, evident to the observer. (73)

What Barba appears to imply here is that the actor's physical performance as perceived by an outside observer will differ depending on the actor's mental attitude behind the physical expression.

The organ of u-topia

Body technique is only one component of the 'theatre's body'. The second is 'the organ of *u-topia*', of 'non-place', residing in the actor's viscera and his right hemisphere. 'It is the super-ego which the presence of a master or masters has imbued us with during the transitions from daily technique to extra-daily performance technique' (Barba, 1988: 291). This organ transforms technique and raises it 'to a social and spiritual dimension' (291).

The elusive third organ

Barba describes the third organ as the 'irrational and secret temperature which renders our actions incandescent' (1988: 291). Whereas the body and the 'super-ego' can be trained, the elusive third organ is 'our personal destiny. If we don't have it, no one can teach it to us' (291). A unity of the three organs of the 'theatre's body', allows the actor to radiate energy, establish 'presence', thus attracting the spectator's attention. Reference to the 'third organ', is vague and does not lead very far. As Watson points out,

> Barba is essentially a creative artist, a poet both in the theatre and in his writings about it. This poetic quality calls for a careful reading of his ideas since he favors poetic metaphors over the more traditional intellectual approach of deductive logic to sustain his arguments. (1993: 18)

Barba argues that *sats*, *presence*, the decided body, the principles of extra-daily behaviour, are all 'descriptions at the pre-expressive level' (1995: 104). The pre-expressive attracts the spectators' attention before meaning is conveyed. 'This is a logical, and not a chronological 'before'' (1995: 9). The relationship between mind and body, the phenomena of *presence*, the pre-expressive, and the three organs of the theatre's body are clearly related to questions at the forefront of current consciousness studies.

Following this outline of Barba's views on *presence*, I want to reassess the views from the perspective of Vedic Science. First I want to address Barba's claim for a co-existence, in the actor, of inner subjectivity and its objective outer expression and subsequent subjective reception by the spectator. Vedic Science can assist in understanding the implications. In higher states of consciousness, pure consciousness is fully developed, and all aspects of the body are fully developed. Thus inner subjectivity can be expressed objectively in the sense that it neither overshadows pure consciousness, nor is subjective to the extent that it is incommunicable, incomprehensible to a spectator. On the contrary, acting from a higher state of consciousness will enable the actor to shape his fully developed subjectivity in such a way as to allow the spectator maximum benefit, taking the individual spectator's state of consciousness into account and tuning his performance to the spectator's level of consciousness. The actor's subjectivity thus becomes the focal point of acting, because it initially decides the objective outer expression. The actor's subjectivity, through the means of objective expression, concurrent with subjectivity, without time lapse, has a direct impact on the spectator's subjectivity.

Secondly, I want to address Barba's three levels of the theatre's body. The actor's body, moulded through technique; the organ of u-topia, which raises mere technique to a social and spiritual dimension; and the elusive third organ, the 'irrational and secret temperature which renders our actions incandescent' (1988: 291). Together, they allow the actor to radiate energy, establish presence, and attract the audience. What Barba poetically alludes to here are various levels of expression of consciousness. The body is the most concrete manifestation of consciousness on the human level. It is tangible, and can be subjected easily to (scientific) observation. For the actor, this level is associated with training, technique and routines. Barba recognises that mere technique is empty if it is not informed by social and spiritual dimensions. These dimensions are characteristic of the level of intuition as described by Vedic Science. Social and spiritual values become an integral part of the actor's mind through training in the presence of masters.

From the perspective of Vedic Science, the third organ of the body of the theatre can be identified as pure consciousness. At least during performance, great performers experience this level, it is active within their mind, and is thus able to create the effects of presence on the stage that are so attractive to an audience. Barba argues that this organ cannot be trained. I disagree. The experience of pure consciousness can be facilitated through various meditation techniques. In addition, as I have argued elsewhere (1999), the techniques of performance themselves (especially as described in the *Natyashastra*) can function as facilitators of the experience of pure consciousness (together with theatre-specific stimuli). An enlightened actor, that is an actor who performs from a higher state of consciousness as defined by Vedic Science, will spontaneously do whatever the performance situation (play and audience) requires. Full flow of energy is a given in that state; any observation which occurs will be part of the process, and not hindering the performance. For Barba, this is a theoretical ideal, based on occasional experiential glimpses. All his practical work, both training and performance, is geared towards attaining this ideal. This work combines all kinds of elements from manifold sources. I believe that this non-systematic approach is mainly responsible that Barba (and he is not alone here!) has so far not really succeeded in developing a set of techniques which allows the systematic development of higher states of consciousness in the theatre.

To sum up: *presence* is a very important aspect of acting. Reassessing this concept against the background of the model of consciousness proposed by Vedic Science allows a clear and cogent understanding of the actor's *presence* on stage as an actor's performative activity on stage suffused by pure consciousness: the more pure consciousness is experienced, the more *present* is the actor.

State (Mnouchkine)

One of the most important skills of acting Ariane Mnouchkine tries to help her actors achieve is their ability to express their character's *state*. *State* is clearly related to *presence*: Mnouchkine explains that *state* is the 'primary passion which preoccupies the actor. So when he is "angry", he must *draw* the anger, he must *act*' (Williams, 1999: 95). Mnouchkine further elaborates:

> An actor is a person who metaphorises a feeling. On the other hand, a 'state' is never lukewarm. This doesn't mean that you can only show extreme states, but it is very difficult to show intermediary states. If one wants to show lukewarmness, that lukewarmness must be extreme. Finally, one can only show successive states, in ruptured discontinuity. (Williams, 1999: 95)

State, then, implies that the actor, at every second of acting, has to be in the *present*-Mnouchkine deplores the baggage Stanislavski-trained actors bring to the stage by delving so deeply into the characters' past. The *present* is the specific passion, or emotion, the *state* that is required at that very moment by the text (or the production's interpretation of the text). The actor can play only one *state* at a time: 'even if he plays it for a quarter of a second, and in the next quarter of a second there's another state' (Williams, 1999: 119).

Mnouchkine knows, she can detect, or sense, when an actor has achieved the right *state*, and she equally knows when the actor has not. However, she maintains that she has no technique of helping an actor achieve it. She concedes she may have a method, but in her case it is an unconscious one, which she does not know (Williams, 1999: 171). It is remarkable, however, that she picks up, in interview, on her abilities of listening and watching:

> I believe that I know how to do that well. I love to listen, and I love to watch the actors-with a passion. I think that's already a way of assisting them. They know that I never tire of listening to them, of watching them, but how do I help them? I don't know. (Williams, 1999: 171)

I want to relate Mnouchkine's concept of *state*, and her reference to listening in their loose context to the method of helping actors achieve being in the present, achieve the right *state*, with some distinct experiences of my own. In summer 2000, I was able to conduct an exploratory study, funded by the Arts and Humanities Research Board, into the potential of using theatre training to achieve an impact on consciousness, in the context of transformation and transportation as defined by Schechner. The abstract of the publication based on the study provides the necessary background information:

The effects of two drama workshops (workshop N, based on the Indian *Natyashastra*, and workshop E, an eclectic one) were compared in an exploratory study. A total of six students participated, experiencing both workshops in counterbalanced order. A variety of psychological measures was taken prior to commencement, immediately following the first and the second workshops, and at a six-month follow-up. Higher scores on self-reported perception and directed attention, greater improvement in mood regulation, greater changes in reported dissociated states and superior time-management were shown following workshop N than following workshop E. Scores on the dissociated scale of the Assessment Schedule of Altered States of Consciousness were higher following workshop E than workshop N. Workshop N was perceived as of greater benefit to life in general whereas workshop E was perceived as of greater benefit to acting. The results are discussed in relation to theories of transformative change and to future work. (Meyer-Dinkgräfe et al., 2002: 29)

Prior to the workshops, I was curious whether any of my theories about the relation between performance and consciousness would be confirmed (and if so, how precisely) during my own workshop experiences. I participated in workshop N twice, so as to achieve the cumulative effects of the longer exposure. During the second workshop, I began to notice the flow of energy in my body. This is, on its own, nothing new, Zarrilli has written about it extensively (1990, 1995, 2000), and I had read, heard, and written about it. What was new was my own direct experience of it. In particular, I noticed the change of energy level depending on whether specific movements central to *Bharata Natyam* were carried out precisely as taught by the workshop leader, or with a certain lack of precision. For example, for the initial pose of *Bharata Natyam*, holding the elbows at a 90 degree angle to the body makes for a strong flow of energy, especially to the head and back, whereas letting the elbows go limp and reducing their angle to the body markedly reduces energy flow to the extent of being barely noticeable. Strong energy flow in extra-daily performance mode (dependent on proper body posture) went along with heightened alertness and focus on the current moment, whereas an energy flow that was not much different from daily behaviour did not have any effect on the mind. For me, this was experiential confirmation that the body posture adopted during performance has a direct bearing on consciousness.

The workshop leader guided us to centre ourselves, equivalent, in terms of Vedic Science described above, to experience the state of pure consciousness. From this state we were asked to proceed towards a specific emotion, express that emotion through the body, return to the state of pure consciousness, and proceed to a different emotion. One of the participants wrote

> After each section we paused in whatever position we were in, feeling the emotion fade and experiencing the body in a state of non-action. Breathing deeply in this position and relaxing the body meant that I felt as though I was creating an almost neutral slate on which the next emotion could be placed (Smith, 2000: 9).

I can describe the emotion resulting from the state of pure consciousness, and at least to some extent suffused by it, only as pure emotion (say, of love), ready to be applied to any desired specific instance of that emotion demanded by a specific context in a play (love for one's wife, son, daughter, mother etc.). One of the participant's entry in her working notebook confirms, in her own terms, my experience:

> (...) I found that what we were creating was the extreme of that emotion. It was difficult to pare it down to appear more natural but could understand how this approach could be extremely useful in dance. I also felt that if I were to work on this technique over a much longer period of time it would indeed be possible to find, not only different manifestations of the same emotion but also create different percentages of it. (Smith, 2000: 10)

What we experienced in workshop N was a method allowing the actor to be in the present, and to easily shift between pure emotions. In workshop N we experienced the impact of this method after only a few hours of practice. It should have much more powerful impact on both actors and spectators if integrated into a longer training programme.

On the basis of my own experience in workshop N, corroborated by comments from the other participants, I would like to argue that what Mnouchkine describes as *state* is emotion suffused with pure consciousness. It should be possible to test this claim empirically: take a number of experienced actors, measure them for a range of psycho-physiological indicators of pure consciousness both during everyday life and during performance. Allow Mnouchkine to indicate whether they are achieving what she calls presence and appropriate *states*. The hypothesis is that high ratings of pure consciousness from empirical measures should correlate significantly with the degree to which Mnouchkine considers such actors as being in the present, and in the appropriate *state*. Alternatively, those actors having worked with Mnouchkine for a long time should rate highly on the measures for pure consciousness. Further research could then further elaborate the possible causal connections: does working with Mnouchkine, do her unconscious, unknown ways of helping the actors achieve presence and the appropriate *state*, not only assist her actors achieve presence and the appropriate *state*, but does that method also, through the theatre activity, lead to transformation (lasting impact on consciousness)?

Translumination (Grotowski)

Presence is the key concept in Barba's theatre theory and practice, and so is *state* for Mnouchkine. Both can be understood, in terms of the model of consciousness proposed by Vedic Science, as acting suffused by pure consciousness, which is nothing else than acting in a higher state of consciousness. The related experience and concept for Grotowski is *translumination*. Grotowski developed this concept in the context of his development of 'poor theatre'. Grotowski sees the 'personal and scenic technique of the actor as the core of theatre art' (1969: 15). Whereas in conventional Western theatre practice the emphasis is on the actor acquiring specific skills (Bradby and Williams, 1988: 124), a 'proliferation of signs' (Grotowski, 1969: 18), Grotowski developed a *via negativa* (way of negation), which 'necessitates the stripping away of "how to do", a mask of technique behind which the actor conceals himself, in search of the sincerity, truth and life of an exposed core of psycho-physical impulses' (Bradby and Williams, 1988: 124). According to Grotowski, the prerequisite for the actor to be able to lay bare the core of his private personality is that he reaches a state of mind characterised by 'passive readiness to realise an active role' (1969: 7). In such a state of mind, the actor is able not to want anything specific; he rather 'resigns from not doing it' (7).

Grotowski developed various training methods to enable his actors to reach that state of mind. The methods were mainly physical, aiming 'to facilitate the activation of (...) body memory: a natural reservoir of impulses to action and expression stored within the physiological make-up of an individual, an intuitive corporeal "intelligence"' (Bradby and Williams, 1988: 123). If this body memory is stimulated externally, 'pure and communicable signs of an archetypal nature may be released' (123). Ideally, the result of such a stimulation of the body memory leads to a state where the actor transcends incompleteness and the 'mind-body split': the 'division between thought and feeling, body and soul, consciousness and the unconscious, seeing and instinct, sex and brain then disappear' (Kumiega, 1987: 128-9). Consequently, the actor achieves totality, 'a certain quality of attention, or consciousness, characterised by a full presence in, and recognition of, the moment' (Kumiega, 1987: 139). The actor who has attained this state is free from the 'time-lapse between inner impulse and outer reaction in such a way that the impulse is already an outer expression. Impulse and expression are concurrent (...)' (Grotowski, 1969: 16). The process leading to such a 'transcendental state of being' which parallels mystical and transpersonal states (16) has to be disciplined: undisciplined 'self-penetration is no liberation, but is perceived as a form of biological chaos' (39).

An actor who has ripened to the ability of enduring the extreme tension involved in completely stripping himself emotionally, psychologically, and spiritually to 'totally reveal his inner self to the audience' (Chaim, 1984: 40), is termed by Grotowski, 'holy actor'. A 'holy actor' has been trained through physical exercises and can produce the transcendental state of consciousness described above. Grotowski does not understand the phrase 'holy actor' in a religious sense: 'It is rather a metaphor defining a person who, through his art, climbs upon the stake and performs an act of self-sacrifice' (Grotowski, 1969: 43). Grotowski's terminology: 'holy actor' for the ideal actor, the actor's activity on the stage as 'self-sacrifice', as 'mounting a stake', points, however, if not to religion, then to the related concept of ritual. As Kott maintains, 'Grotowski stubbornly and persistently tried to turn theatre back into ritual (...)' (1990: 203-4). Similarly, Bates claims that for Grotowski acting is a 'ritual testing of the soul, a stretching of the limits of human communication' (1986: 39). This aspect of Grotowski's theory is closely related to his views on the actor-spectator relationship. For Grotowski, theatre originally had a function close to that of ritual: theatre liberated the spiritual energy of the congregation or tribe by incorporating myth and profaning or rather transcending it. The spectator thus had a renewed awareness of his personal truth in the truth of the myth, and through fright and a sense of the sacred he came to catharsis. (Grotowski, 1969: 22-3)

In contemporary society, Grotowski maintained, the relation of spectators to myth is different. Therefore, instead of aiming at an identification with the myth, theatre has to confront the spectator with it. Creating a shock makes the 'life-mask crack and fall away' (23).

The extreme of the actor's gift of his core to the spectator, 'exposure carried to outrageous excess', returns the spectator to a 'concrete mythical situation, an extreme of common human truth' (23). As Roose-Evans puts it, 'If Brecht wanted to make the spectator think, Grotowski's aim is to disturb him on a very deep level' (1989: 147).

The confrontation with myths is closely related to Jung's concept of archetypes. At the depth of human psyche lies the collective unconscious. It is a 'storehouse of latent memories of our human and prehuman ancestry. It consists of instincts and archetypes that we inherit as possibilities and that often affect our behavior' (Ryckman, 1985: 65). The archetypes in particular are 'themes that have existed in all cultures throughout history' (65). Jung holds that these collective memories are 'universal in nature because of our common evolution and brain structure' (65). In confronting spectators with modern versions of myth, Grotowski enlivened archetypes in their collective unconscious.

Different archetypes are not equally developed within the psyche (67). This accounts for differences in the effect of Grotowski's work on different spectators. Gilman describes how such deep disturbance, aimed at renewing the spectator, was so forceful that

> the theater (...) has felt itself in the presence of something very like a redemption (...). Almost every moment and sound is what can only be described as 'pure', without precedent or predictability, yet wholly inevitable, accurate, created, true (...) In having passed beyond all hitherto known means of expression and beyond representation, they place us in the presence of emotions and consciousness themselves, in the presence, that is to say, of a creation and not an image of one. (Gilman, 1970: 206, 216)

Not every spectator responded favourably to Grotowski's approach: Davy remarked on the performance's infantilism, coarseness, delusion(s) of originality, ugliness, and nihilism (1989: 136). Indeed, Grotowski did not present plays for mainstream audiences: he was concerned with a spectator as a spiritual seeker, who wished to improve by self-analysis through 'confrontation with the performance' (Grotowski, 1969: 40). Grotowski tried to achieve for the spectator the same 'translumination' that the actor experiences when he is fully and only present in the moment, in the state of transcendence. Grotowski's method here was to minimise, as far as possible, the distance between actor and spectator, both physically and psychologically (Chaim, 1984: 41). Critic Irving Wardle's comment in his review of *The Constant Prince*, a major production of the Laboratory Theatre, points to a difficulty in this attempt: Wardle noted the 'immense gap between these productions and any common experience. They start on a note of intensity and ascend from there without relief' (Kumiega, 1987: 148). Grotowski himself admitted 'that he was impotent to influence directly the spectator's spiritual and psychic responses to the acts witness' (Kumiega, 1987: 147).

Innes argues that Grotowski uses 'archetypal ideograms (...) to awaken latent emotions in the spectator through subconscious associations' (1981: 163). Reaching the spectator's latent emotions may indeed be one channel in which Grotowski's theatre affects the spectator. However, Grotowski's ultimate goal for both actor and spectator, the transcendental state of consciousness, or 'translumination' (Kumiega, 1987: 139) close to, if not identical with, 'mystical and transpersonal states of consciousness and experience' (Grotowski, 1969: 16, 125, 162), surely lies beyond the already quite subtle level of the emotions. As Kumiega points out, one characteristic of this experience is that the division between thought and feeling disappears. While translumination is experienced by the performer, two elements coexist creatively, which appear, at first sight, to be opposed and mutually exclusive: spontaneity and discipline: 'what is elementary feeds what is constructed and vice versa' (89). Grotowski insisted on his actor's physical discipline, which they gained through regular exercise. The idea that the actor can reach to the unconscious, the source of archetypes, by stimulating the body memory, goes back to the James-Lange theory of emotions. William James's and C. G. Lange's originally independent, later co-authored, studies postulate emotions as 'perceptions of physiological disturbances', e.g. 'we do not cry because we feel sad, but we feel sad because we cry' (Calhoun and Solomon, 1984: 26). The physiological reaction is central to emotion, but in a reversed order: in the above example, '"feeling sad" is not the cause of this reaction, but instead our experience of that reaction' (26). Critics of the James-Lange theory have pointed out that the authors 'leave largely unspecified how events and objects in our environment come to produce these physiological disturbances' (26). The most severe criticism is that the physiological changes are so unspecific that it becomes difficult to distinguish between many different emotions and their nuances merely on the basis of unspecific physiological reactions (Frijda, 1986: 125). In recent years, however, studies of voluntary facial action have shown emotion-specific changes in the autonomous nervous system (Levenson et al., 1990). In addition, stimulation of emotional states in the actor and spectator by specific movements of the actor's body is also characteristic, at least in part, of the Indian theories of acting as stated in the *Natyashastra*. Kumiega has asserted that body memory stimulates the emotions (121). However, as argued above, Grotowski's ultimate aim is to reach beyond the emotions.

Grotowski closed the Laboratory Theatre in 1970. According to Kott, Grotowski realised that his attempts to turn theatre back into ritual 'is sacrilege, pillage of the *sacrum*' for true believers, and 'for non-believers a form of cheating' (1990: 204).

In the following years, Grotowski developed paratheatrical activities. Here, he was able to fully explore his role as therapist in a process of social healing. Grotowski had aimed for his Laboratory Theatre to have a healing effect on the spectators. However, he had direct access only to the actors, and could only hope that the effect on the spectators would be according to his intention. In the set-up of paratheatrical events, there was no longer a distinction between actor and audience:

> Grotowski developed a total concentration on the internal process of self-discovery in groups of the public as participants. In effect they were subjected to an extended session of psychotherapy based on the acting exercises developed by the Theatre Laboratory, (....) (Innes, 1981: 175)

The assessment of Grotowski's theory in the context of Western influences leads to the following open issues which have to be addressed from the perspective of Vedic Science:

> How to account for experiences of the actor's 'translumination' and its effect on the spectator?

> How to account for the paradox of coexistence of discipline and spontaneity in the actor?

Grotowski aims for a state of consciousness and body where the actor transcends incompleteness and the mind-body-split, where he achieves totality, full presence, where he becomes a *holy actor*. Such *translumination* is clearly an experience of not only cosmic consciousness, characterised by a separation of pure consciousness and activity, but an experience of unity consciousness as defined by Vedic Science: subject and object are experienced as a unity, the striking duality of pure consciousness and expressed levels of consciousness, characteristic of cosmic consciousness, disappears. For the duration of the experience of cosmic consciousness or unity consciousness, all action, performative or other, is fully spontaneous, there is no longer a time lapse between inner impulse and outer action. At the same time, all activity in those states of consciousness will be fully disciplined in the sense that there will be no entropy, no waste of energy, actions will lead to the intended result following the principle of least action. The coexistence of spontaneity and discipline is characteristic of higher states of consciousness. Pure consciousness is a field that connects all human beings. If the actor performs from that level, he will necessarily affect the level of pure consciousness of the spectators, independent of whether or not they, too, are alert on the level of pure consciousness.

Physical Presence and Neutrality (Artaud)

In this section I want to discuss an issue relating to Artaud's theories on acting against the context of the Vedic Science model of consciousness: the paradox of the actor's simultaneous physical presence and neutrality. The aim is to develop a new understanding of Artaud's ideas, and potentially to new developments in theatre practice.

According to Artaud, theatre that wants to overcome the stalemate and renew its magic needs specific modes of acting different from traditional performance practices. Artaud conceptualised language that is physical, 'aimed at the senses and independent of speech' (25). This physical language, also referred to as 'poetry for the senses' (25) affects primarily the senses, although Artaud pointed out that it might, at later stages, amplify its full mental effect 'on all possible levels and along all lines' (26).

The effectiveness of physical language on the stage depends primarily on the actor, on the effectiveness of his acting. In his emphasis on a physical language of the theatre, Artaud compares the actor to a physical athlete, with a major difference: in the case of the actor, not actual physiological muscles are trained, but affective musculature 'matching the bodily localisation of our feelings' (100). For Stanislavsky, the solar plexus was the physiological seat of the emotions; Artaud regards the rhythm of breathing as the crucial aspect of the actor's physiological counterpart of affective musculature, maintaining that 'we can be sure that every mental movement, every feeling, every leap in human affectivity has an appropriate breath' (101).

Artaud develops his argument further in demanding that together with breathing, the actor has to have a directly related belief in the soul's flowing substantiality: 'To know that an emotion is substantial, subject to the plastic vicissitudes of matter, gives him [the actor] control over his passions, extending our sovereign command' (102).

The actor, then, must develop his affective musculature just as an athlete must train his physiological muscles. Such development will enable the actor to do justice to the importance placed on his acting in the performance. However, the actor must also be 'a kind of neutral, pliant factor since he is vigorously denied any individual initiative' (75). The paradox of the actor's simultaneous physical presence and neutrality repeats in different terminology and on the physical level rather than the emotional, Stanislavsky's paradox within the actor, the actor's art of being both deeply emotionally involved (Artaud's physical presence) and yet still in conscious control of the acting through his ability to witness his own acting (Artaud's demand for the actor's neutrality).

An actor in a higher state of consciousness as defined by Vedic Science will have developed fully not only his consciousness, but also his physiology-a perfectly functioning physiology is the prerequisite for the mind's ability to reflect pure consciousness on the individual level. Artaud's reference to the actor's neutrality can be explained, with reference to Vedic Science, in two ways: first, it applies to the 'neutral' feature of pure, contentless consciousness, the 'witnessing' function characteristic of cosmic consciousness. Second, 'neutral' refers, on a more practical level, to the actor's ability, growing on the path to and perfected in the state of cosmic consciousness, to adopt any shade of intensity on the stage, depending on the circumstances and requirements of the given production.

The Actor and the Marionette

So far in this chapter, I have used the model of consciousness proposed by Vedic Science to deepen our understanding of several important aspects of acting: the actor's emotional involvement, the actor's *presence* from the perspectives of Artaud and Barba, Mnouchkine's concept of *state*, and my own experiences in relation to it, and Grotowski's concept of *translumination*. In addition to demonstrating the explanatory potential of the model of consciousness proposed by Vedic Science, I argued that *presence*, *state* and *translumination* are not only cogent concepts, but, at least equally important, terms to describe specific experiences of actors and spectators: while different in contents, they have the fundamental experience of pure consciousness in common. The experience of pure consciousness can be trained systematically; thus I conclude that *presence*, *state* and *translumination* can be trained as well, contrary to, for example, Barba's opinion.

In the final section of this chapter on the relationship between acting and consciousness, I want to refer to one aspect of the relationship between the human performer and the puppet or marionette in terms of Vedic Science. Human beings were at times considered lacking in mind and body to reach any ideal state of perfection in performative activity. The ideal was conceptualised in the form of the marionette first and foremost by Heinrich von Kleist. I survey his major positions against the background of Vedic Science to see whether his claims for superiority of the marionette may have further implications for the theatre of the future.

In a series of newspaper articles, entitled *Über das Marionettentheater* (1810), Heinrich von Kleist (1777-1811) argued that the marionette has advantages compared with even the best of human dancers: first, it can achieve an unsurpassed level of grace because it always moves from the centre of movement. In contrast, in human movement the focus of attention is hardly ever at the centre of movement, but elsewhere in the body. Kleist locates the reason for human inability to reach unity of centre of movement and focus of attention in the interference of self-awareness, self-reflection. Only if cognition has passed through the infinite, grace returns. This is possible in the human body which has no consciousness at all (the marionette) or infinite consciousness (God). The second advantage of the marionette is that it is not subject to the laws of gravity which impede perfect movement of the human performer. Whereas the first advantage implies consciousness, the second relates, at first glance, predominantly to the body. Thus, consciousness and body gain a central position for performance. I want to reassess the implications of Kleist's argument for contemporary performance theory and practice. The survey of the current debate in consciousness studies, deals mainly with ordinary states of consciousness. Infinite consciousness, suggested by Kleist, is a phenomenon discussed in terms of altered states of consciousness (ASC), especially the phenomenon of *pure consciousness*, which is said to be an experience of infinity. The model of the mind proposed by Vedic Science, allows a reassessment of the advantages of the marionette over the human performer argued by Kleist, i.e. the lack of two impediments, self-consciousness and gravity.

In my survey of Indian philosophy and its reassessment in the form of Vedic Science by Maharishi Mahesh Yogi, (see appendix 2) I pointed out that cosmic intellect, *buddhi*, causes the unity of *samhita* to express a diversity within itself, thus giving rise to the entire creation, whose purpose is to regain unity. *Ayurveda*, the Indian discipline of medicine, states that it is a similar 'mistake of the intellect' (*pragyaparadha*) which is responsible for illness in the body: primordial imbalance occurs when the intellect becomes absorbed in the diversified values (*rishi, devata, chhandas*) to the exclusion of the unified value, *samhita*. In terms of human consciousness: as long as pure consciousness is not permanently experienced in daily life, the intellect is bound to get absorbed in any field of daily activity, allowing sensory impressions and other activities of the waking mind to overshadow the experience of pure consciousness. Reflection of one's own activity can be one of the activities the intellect gets absorbed in. This is self-consciousness, according to Kleist so detrimental to performance because it impedes natural, spontaneous flow of energies, appreciated as grace. In a higher state of consciousness, as described by Vedic Science, pure consciousness co-exists with waking consciousness. In cosmic consciousness this co-existence is experienced as total dualism: fully committed activity of the waking, dreaming or sleeping mind is witnessed by pure consciousness. Via refined cosmic consciousness, pure consciousness and activity are experienced as unity in unity consciousness.

In such higher states of consciousness, the intellect, responsible in the ordinary waking state of consciousness for the detrimental effect of self-reflection, has become an integrated part of consciousness. The intellect had been absorbed in diversified values of daily life; it had lost touch with, or, to be more precise, it had lost its memory of, the value of unity, *samhita*. Higher states of consciousness are characterised by the permanent experience of pure consciousness, as separate from activity in cosmic consciousness and unified with activity in unity consciousness. Detrimental self-reflection could be interpreted as a conscious, intentional effort to experience pure consciousness. The fact that it is intentional, i.e. not spontaneous, is exactly what makes it an impediment against spontaneity in any action it is involved in, including performance. If pure consciousness, as one characteristic of living a higher state of consciousness, is experienced spontaneously, self-reflection is no longer needed and will automatically subside. Mind and body are functioning together as a unit, without impediment, energies can flow freely. In Kleist's terms, unity of the centre of movement and focus of attention will be achieved, grace restored. All this is possible, the argument implies, on the level of human mind and body. I will deal with the implications of this conclusion at a later stage. First I have to address the second impediment proposed by Kleist:

The preceding reassessment of Kleist's argument from the perspective of Vedic Science suggests that development of higher states of consciousness, open to all human beings including performers, enables performers to reach a very high level of mind/body co-ordination which Kleist would attribute to the marionette or to a being with infinite consciousness, whom he can associate only with God. The second major impediment, gravity, constitutes an even more challenging phenomenon, because our contemporary mindset implies that by necessity and law, human beings are subject to gravity. A contemporary performer, then, appears to have no choice but to spend much energy trying to overcome gravity to achieve 'soaring feats of lightness and grace' (Watson, 1993: 34). The marionette, Kleist argues, is not hindered by this law of nature, and therefore, its grace is infinitely higher and more appealing to the audience. The *Yoga Sutras* by Patanjali are a major text of Indian *Yoga* philosophy. Dating from around 350 to 250 BCE (Karambelkar, 1986: xii), the aspect of the text relevant to the present discussion concerns the *vibhutis*, extraordinary abilities achieved through specific meditative practices, which imply a subtle impulse on the level of pure consciousness. One of those abilities is 'moving through space', 'flying' (99).

Quantum physics has attempted to explain this phenomenon, which appears to defy current common sense and traditional Newtonian laws of gravity. Vedic Science identifies the field of pure consciousness with the Unified Field as proposed in quantum physics (Hagelin, 1987). By setting an impulse on the level of pure consciousness, the unified field within the human being, it is possible, Hagelin argues, 'to modify the local curvature of space-geometry described in general relativity in such a way that the body flies up, or to the left, or forward, or in any possible direction' (Wallace, 1993: 174).

The *vibhuti* technique which enables flying, described by Patanjali, represents one among many techniques meant to assist the practitioner to develop higher states of consciousness. It is not an end in itself; however, the person who has established a higher state of consciousness permanently will have immediate access to any of those abilities. Whereas from the perspective of the person who is bound in ordinary waking consciousness with all its restrictions, separated from the experience of pure consciousness, those abilities appear extraordinary, they are a normal aspect of the range of consciousness open to anyone who has permanently established a higher state of consciousness. The path of development includes initially short, and in due course longer glimpses, experiences of such abilities, until the higher state of consciousness has been established on a permanent basis.

The marionette, Kleist maintains, is not subject to the law of gravity. My preceding argument leads to the conclusion that the human performer is not necessarily bound by that set of laws either. A performer who achieves a temporary experience or approximation of experience on the path of development towards permanent higher state of consciousness, or has permanently established higher state of consciousness, is beyond the law of gravity and can achieve the kind of grace which Kleist attributes to the marionette.

The reassessment of Kleist's essay on marionettes from the perspective of Vedic Science has shown that in theory the development of higher states of consciousness enables human performers to be as graceful in their movements as the marionette, because the two impediments Kleist indicates, self-reflexive consciousness and the body's subjection to the laws of gravity, no longer exist in a performer who during performance briefly experiences, or permanently lives (in) a higher state of consciousness.

A major question results from this theoretical conclusion: what are the implications for contemporary performance practice and training? Performative means have to be developed which ensure that the performer is enabled to experience higher states of consciousness during performance. The means of histrionic representation described in the classical Indian treatise on drama and theatre, the *Natyashastra*, might be interpreted as functioning as yogic techniques, conditioning the mind and body to function in higher states of consciousness. Other traditions of performance may offer similar techniques that need further research. These performative means have to be assisted by extra-performative means, such as meditation. Hypotheses resulting from this theory can be tested empirically, using psycho-physiological parameters known in neuroscience, etc. The methodological approach to testing the practical implication of higher states of consciousness in the theatre has to be carefully chosen: a 'pick and mix' approach, taking at random, on a trial-and-error basis, all kinds of techniques and ideas from whatever source one can lay one's hands on, in the hope of achieving the goal, may be interesting but inconclusive in its results. In contrast, it may be more useful to critically select one distinctive approach and study it in depth. If Indian philosophy and aesthetics provide the concepts on which the research approach is based, the assistance of an enlightened Indian spiritual master, a person who not only theoretically writes about, but actually lives higher states of consciousness, may be advisable. I want to critically assess this potential of Indian theatre aesthetics in theory and practice in the next chapter of this book.

4: Indian Theatre Aesthetics

In this chapter, I introduce the theatre aesthetics of the fundamental Indian text on drama and theatre, the *Natyashastra,* reassess these against the model of consciousness proposed by Vedic Science, and review the influences of Indian theatre aesthetics on Artaud, Grotowski, Barba and Brook in arriving at their concepts of theatre and their theatre practice. In the course of this argument, I also address the question if, to what extent, and how, performance that follows the guidelines of the *Natyashastra*, may serve to enhance the development of higher states of consciousness in actors and spectators.

Date and Origin of the *Natyashastra*

The *Natyashastra* mentions some other texts and their authors. It must be concluded that other sources existed prior to the *Natyashastra* itself, but no manuscripts of those earlier sources have been found so far. The authorship of the *Natyashastra* is ascribed to Bharata. However, there is no historical evidence outside the *Natyashastra* for his existence. Moreover, several critics argue, based mainly on linguistic studies of the text, that the *Natyashastra* is not a homogeneous composition of one author, but a compilation of dramatic theory and instructions for the actor of how to put the theory into practice. Critics disagree as to whether there was one original text by one author with was changed over the years, or whether the text was from the beginning a compilatory effort of several authors. Srinivasan finds an irreducible heterogeneity in the text and argues that 'we have every reason to conclude that these disparate materials are not later accretions to the *Natyashastra* known to us' (1980: 1). A major difficulty in textual matters is that there are many manuscripts of the *Natyashastra* which differ considerably among each other as to content, numbering of stanzas and chapters, some even in ascribing the author (Kale, 1974: 5). As uncertain as the authorship of the *Natyashastra* is its date, placed between the first century BCE and the eighth century CE (5).

Scope

The scope of the material covered in the *Natyashastra* is vast. There are thirty-six chapters, beginning with the origin of drama, and encompassing dramatic theory as well as practical instructions to the actors of how to achieve aesthetic experiences in the spectators. The term *shastra* implies a holy text, and in the *Natyashastra* itself Bharata claims that *Natya*, drama, was created by the creator, Brahman, as a fifth Veda, taking recitative from the *Rigveda*, the song from *Samaveda*, the histrionic representation from the *Yajurveda*, and the sentiments from the Atharvaveda (Ghosh, *Natyahastra* [NS], 1950: 4).

For the orthodox in India thus the *Natyashastra* has the combined force and authority of a divinely revealed *shruti*, the sage-expounded *smritis*, and the broad

Table 3: Rasa

```
┌─────────────────────────────────────────────────────────────┐
│       situation in the play = determinant = vibhava          │
└─────────────────────────────────────────────────────────────┘
                             │
                             ▼
                  ┌──────────────────────┐
                  │ Natyashastra prescribes │
                  └──────────────────────┘
                             │
                             ▼
┌─────────────────────────────────────────────────────────────┐
│          means of acting = consequent = anubhava             │
└─────────────────────────────────────────────────────────────┘

        ┌──────────────┐                  ┌──────────────────┐
        │    words     │                  │   temperament    │
        │   vacika     │                  │    sattvika      │
        └──────────────┘                  └──────────────────┘

            ┌──────────────┐      ┌──────────────────┐
            │   gestures   │      │   costume and    │
            │   angika     │      │ make-up aharya   │
            └──────────────┘      └──────────────────┘

┌─────────────────────────────────────────────────────────────┐
│          means of acting combine to create                   │
└─────────────────────────────────────────────────────────────┘

   ┌──────────────────┐                  ┌─────────────────────┐
   │ dominant states  │                  │   temperamental     │
   │   sthayibhava    │                  │ states, sattvikabhava│
   └──────────────────┘                  └─────────────────────┘

              ┌──────────────────┐
              │ transitory states │
              │  vyabhicaribhava  │
              └──────────────────┘

┌─────────────────────────────────────────────────────────────┐
│            states combine to create                          │
└─────────────────────────────────────────────────────────────┘
                             │
                             ▼
                      ┌─────────────┐
                      │    RASA     │
                      └─────────────┘
```

based popular tradition of the *Puranas* (Kale, 1974: 1). It is therefore no wonder that the *Natyashastra* must still be regarded as the primary source for Indian aesthetics, and indeed all the later Indian theorists of dramaturgy expressly refer to the *Natyashastra*.

Rasa

The key concept in the aesthetic theory presented in the *Natyashastra* is *rasa*. This term occurs frequently in Vedic texts, where it has various meanings:

> In *Rig Veda* the word, *rasa*, is found occurring in the sense of water (...), Soma juice (...), cow's milk (...), and flavour. The *Atharva-Veda* extends the sense to the sap of grain and the taste, the latter becoming very common. In the *Upanishads rasa* stands for the essence or quintessence and self-luminous consciousness though the sense of taste is at places conveyed (...) In Sanskrit other than the Vedic, the word, *rasa*, is used for water, milk, juice, essence, tasteful liquid, etc. (Mishra, 1964)

The material aspect of the meaning of *rasa* is emphasised in *Ayurveda*, the ancient Indian system of holistic medicine. Here, *rasa* denotes 'a certain white liquid extracted by the digestive system from the food. Its main seat is the heart' (Pandey, 1950: 10), and the *Rasayanashastra*, is a treatise on chemistry, which 'moves round the pivot of *rasa*. Mercury, which is called *rasa*, plays here a very important part' (Mishra, 1964: 198). The spiritual aspect of the meaning of *rasa* is emphasised in Shankara's commentary of the Upanishadic use of the term: '*Rasa* is here used to mean such bliss as is innate in oneself and manifests itself (...) even in the absence of external aids to happiness. It emphasises that the bliss is non-material, i.e. intrinsic, spiritual, or subjective' (Rhagavan, 1988). As such, the experience of *rasa* has been likened to the experiences of yogis by Abhinavagupta, the major commentator of Bharata's *Natyashastra*.

In the context of Indian aesthetics, *rasa* is understood as the actor's and especially the spectator's aesthetic experience. In an aesthetic context, *rasa* is translated as 'sentiment'. The *Natyashastra* differentiates eight sentiments: erotic, comic, pathetic, furious, heroic, terrible, odious, and marvellous (NS 102). Some later writers on Sanskrit poetics add one more *rasa* to this number, *santa*. The concept of *rasa* is phrased in the *Natyashastra* in form of a short statement, a *sutra*: *Vibhava- anubhava- vyabhicaribhava- samyogad rasa- nispattih*. The translation is '*Rasa* is produced (*rasa-nispattih*) from a combination (*samyogad*) of Determinants (*vibhava*), Consequents (*anubhava*) and Transitory States (*vyabhicaribhava*)' (NS 109). Determinants (*vibhava*) are characterised as situations that cause the emergence of *rasa*. For example, the erotic *rasa*

> has two bases, union (...) and separation (...). Of these two, the Erotic Sentiment in union arises from Determinants like the pleasures of the season, the enjoyment of garlands, unguents, ornaments [the company of] beloved persons, objects [of senses], splendid mansions, going to a garden, and enjoying [oneself] there, seeing

the [beloved one], hearing [his or her words], playing and dallying [with him or her]. (NS 108-9)

Consequents (*anubhava*) are defined as means of histrionic representation. In the above example, the erotic *rasa* in union should be represented on the stage by 'Consequents such as clever movement of eyes, eyebrows, glances, soft and delicate movement of limbs and sweet words and similar other things' (NS 109).

The *Natyashastra* lists altogether thirty-three transitory states (*vyabhicaribhava*): discouragement, weakness, apprehension, envy, intoxication, weariness, indolence, depression, anxiety, distraction, recollection, contentment,

shame, inconstancy, joy, agitation, stupor, arrogance, despair, impatience, sleep, epilepsy, dreaming, awakening, indignation, dissimulation, cruelty, assurance, sickness, insanity, death, fright, and deliberation (NS 102). In the example of the *rasa* of love, the *Natyashastra* states that 'Transitory States in it do not include fear, indolence, cruelty and disgust' (NS 109).

To the concern of critics, the *rasa-sutra* on its own appears not to mention all elements that work together to create *rasa*. It does not mention, that is, dominant states (*sthayibhava*) and temperamental states (*sattvikabhava*). The *Natyashastra* lists eight dominant states (*sthayibhava*): love, mirth, sorrow, anger, energy, terror, disgust, and astonishment (NS 102). There are eight temperamental states (*sattvikabhava*): 'Paralysis, Perspiration, Horripilation, Change of Voice, Trembling, Change of Colour, Weeping and Fainting' (NS 102-3). The text explains the relationship between *rasa* and determinants, consequents, dominant states, transitory states and the temperamental states through an analogy: just as various ingredients such as vegetables and spices, when mixed, produce a flavour, so the combination of the 'Dominant States (*sthayibhava*), when they come together with various other States (*bhava*) attain the quality of the Sentiment (...)' (NS 105). All the eight sentiments, the eight dominant states, the transitory states and the temperamental states are described in the *Natyashastra* in detail with reference to the determinants, the consequents, and their relation to the sentiments.

The *Natyashastra* places much emphasis on the means of histrionic representation (*abhinaya*). They are the techniques used by the actor to portray the consequents. 'From the point of view of the playwright or the character it is *anubhava*, and from that of the actor it is *abhinaya*' (Marasinghe, 1989: 198). Four kinds of *abhinaya* are differentiated: gestures (*angika*), words (*vacika*), costume and make-up (*aharya*) and the representation of the temperament (*sattvika*). To each of these aspects the *Natyashastra* devotes several chapters. Gestures are treated in chapters on the movements of minor limbs, hands, other limbs, dance movements, and gaits. The movements are also specifically related to the space of the stage (NS, chapter 14). *Vacika abhinaya*, representation through words, is covered directly in chapters on prosody, metrical patterns, dictions of play, rules of the use of languages, and modes of address and intonation; more indirectly in chapters on the construction of the plot. Other chapters provide details about costume and make-up, thus referring to *aharya abhinaya*, others about the representation of the temperaments (*sattvika abhinaya*). The means of histrionic representation (*abhinaya*) are variously combined to give rise to four different styles of dramatic performance (*vritti*), the verbal (*bharati*), the grand (*sattvati*), the graceful (*kaisiki*) and the energetic (*arabhati*). Finally, the practice of representation in a dramatic performance is twofold: realistic (*lokadharmi*) and theatrical (*natyadharmi*). The means of histrionic representation, *abhinaya*, belong to the category of *natyadharmi*.

Within this broad scope of material covered in the *Natyashastra*, the following information can be gathered about the actor: the actor is the agent responsible for creating an aesthetic experience, *rasa*, in the audience. He does this by his acting skills; the traditional view thus is that the majority of chapters in the *Natyashastra* represents a 'how-to-do-it' manual for the actor, describing in minute detail all the different techniques of the *abhinaya*, the means of histrionic representation, especially those involving gestures (*angika abhinaya*), costume and make-up (*aharya abhinaya*), representation of the temperament (*sattvika abhinaya*), and the particulars of verbal representation (*vacika abhinaya*). The text contains repeated instructions of how to combine elements of those four performance categories to convey the emotions of the characters to the spectators, to arouse the adequate *rasa* in the spectators.

In the *Natyashastra*, the focal point of the actor's emotional involvement with the character he plays is indeed the representation of the temperament (*sattvika abhinaya*). This mode of representation has its special function in conveying the temperamental states (paralysis, perspiration, horripilation, change of voice, trembling, change of colour, weeping and fainting) (NS 143). In ordinary life, such states are involuntary and would be classified by contemporary Western psychology as directed 'mostly by the effective motor region of our nervous system' (Ambardekar, 1976: 26). The *Natyashastra* explains that this way of acting is accomplished by concentration of the mind. 'Its nature (...) cannot be mimicked by an absent-minded man' (NS, 143). This statement appears to imply that the actor has to fully identify with the character he plays. Identification could then be understood to be equivalent to the concentration of the mind requested in the *Natyashastra* for a satisfactory performance of the temperamental states. However, the *Natyashastra* states in the same paragraph that 'tears and horripilation should respectively be shown by persons who are not [actually] sorry or happy' (NS 143). This is a contradiction to the requirement of a concentrated mind; it is difficult to understand how the actor's mind can be so concentrated to produce 'real' tears, horripilation, etc. for the audience to see, without that actor's involvement in the character's emotions, those emotions shown to the spectators as the cause for the tears or horripilation.

This contradiction between involvement and non-involvement has been variously discussed by later commentators and critics of the *Natyashastra* up to the present. Abhinavagupta, for example, summarises the positions of Bhatta Lollata and

Srisankuka before presenting his own view of the nature of *rasa* and the actor's role in achieving it. According to Bhatta Lollata,

> the aesthetic experience (...) is a matter of mere appearance occasioned by false identification. It is analogous to the experience of a man who experiences fear because he erroneously takes a rope for a snake. (...) The actor creates an illusion; he is a master of *maya*. The spectators are subject to his *maya* (...) [which] is productive of *rasa*. (Dhayagude, 1981: 14)

In creating this illusion, *maya*, the actor, according to Bhatta Lollata, is identified with the hero, and *rasa* is a characteristic of the character (172). Srisankuka disagrees with this latter opinion. Using popular plays about Rama, hero of the Indian epic *Ramayana*, as an example, Srisankuka argues that the actor does not identify with the character, because

> an actor who appears on the stage as Rama is obviously not identical with the real Rama. Nor is he 'non-Rama'. Since the spectators take him to be Rama, he is not different from Rama either. He cannot be said to be 'similar' to Rama since the spectators do not know the real Rama. The cognition involved in the experience 'enacted' Rama is unique. (15)

Abhinavagupta himself regards the actor as an instrument in conveying *rasa* to the spectators. The actor is not involved in the emotions of the character he plays. Moreover, 'the moment he starts enjoying himself the emotion he is playing he ceases to be an actor and becomes a *sahridaya* [connoisseur of art]' (Bhat, 1984: 48). Abhinavagupta analyses the Sanskrit term for actor, *patra*, to substantiate this point. It means both 'character' and 'carrier-pot'. The first meaning refers to the actor proper. The latter meaning implies that the actor, just as the pot, is only the carrier of relish: 'the kettle does not know the taste of the brew' (48). Starting with the contradiction in the *Natyashastra*, we find that Bhatta Lollata appears to defend, if vaguely, an identification and involvement, whereas Srisankuka and Abhinavagupta argue against such an involvement. Among contemporary critics, Jhanji points out that 'to say that the actor does not feel anything *qua* himself does not imply that he does not imaginatively reconstruct the emotive experience of the character he portrays' (1989: 35). In support of this argument he mentions Bharata's emphasis on the *sattvika abhinaya*, the means of histrionic representation dealing with the temperamental states. He interprets these means as 'internalisation of emotive experience on the part of the actor' (35). This view presents a compromise: Jhanji accepts Abhinavagupta's idea of the actor's non-involvement. He then explains the actor's ability to get his body to function in a mode that is the domain of the involuntary nervous system by reference to 'internalisation of emotive experience'. However, this concept would need a thorough explanation in itself as to how it might be able to account for the phenomenon it has been used to explain.

In her study of the technique of *abhinaya* Pandya attempts to explain the actor's ability to present temperamental states with reference to the term *sattvika*, and the concept of *sattva*. Thus, she defines *sattva* as 'the capability of an individual to bring into being the pleasures and pains experienced by others, making them his own' (Pandya, 1988: 256). This capability applies both to the author, the actor, and the spectator. Through *sattva* the author experiences the pleasures and pains of the character he creates and is thus able to draw the character. 'The actor (...) with the help of *sattva* makes theses experiences his own and presents them on the stage while the sympathetic spectators enjoy the representation through the same medium, i.e. *sattva*' (256). Dalal interprets *sattva* similarly. Referring to Dhanika, a later Sanskrit theorist of drama and poetry, he states that *sattva* 'is a mental condition which is highly sympathetic to the joys and sorrows of the others' (1973: 36). She adds that this mental state arises when the mind 'is in a state of composure' (36). Bhat takes both the mental and the physical aspect into account when he defines *sattvika abhinaya* as 'a physical manifestation of a deep mental state' (1981: 51). Marasinghe defines *sattva* as 'a certain law (*dharma*) which governs the expression of the inner state of a person' (1989: 188).

Issues for Further Debate

The concept of *rasa* is central to understanding Indian theatre aesthetics as described in the *Natyashastra*. The majority of current attempts at making sense of *rasa* are based on Western concepts of the mind. In order to enable a cogent comparison of any Western aesthetic theory with its counterparts in Indian aesthetic theory, the latter has to be understood on the basis of the same underlying model of mind and consciousness. In particular, the following issues have to be addressed:

a) Is the actor to be emotionally involved or not while acting? The *Natyashastra* is not conclusive on this subject. In requesting the actor to be of utmost concentrated mind, it appears to suggest involvement. In stating that the temperamental states (*sattvika bhava*) should be shown by persons (i.e. actors) who are not actually feeling the emotions that cause those states, the text appears to suggest emotional non-involvement on the part of the actor.

b) How exactly does the actor achieve (process of *sattvika abhinaya*) the histrionic representation of those temperamental states (*sattvika bhava*)? The problem here is that the temperamental states belong to the domain of the autonomous nervous system. This part of the nervous system is in charge of involuntary neuro-muscular activities, commonly understood to be beyond the influence of the will. How could an actor influence this domain, independent of whether or not he is emotionally involved in the emotions of the character he is portraying.

c) A brief survey of previous attempts to clarify the problem raised in item (b) suggests that major importance will have to be placed on an adequate interpretation of the concept of *sattva* in its different occurrences in the technical terms used in the *Natyashastra* and later Indian aesthetics, such as *sattvika abhinaya* and *sattvika bhava*.

d) In this context, the frame-concept of the entire *Natyashastra*, *rasa*, has to be re-assessed, especially regarding the following sub-areas of interest:

I. What is the nature of the aesthetic experience called *rasa*?
II. What importance does the number of *rasas* have on the understanding of the *rasa*-concept in general, and with reference to items (a) to (c) stated above. In detail this means an investigation of
> • whether there is a difference in concept between the eight sentiments (erotic, comic, pathetic, etc.), originally found in the *Natyashastra* and the ninth sentiment later added to that enumeration;
> • whether there is a difference in concept between the eight or individual sentiments on the *Natyashastra* and later additions, rendered as *rasa-s*, and the eight or nine *rasa-s* and one *rasa* in the singular, on a different (possibly hierarchically higher) conceptual level.
III. Is the spectator's aesthetic experience as described by the concept of *rasa* like, or equal to, or unlike the spiritual experience of a yogi? Is there any parallel between an actor's experience while acting with the spectator's? Is there a spiritual dimension involved in acting, parallel to the yogic practices that lead to yogic experiences?

Based on a thorough discussion of items (a) to (d), the meanings of the crucial terms in the *rasa-sutra*, *samyogad*, traditionally rendered as 'combination', and *nispattih*, traditionally rendered as 'produced' have to be subjected to a reassessment.

The Perspective of Vedic Science

The discussion of the *Natyashastra* from the tradtional Indian and Western critical perspectives led to a number of open issues, which I want to address in this part of the chapter. For that purpose, I place the *Natyashastra* in the context of *Gandharva-Veda*, that part of Vedic Literature that deals with dance, drama and music. Subsequently, I subject the major aesthetic concept (or experience) of *rasa* to a reassessment from the perspective of Vedic Science.

Gandharvaveda, consciousness and the primoridal sound

The aspect of Vedic literature that deals with theatre is *Gandharva-Veda*. The term is a combination of *Gandharva*, divine musician, and *Veda*, knowledge. It is part of a group of four disciplines, called *Upaveda*, which focus on four major areas of practical life. Apart from *Gandharva-Veda*, this group comprises *Ayurveda* (medicine), *Sthapatya-Veda*, (architecture) and *Dhanur-Veda* (politics). *Gandharva-Veda* is closely related to *Ayurveda*, representing on of its methods of therapy. *Gandharva-Veda* incorporates the major treatises on music theatre, the *Natyashastra*, ascribed to Bharata; the *Narada-Shiksha* by Narada, and the *Sangita Ratnakara* by Sharngadev. All three texts of *Gandharva-Veda* cover, in various scope, three aspects of music: song (*gitam*), instrumental music (*vadyam*), and dance, theatre arts (*nrittam*). Within the concept of *samhita*, *rishi*, *devata* and *chhandas*, *Gandharva-Veda* as a whole is dominated by the *rishi* element. It also represents the *rishi element* in relation to the four *Upaveda*, with *Ayur-Veda* representing *samhita*, *Dhanur-Veda* representing *devata*, and *Sthapatya-Veda* representing *chhandas*. Within *Gandharva-Veda*, the *Natyashastra* represents the *rishi* value, *Narada-Shiksha* the *devata* and *Sangita Ratnakara* the *chhandas* value. *Sangita* is the total work of art, combining as *rishi* value *gitam* (song), as *devata* value *vadyam* (instrumental music) and as *chhandas* value *nrittam*, dance and theatre arts.

According to the *Gandharva-Veda*, dance originally symbolises the subtle, rhythmical dynamics of transformations from one note to the other, a manifest expression of unmanifest processes in *samhita* on which the entire creation is based. Primordial sounds are qualities of consciousness. Thus the expressed values of consciousness, the individual dance movements, each represent a specific quality of consciousness (Hartmann, 1992: 62). A performer who has full command of consciousness, i.e. who has established at least cosmic consciousness, will automatically, without time lapse between impulse and expression, use the gesture, or combination of gestures, that is the manifest equivalent of the quality of consciousness required in a given situation of performance dictated by the contents of performance and the outer conditions of performance, e.g., performance space and audience. Thus the description of *angika abhinaya*, gestural means of histrionic representation, is a description from an enlightened consciousness of what a fully developed actor will spontaneously, and with full discipline of mind and body, do to create a specific effect on the spectator in a given theatrical situation. The inner dynamics of the primordial sound of *nada* begins to vibrate in every cell, gaining such strength that it finally takes hold of the entire body and causes it to dance (62). The art of dancing was developed into the art of theatre. The intention of this development was, as described in the *Natyashastra*, to enable people who had lost touch with their unmanifest source to gain familiarity with Vedic truths.

A reassessment of *rasa*

Theatre, in the sense of dance-drama, functions not only on the level of symbolism of theatrical action, but also through language (*vacika abhinaya*), costume and make-up (*aharya*) and representation of the temperament (*sattvika-abhinaya*). Costume and make-up will function mainly through the sense of sight, affecting the emotions. The symbolic nature of theatre affects mainly the intellect. Gestures (*angika abhinaya*), function through the sense of sight, and language (*vacika abhinaya*) through the sense of hearing. Both gestures and language arise from the level of pure consciousness, and will ultimately affect the spectator on that very same level of pure consciousness. The fully developed actor, then, achieves his effects on the spectator by stimulating the spectator's senses, his intellect, the emotions, and both through stimulating all these, and unmediated, the actor reaches to the spectator's pure consciousness, which is the ultimate target of his art and skill. In meditation, the aim might be to reach the experience of pure consciousness on its own. However, as Vedic Science shows, the ultimate aim of meditation is not pure consciousness on its own, but the coexistence of pure consciousness with waking, or dreaming, or sleeping, a state called cosmic consciousness, which develops further to refined cosmic consciousness and ultimately unity consciousness. What theatre in the Vedic sense aspires to is to provide the spectators with experiences of at least cosmic consciousness, initially only lasting for a short time, eventually longer. Repeated exposure to Vedic theatre will train the mind to naturally experience pure consciousness together with sensory impressions.

One of the characteristics of pure consciousness, or *sat chit ananda*, absolute (*sat*) bliss (*ananda*) consciousness (*chit*) is bliss. Any experience of pure consciousness will have that quality. Thus the specific experience in the theatre, an aesthetic experience, if it allows the spectator's mind to reach pure consciousness, will suffuse the impressions gained by the senses with the underlying quality of bliss. Neither the sensory impressions nor the bliss, however, will overshadow pure consciousness: when the spectator experiences temporary cosmic consciousness while watching a play, his pure consciousness is separate from the sensory impressions, and bliss is a quality of pure consciousness itself. In cases of temporary experiences of unity consciousness through the stimuli of the performance, the spectator will experience the events acted on the stage, the actors, and even the fellow-spectators, as expressions of the same pure consciousness that also forms his own basis. There is an experience of unity, all in terms of pure consciousness, which is not overshadowed.

The nature of the aesthetic experience, *rasa*, is thus the experience of pure consciousness together with performance-specific theatrical contents of the mind (in the broad definition of Vedic Science). Through repeated exposure to the experience of pure consciousness, brought about by actor's art in the theatre, the spectator's consciousness is trained to uphold pure consciousness for longer periods of time, ultimately indefinite, not only in subsequent theatrical performances, but also in daily life outside the theatre. The *Natyashastra's* claim of its original purpose, to restore the golden age which had given way to the silver one, thus becomes more than a rhetorical claim for usefulness.

Rasa has been re-defined from the spectator's perspective as a combination of blissful pure consciousness and the specific impressions on the mind provided by a theatrical performance. Abhinavagupta held that the actor does not experience *rasa* himself. From the point of view of Vedic Science, this assumption needs a re-assessment. What affects the spectator are the actor's means of histrionic representation, gestures, words, representation of temperament and costume and make-up. For the enlightened actor, gestures and words, it has been shown, will proceed spontaneously from his pure consciousness, transforming itself without time lapse into objective expression, which is then subjectively experienced by the spectator, affecting his senses, intellect, emotions, and through those his pure consciousness. Pure consciousness has been discovered to be a field that connects all individuals. If the actor, then, operates from the level of pure consciousness, he will affect the spectator not only on the expressed levels of the mind, but also directly on the level of pure consciousness. The enlightened actor has the continuous experience of the bliss characteristic of pure consciousness. If he produces from within that pure consciousness the expressed means of histrionic representation, he combines bliss with expressions of *abhinaya*, which make up the experience of *rasa*. Thus the actor establishes *rasa* within himself in the process of stimulating the experience of *rasa* in the spectator.

In Bharata's *Natyashastra*, eight *rasas* are mentioned, the erotic, comic, pathetic, furious, heroic, terrible, odious, and marvellous (NS 102). A ninth *rasa* is added to this list by later theorists. Abhinavagupta describes it as follows:

> Now *santa*, which has sama for its *sthayibhava*, and which leads to *moksha*, arises from *vibhavas* such as knowledge of the truth, detachment, purity of mind, etc. It should be acted out by the *anubhava* such as *yama* and *niyama*, meditation on the Self, concentration of the mind on the self (*dharana*), devotion (*upasana*), compassion towards all creatures, and the wearing of religious paraphernalia (*lingagrahana*). Its *vyabhicaribhavas* are disgust with the world (*nirveda*), remembrance, firmness of mind, purity in all the four stages of life (*asrama*), rigidity (of the body) (*stambha*), horripilation, etc. The following Aryas and Slokas exist on this subject: *Santa Rasa* has been taught as a means to the highest happiness (*naihsreyasa*). It arises from a desire to secure the liberation of the pure consciousness and leads to knowledge of the truth. *Santa Rasa* should be known as that which brings happiness and welfare to all beings and which is accompanied by the stabilization (*samsthita*) in the Self that results from the curbing of the organs of perception and the organs of physical activity. *Santa Rasa* is that state wherein one feels the same towards all creatures, wherein there is no pain, no happiness, no hatred and no envy. *Santa* is one's natural state of mind (*prakrti*). Other emotions such as love, etc. are deformations of that original state. The deformations arise out of this natural state of the mind and in the end again merge back into it. The emotions arise out of *santa* depending on their particular respective causes. And when the specific causes cease to function, they all merge back into *santa*. Those who know dramaturgy see nine *Rasas* along with their characteristics in this manner. (Masson and Patwardhan, 1969: 92-3)

Santa is called 'one's natural state', which is termed *prakriti*. This refers to *samkhya* philosophy, where *prakriti* is a major principle of creation. *Prakriti* is primordial nature, everything arises from it (Sinha, 1971: Sutra 118). The three *gunas*, *sattva*, *rajas*, and *tamas*, the creating, stimulating and restricting powers, are in balance on the level of *prakriti*, so that no structures can come into existence. *Prakriti* is faced by the other major principle, *purusha*. In other Vedic texts, this principle is referred to as *atman*, pure consciousness. It is characterised as eternal, pure, conscious, liberated, and self-sufficient (Sutra 37-8), without action (Sutra 229) and a witness (Sutra 205). The principles of *purusha* and *prakriti* function both on the cosmic and on the individual human levels. *Purusha* is experienced as pure consciousness, and *prakriti* represents the dynamism within *purusha*, within pure consciousness, a dynamism that will eventually lead to all possible manifestation.

The characteristics of *santa rasa* match with the descriptions of pure consciousness as contentless: the individual experiencing *santa rasa* feels 'the same', i.e. nothing, 'towards all creatures'. There is no pain, no happiness, no hatred, and no envy. The effects that experiencing *santa rasa* bring to the spectator are 'happiness and welfare', 'highest happiness', 'stabilization of the Self'. The ingredients leading to the experience of *santa rasa* are also related to the process of gaining liberation: (*moksha*): the dominant emotion (*sthayibhava*), the determinants (*vibhava*), the consequents (*anubhava*), and the transitory states (*vyabhicaribhava*).

Santa rasa is called the natural state of the mind, in the sense that it is the basis of all other states. Seen from the perspective of Vedic Science, *santa rasa* is equivalent to the experience of pure consciousness evoked in actor and spectator through theatre; the other eight *rasas* represent the influence of the expressed stimuli of theatre, leading to an aesthetic experience dominated by love, mirth, sorrow, anger, energy, terror, disgust, and astonishment (NS 102). The fully developed actor is best able to create *santa rasa* and a specific expressed *rasa* in the spectator. Again the assumption applies that the actor, too, not only the spectator, experiences *rasa*.

These considerations necessitate a re-assessment of the *rasa-sutra*: *Vibhava-anubhava-vyabhicaribhava-samyogad rasa-nispattih*. The translation provided by Ghosh is: '*Rasa* is produced (*rasa-nispattih*) from a combination (*samyogad*) of Determinants (*vibhava*), Consequents (*anubhava*) and Transitory States (*vyabhicaribhava*)' (NS 109). Ghosh translates the term *vibhava* from the expressed context of the theatrical situation as 'determinant', given situations found in the playtext in which specific means of histrionic representation have to be used. In view of the fact that *santa rasa* is pure consciousness, and taking into consideration that *vibhava* also means 'pure consciousness' (Shankar, 1992), the use of the term *vibhava* in the context of the *Natyashastra* refers to situations structured as possibilities in the dynamism of pure consciousness. Such latent situations, present as potentialities on the level of pure consciousness, take their shape in the theatrical context as *anubhava*. Ghosh again renders this term on the expressed level, as 'consequent', means of histrionic representation doing justice to the 'Determinants'. *Anubhava* also means the experience of multitude after arising from pure consciousness (Shankar, 1992). In other words, the potentialities of *vibhava* are experienced by the actor and in turn by the spectator as taking a specific shape in the theatrical context. Manifestation progresses further by 'adding the ingredient' of *vyabhicaribhava*, translated by Ghosh as 'transitory states [of emotion]'. Indeed, *vyabhicaribhava* means the spreading, the expression of that experience of multitude implied by *anubhava* (Shankar, 1992). *Samyogad* has been translated by Ghosh as 'combination', taking recourse to the illustration provided by the *Natyashastra* itself, which compares the functioning of the different elements in creating *rasa* to adding diverse ingredients to cook delicious food. *Samyogad*, however, means not so much a combination, an adding together, but implies a unity (Shankar, 1992). Only when pure consciousness (*vibhava*), the experience of the multitude after coming out of pure consciousness (*anubhava*) and the spreading, or expression of that experience form a unity will *rasa* be produced in actor and spectator alike.

To summarise: *rasa* is an aesthetic experience for both actor and spectator, consisting in the coexistence of pure consciousness with aesthetic, theatre/performance-specific contents, sensory impressi-ons, stimuli for the mind, the intellect, and the emotions. As time is non-existent on the level of pure consciousness, the basis of theatrical activity in the case of the enlightened actor, creation of *rasa* in the actor will be simultaneous with the stimuli creating *rasa* in the spectator being emitted by the actor. The time lapse between the onset of those stimuli and their taking effect in the consciousness of the spectator, and the degree to which they take effect, depend on the 'openness' of the spectator's consciousness. Repeated exposure to such experiences will train the spectator in responding to *rasa*-inducing stimuli faster, and to a larger degree. In due course, experiences of pure consciousness together with other (i.e. not necessarily aesthetic) contents of the expressed mind will be the natural consequence of the training process.

Now that I have introduced the theatre aesthetics of the *Natyashastra* in the context of Vedic Science, I proceed to assess the influence of this body of knowledge, in combination with general aspects of Indian philosophy, on eminent nineteenth- and twentieth-century theatre artists, Stanislavsky, Artaud, Grotowski, Barba and Brook.

Stanislavsky: general points of contact

Stanislavsky argued that the solar plexus is the seat of emotion in the same way that the brain is the seat of consciousness. In addition, for Stanislavsky the solar plexus is the radiating centre of *prana*, the vital energy of life. According to Vedic literature, *prana* or life-energy is a direct emanation of Brahman, absolute consciousness (Vires-waranananda, 1970, 252). It is located in the heart lotus, equivalent to the solar plexus (Venkatesananda, 1984, 282). Prana itself gives rise to several functions of the body: 'It enables the eyes to see, the skin to feel, the mouth to speak, the food to be digested, and it performs all the functions in the body' (282). Thus the function of *prana* appears to be related to the functioning of the body as a manifestation of consciousness. Stanislavsky believed that not only external, visible movements are manifest, but also 'inner, invisible acts of spiritual communion' (1986: 205). In consequence, Stanislavsky asks the actor: 'In addition to the consciousness, explicit discussion and intellectual exchange of thought, can you feel a parallel exchange of currents, something you draw in through your eyes and put out again through them?' (214). Stanislavsky termed this current of energy, derived from the Hindu concept of *prana*, 'irradiation', and likened it to 'an underground river, which flows continuously under the surface of both words and silence and forms an invisible bond between subject and object' (214). We have seen that according to Vedic literature, *prana* or life-energy is a direct emanation of

Brahman, absolute consciousness, located in the heart lotus, equivalent to the solar plexus. The function of *prana* appears to be related to the functioning of the body as a manifestation of consciousness more than specifically related to the emotions; a misunderstanding in Stanislavsky's sources or on his own part seems likely, associating an energy which is centred in the heart with the emotions, which are traditionally associated with the heart.

Stanislavsky described the unconscious objective as the best and most desirable, and he states: 'The Hindus call such objectives the highest kind of superconsciousness' (Stanislavsky, 1961: 52). In terms of Indian philosophy, pure, contentless consciousness is called *samadhi*. In the individual process of development of consciousness, occasional glimpses of pure consciousness are called *savikalpa samadhi*. Such temporary pure consciousness is differentiated from permanent pure consciousness, or *nirvikalpa samadhi* (Haney, 1991: 297).

Kramer has tried to compare the theatre aesthetics of the *Natyashastra* with Stanislavsky's system, acknowledging that drawing such parallels makes no claim at establishing direct influence. According to Kramer, the determinant (*vibhava*) causes a specific emotional state (*bhava*) which in turn causes a consequent (*anubhava*). This, according to Kramer, parallels Stanislavsky: 'given circumstances cause emotions causes behavior' (1991: 56). The assumptions on which Kramer bases his parallels, however, require a reassessment. The causal chain 'determinants-emotional state-consequents' is not appropriate. Rather, the mechanism is as follows: in specific situations laid down in the play (determinants), the actor has to use specific means of histrionic representation (consequents) to create specific dominant emotional states (*sthayibhava*). Those dominant emotional states combine with transitory states (*vyabhicaribhava*) and temperamental states (*sattvikabhava*). The end product of this combination process is the aesthetic experience, *rasa*. Although Stanislavsky comes close, the parallel as argued by Kramer cannot be maintained.

Kramer links the temperamental states *sattvikabhava* to Stanislavsky's 'Magic If' and 'sense of truth', since 'sattva' can be understood, Kramer argues, as 'the mental capacity of the actor to identify himself with the character and his feelings' (56). Similarly, the 'Magic If' or 'sense of truth' allows 'the actor to convince himself that the circumstances are real to the character, even though, as an actor, he knows that they are not' (57). The discussion of the concept of *sattva* has shown, however, that the concept of 'sattva', whatever its exact definition, certainly refers to a state of mind that is beyond the emotions, the field of operation of the 'magic If'.

The comparison of aesthetic concepts, theories of acting in the *Natyashastra* and in Stanislavsky's system was inspired by Stanislavsky's apparent influence by Indian philosophy. Kramer's essay highlights the difficulties of this approach: scholarship currently lacks a consistent model of human consciousness, of the human mind, that allows a precise understanding of the assumptions of consciousness informing the aesthetics of the *Natyashastra*, and thus enables a coherent comparison with Stanislavsky's concepts.

Artaud: The Balinese inspiration

In arriving at his concept of *Theatre of Cruelty* Artaud was strongly influenced by seeing a performance of a Balinese dance/theatre company (see chapter six for a reassessment of Artaud's concept against the background of Vedic Science). Artaud seems to have attended the performance at the French Colonial Exhibition on August 1, 1931, because he wrote a very enthusiastic letter about this experience to the director Louis Jouvet the next day (Schumacher, 1989: 92). Inspired by his experience, Artaud also wrote a short article, *On the Balinese Theatre*, which was published in *Nouvelle Revue Francaise* No. 127, on 1 October 1931.

Artaud regards Balinese theatre as different from European theatre in its emphasis not on psychology but on 'dance, singing, mime and music' (1974: 38). Artaud describes these forms of theatrical expression further by referring to

> angular, sudden, jerky postures (...), syncopated inflections formed at the back of the throat, (...) musical phrases cut short, (...) sharded flights, rustling branches, hollow drum sounds, robot creaking, animated puppets dancing. (38)

Hayman notes that most of these images are non-human (Hayman, 1977: 77). Artaud's profound experience of Balinese dance, singing, mime and music led not only to the vivid description just quoted. It set the foundation for the theory that theatre need not exist on the basis of words, of dialogue alone. Rather, the Balinese experience opened his eyes to the potential of a 'new bodily language' (77) which is based on signs. Those signs function on an intuitive level. Because they are so strong and powerful, the spectator who is affected by them does not have to react on a logical, discursive level of language—his/her intuitive reaction is sufficient, this reaction alone is aimed at in Balinese theatre. Artaud felt that it was possible, through this kind of bodily language practised by the Balinese performers, to 're-establish theatre as pure and independent creativity' on the level of the spectator's consciousness. At the same time, Artaud maintains, Balinese performance is based on realism. The performers skilfully make use of a wide range of theatre conventions, such as eye-rolling, pouting lips, twitching muscles, heads moving horizontally. All these means of histrionic representation produce 'studiously calculated effects which prevent any resorting to spontaneous improvisation' (39).

Artaud again compares the experience of Balinese with that of European theatre. To the earlier difference of Balinese theatre as pure and independent creativity, and European psychological theatre he now adds the difference of verbal European theatre and total Balinese theatre, a theatre which combines 'everything that exists spatially on the boards or is measured and circumscribed in space, having spatial density (moves, forms, colours, vibrations, postures, shouts)' (40) with the spiritual dimension also lacking in European theatre, which Artaud associates with the indeterminable, the dependence on the suggestive power of the mind.

Artaud sets one-sided, dialogue-dominated European theatre against Balinese theatre, in which all theatrical elements are connected in a perfectly ordered fashion. Whereas European theatre mainly serves entertainment purposes, defined by Artaud as 'useless artificiality, an evening's amusement' (44), Balinese theatre, for Artaud, takes on the dimension of a religious ritual ceremony. In the play staged in the Balinese theatre Artaud saw, the aim was not to imitate reality. Rather, it aimed at specific experiences in the spectator's consciousness. Artaud seemed unable to clearly pinpoint these experiences, and there is an apparent contradiction in his writings on the matter. In the article for *Nouvelle Revue Francaise* he had argued that the signs shown on the stage function on an intuitive level. In later comments on Balinese theatre, he holds that

> the things this theatre makes tangible are much less emotional than intellectual, enclosing them as it does within concrete, though almost constantly esoteric, signs. Thus we are led along intellectual paths towards reconquering the signs of existence. (46)

Artaud's thoughts about the mechanisms of the effects of Balinese theatre on its spectators do not even stop at the contradictory preferences for intellect or intuition or emotion. At times, a level beyond all those is indicated, when Artaud talks about a trance-like state being induced in the spectator, and observes that the spectator's thoughts (intellect) and feelings (emotion and intuition) are dissolved and thus returned to their pure state. Artaud here evokes, in poetic language, a state of consciousness beyond intellect, emotions, feelings, intuition, and Artaud holds that this state can be experienced through exposure to Balinese theatre.

Artaud's views on Balinese theatre are controversial: allegedly, he got the facts wrong on which he bases his conclusions. Grotowski, for example, points to a major mis-reading:

> Artaud deciphered as 'cosmic signs' and 'gestures evoking superior powers' elements of the performance which were concrete expressions, specific theatrical letters in an alphabet of signs universally understood by the Balinese. (1969: 89)

On a surface level, this criticism is accurate. Whether Artaud did not know about the codification of the signs used in Balinese drama or not, he at least does not indicate that he did. However, does the existence of a theatrical alphabet which the Balinese understand intellectually, rule out that the practical use of this alphabet in performance has direct or indirect effects on the spectator's consciousness independent of whether he or she knows intellectually what a particular letter is supposed to *mean*? Artaud attended one Balinese performance without much prior knowledge or any experience of this art form. His direct experience, unmediated by prior knowledge or experience, was influential for his thinking, and it is those unmediated experiences that he tried to conceptualise. Lacking any background in specifically Balinese performance aesthetics, he used whatever knowledge he had at his disposal, including Freudian psychoanalysis and mystic theories of Cabbala and Gnosticism, and thus arrived at the phrases criticised by Grotowski, e.g.

'cosmic signs' or 'gestures evoking superior powers'. The argument here is that the intellectual level of meaning created in Balinese theatre through signs universally understood by the indigenous spectators, can co-exist with a different level on which the signs (which produce meaning on the first level) produce effects on a level that goes beyond that of meaning, intellect.

To return to Artaud and Balinese theatre: the signs of Balinese theatre are codified, based, as they are, in the *Natyashastra*. Many Balinese spectators will *know* (intellectually) what the signs mean, and can thus follow the danced storylines. However, the signs (the means of acting, deriving from the *Natyashastra*) function on levels beyond *knowing*: they affect all levels of consciousness, including pure consciousness. To repeat the point I made above, and which I wanted to support by summarising my research into *rasa* and the *Natyashastra:* the intellectual level of meaning created in Balinese theatre through signs universally understood by the indigenous spectators, can co-exist with a different level on which the signs (which produce meaning on the first level) produce effects on a level that goes beyond that of meaning, intellect. Remember: Artaud talks about a trance-like state that is induced in the spectator, and observes that the spectator's thoughts (intellect) and feelings (emotion and intuition) are dissolved and thus returned to their pure state. Artaud holds that this state can be experienced through exposure to Balinese theatre. Because Artaud allegedly misunderstood some details of Balinese theatre, his intuition that Balinese theatre could achieve such a 'pure state', an experience of *rasa*, tended to be overlooked. My reassessment, based on consciousness studies and a reassessment of the *Natyashastra's* aesthetics, summarised above, suggests that Artaud was on the right track with his intuition here, just as he was with the ideas about language of nature (see chapter six) and the apparent paradox of neutrality and presence (see chapter three).

A further highly controversial point in Artaud's understanding of Balinese theatre is the role of the director. Basis of the controversy is the following passage:

> This theatre does away with the playwright to the advantage of what in Western theatre jargon we call the producer. But the latter becomes a kind of organiser of magic, a master of holy ceremonies. And the material on which he works, the subjects he makes thrilling are not his own but descend from the gods. They seem to stem from primal unions in Nature promoted by a double Spirit.
>
> What he sets in motion is MANIFEST
>
> A Kind of ancient Natural Philosophy, from which the mind has never been separated. (Artaud, 1974: 43)

This statement is criticised because it allegedly misrepresents facts of Balinese theatre, and thus shows Artaud's misunderstanding. Indeed, traditional performances in Indonesia as a whole do not have a written text, nor are the songs to be played during a show preplanned by the troupe. The genre's set dramatic structure in conjunction with the scenario and rules of type allow performers to generate the text and song sequence in performance. (Brandon, 1993: 119)

Improvisation is thus an integral part of Balinese theatre, and the role of the director, central to Artaud's argument, appears minimal. Such a misrepresentation of elements of an other culture then form the basis of accusing Artaud of cultural imperialism: taking up misunderstood aspects of the foreign culture to form an image of, and an opinion about that culture, and to misguidedly try to enrich one's own culture with those elements taken from their proper original context.

When Artaud talks about the re-establishment of theatre as pure and independent creativity, he adds that the products of this kind of theatre are hallucination and terror (1974: 38). In a classification of states of consciousness, these would certainly range among maladaptive states, states that one would not normally wish to experience. An emphasis on the need for humans to confront and control the darker side of their psyche is generally characteristic of Artaud's theories. In his view, the Balinese theatre allows us to reach such levels of the mind, which are located beyond verbal speech.

Grotowski's retreat from Indian material

Grotowski had become acquainted with Eastern philosophy early on in his life, and to recover from an illness that interrupted his studies at the State Institute of Theatre Art in Moscow in 1956, he spent two months travelling in Central Asia. Oriental philosophy was the topic of a series of weekly talks he held in the Student Club in Cracow where he trained as a director and where he directed his first productions in professional theatre. Those talks were about 'Buddhism, Yoga, the Upanishads, Confucius, Taoism and Zen Buddhism' (Kumiega, 1985: 6).

In the early stages of training at the Laboratory theatre, the actors experimented with training forms and techniques from Oriental and Asian theatre, and they exercised yoga. The Theatre of Thirteen Rows was founded by Grotowski in 1959, and the second season of the theatre began with Grotowski's adaptation of an Indian classic, *Shakuntala*. The play originates in the fourth or fifth century CE and deals with love in a highly poetic way. Grotowski's adaptation of this play used major cuts, and insertions of other Indian texts, including the Kama Sutra (29). Rather than attempting to recreate an Indian production of the play in his theatre in Poland, Grotowski emphasised the difference of this kind of play, the difference of cultural codes, which would allow his actors to be free of the expectations of performance associated with any Western literary text presented on stage. Kumiega argues that this production already contained some of the ingredients of Grotowski's later theatre theory and practice, i.e. fascination with ritual, experiment with architectural space, the actor-spectator relationship, investigation into a theatrical system of signs, and questions of actor training (1987: 32).

Grotowski's fascination with Indian theatre is evident not only from his choice of an Indian classic, in a non-Indian production, but also from his reference to the Indian God Shiva, the Cosmic Dancer, Nataraja, who creates all that exists while dancing: 'If I had to define our theatrical researches in one sentence, one phrase, I would refer to the myth of the Dance of Shiva' (115). Grotowski defined the essence of what he was searching for by quoting Shiva: 'I am the pulse, the movement and the rhythm' (115.). Byrski, assessing Indian influences on Grotowski, argues that both classical Indian theatre and the theatre created by Grotowski strive to achieve non-ordinary states of consciousness in both actors and spectators (1972). Furthermore, both forms of theatre require a specifically trained audience.

However, Grotowski eventually abandoned such experiments, concluding that non-Western aesthetic was completely alien to him: 'I do not think that we can adopt from them any techniques, or that they could inspire us directly' (Kumiega, 1987: 116). Grotowski realised that Oriental or Asian theatre forms are characterised by achieving a state of sacred theatre, in which spontaneity and discipline co-exist and mutually reinforce each other. He considered such a state desirable for a Western actor, but felt that techniques that allow, say, an Indian actor to achieve this co-existence, will not work for a Western actor.

Grotowski's problems with intercultural theatre practice are rooted in the way he understands and uses Indian material: *Mudras* are first described in the *Natyashastra*. The *mudras* are not isolated means of histrionic representation: in specific situations in a given play, specific means of histrionic representation have to be used to create a specific emotional and aesthetic experience in the spectators. The *Natyashastra* functions on two levels: it is both a description of what a 'perfect' actor, an actor who has reached a state of enlightenment, or *moksha*, liberation, will automatically, spontaneously do to create a specific emotion, a specific aesthetic experience in a specific audience. For an actor who is not yet 'perfect', the techniques described in the *Natyashastra* are a means to achieve perfection, enlightenment, *moksha*, parallel to reaching this state through yoga or meditation practices. Thus, though the *mudras* and other means of histrionic representation are apparently fixed codes, laid down and described as such in the text of the *Natyashastra*, they originate in the very moment they are created by the enlightened actor. Grotowski's argument that Indian signs are fixed thus loses its ground.

We saw that Grotowski was disillusioned with yoga as leading to introverted concentration harmful to the actor. There are techniques that are meant for people who have consciously chosen the way of life of a monk, in a monastery. Renouncing the world, they hope to gain enlightenment. However, this is not the only path to the same goal: there are also methods specifically for the individuals who have to deal with everyday activities; in this case, the meditative practices do not draw the person's mind inwards with the result of such individuals becoming incapable of ordinary day-to-day activities. Rather, the techniques are geared to produce deep physical relaxation together with refined states of consciousness during the meditation, allowing the mind to access levels of consciousness otherwise not open to experience. Such subtler levels of the mind reverberate with energy, which is taken out into the activity after meditation. Thus, meditative practices intended for householders as opposed to monks will support the householder's activity. Indeed, activity is an integral part of the development to enlightenment: in alternating meditative experience of *samadhi* with ordinary activity, the nervous system is trained to maintain a state where *samadhi* can co-exist together with the ordinary state of consciousness (Orme-Johnson, 1987: 336). Such co-existence is not an intellectual understanding, but a profound holistic experience, is the aim of both the monk and the householder. What differs are the paths adopted by the different types of individuals to obtain that state of liberation.

When Grotowski found that the practices he used tended to block his actors from activity, then it must be assumed that he used practices intended for monks, rather than techniques which would indeed support the actor's activities, thus providing the service that Grotowski had hoped to gain from having his actors train in those methods.

Barba: Theatre Anthropology

Barba locates the equivalents of *energy*, *life*, *power*, and *spirit* in the performance traditions of various Asian cultures.

Country	Terms
Japan	Ki-ai, kokoro, io-in, koshi
Bali	Taksu, viraqsa, chikara, bayu
China	Kung-fu, shun toeng
Sanskrit (India)	Prana, shakti

Barba argues that the behaviour appropriate for an actor on the stage must be different from that of daily life (*extra-daily behaviour*). This view is supported by the *Natyashastra*. Barba derived one of the major concepts of his theatre anthropology from the theatre aesthetics of the *Natyashastra*: the *Natyashastra* differentiates between *lokadharmi* and *natyadharmi*, realistic and theatrical forms of representation; on this basis, Barba developed his concepts of daily behaviour (equivalent, in his view, to *lokadharmi*), and extra-daily, performative behaviour (equivalent, Barba argues, to *natyadharmi*). A close look at the *Natyashastra*, however, shows that this parallel is limited. In the *Natyashastra*, both terms refer to practices of representation which can be employed in performance. The realistic style, *lokadharmi*, is defined as follows:

If a play depends on natural behaviour [in its characters] and is simple and not artificial, and has in its [plot] professions and activities of the people and has [simple acting and] no playful flourish of limbs and depends on men and women of different types, it is called realistic (*lokadharmi*) (Ghosh, 1950: 245-6).

Those two verses defining *lokadharmi* are followed by twelve verses on *natyadharmi*, providing a detailed description of theatrical circumstances in which theatrical representation is appropriate. The emphasis on *natyadharmi* might lead to the conclusion that it is more important in *natya* than *lokadharmi*, and indeed all the numerous descriptions of the means of histrionic representation in the *Natyashastra*, *abhinaya*, belong to the category of *natyadharmi*. However, whatever the emphasis, *lokadharmi* is part of the actor's theatrical practice. Although it is thus possible to differentiate daily from extra-daily behaviour on the basis of the concepts of *lokadharmi* and *natyadharmi*, the important difference is that in Barba's theory, daily behaviour is outside the realm of performance; even more, it is the kind of behaviour that the performer has to *overcome* to become a good performer. In contrast, *lokadharmi* and *natyadharmi* both pertain to the performance.

Barba likes the concept of masters of performance: it is deeply rooted in Eastern performance practice, where training is not undergone rather impersonally, and a for a relatively short period of time, as today in the West, but over many years, often from early childhood, and focused on one master teacher, guru. The concept of *guru* needs clarification. It dates back to the Vedic times, when the Guru was a Brahmin teacher who ensured oral tradition of Vedic hymns. He usually was a married man whose home became the home of his pupils: 'Students who were qualified by birth had to be accepted and, once installed, they became the Guru's responsibility' (Brent, 1971: 2-3). During the minimum period of eight years of training, the students would learn the Vedic hymns by heart, and they would serve their Guru (3-5). In the course of time, the concept of 'Guru' broadened. Leaders of religious sects, often claiming descent from a deity, were called adi-Guru; the heads of monasteries performed the function of a Guru. The Sad-Guru, finally, is for many the 'real Guru' (18). He has reached *moksha*, liberation, and he leads others on the path to enlightenment. The guru in the context of the arts originally (and ideally) combines the teaching of the appropriate techniques of the art with his disciple's spiritual development. In recent times, however, such a close relationship of master and student cannot be found any more: the Indian diaspora in Western countries has to adopt to the style of living dominating those societies, rendering it impossible to allow the kind of intensity of training at the basis of the *guru-shishya parampara*. A few hours of training on one day of the week is the norm. In India itself, packaged one- to three-year courses have become more and more popular, offered by major training schools. In comparison with many years of training with one guru, little time is left, and that is spent predominantly on technique, at the expense of the spiritual dimension inherent in the special guru-disciple relationship.

Brook's *Mahabharata*

The year 1985 saw the first performances of Peter Brook's production of his and Jean Claude Carrière's adaptation (or version) of *The Mahabharata*. The classical Indian epic is 15 times the length of the Bible, eight times the length of the *Iliad* and *Odyssey* combined, or more than 30 times the length of *Paradise Lost* (Williams, 1991: 19). Brook's production lasted for nine hours, his TV/film version was six hours in length. The production caused a stir in the worlds of entertainment and academia, hailed by theatre critics as one of the major productions of the twentieth century, and predominantly judged a failure by theatre scholars, especially those from India, who, on the whole, felt offended by the way Peter Brook treated 'their' national religious Epic. The debate is well documented in a purpose-published collection (Williams, 1991).

I did not have the chance to see the original theatre production on stage. Instead, I encountered Brook's production through the TV/film version, which I first saw in Norway (on the Swedish channel, with Swedish subtitles) in 1990. I was genuinely impressed by the production: I found that it provided me, while watching, with experiences I would otherwise have associated only with my experiences while practising meditation. I was thus quite disappointed by the scholarly response to it. How to put my own, subjective experiences with Brook's *Mahabharata* into context.

At this stage of reading this section of the book, some readers may feel alarmed at my use of the first-person perspective. This may not come across as scholarly, or scientific. Certainly when I studied English literature in the late 1970s, at a German university, I would have been penalised for this unscientific approach. Within the German university system, literature is (supposed to be) studied and taught as a science (Literatur*wissenschaft*). Referring to myself is subjective, and thus not scientific-science understood here as the attempt of being as objective as possible, safeguarded, among others, by strict exclusion of the subjective.

If you were or are alarmed at my so far subjective approach, then this demonstrates the science-orientation of literary scholarship. If, however, you were or are not alarmed, but feel comfortable with my approach, wondering where it may lead, you represent a tendency in at least part of science to take the subjective more seriously. In the booming consciousness debate outlined in the introduction, so-called *First-Person Approaches* have received a broad base of discussion, with numerous publications bearing witness to this. Thus one of the leading philosophers in the consciousness studies field, David Chalmers, argues:

> the development of more sophisticated methodologies for investigating first-person data and of formalisms for expressing them is the greatest challenge now facing a science of consciousness. Only by developing such methodologies and formalisms will we be able to collect and express first-person data in such a way that it is on a par with third-person data, so that we can find truly systematic and detailed connections between the two. (1999)

I have decided to take my 'feeling', my 'first person experiences' regarding Brook's *Mahabharata* seriously. In a first stage of developing a discourse in which to express those feelings and experiences in such a way that they make sense to others, I have argued elsewhere that the theoretical approaches adopted by a majority of critics do not do justice to the work of art almost by definition. Those approaches are clearly set within the confines of the Western mindset with its predominance and superiority of reason, the intellect, concepts, historicity, and understanding, over levels of the mind that in the context of the *Western* mindset are considered inferior, such as intuition, anything that cannot be expressed clearly in words, hunches, myth, archetypes, the spiritual, the universal. It is striking that most Indian commentators on *The Mahabharata*, especially Rustom Bharucha, follow the same pattern.

Since the majority of the critical debate surrounding Brook's *Mahabharata* has revolved on Bharucha's essay 'A View from India', I will in turn focus on the argument he presents.

According to Bharucha, Brook fails to expressly make clear the implications of various important philosophical concepts informing the action and motivation of *The Mahabharata's* characters. *Dharma*, for example, Bharucha insists, is mainly absent in Brook's conception of character, or else, it is travestied through:

a mish-mash of cultures with an overriding aura of 'Indianness';

a total avoidance of historicity, or social transformation underlying *The Mahabharata* from a tribal to a brahmin-dominated caste society;

a monochromatic presentation of characters with no sense of their evolution through different stages in life;

a failure to suggest that this life is just part of a series of rebirths, relivings of past transgressions, that can cease only through *moksha*. (Bharucha, 1991: 233)

The implications of the caste system, especially those surrounding *kshatrya*, inadequately rendered as 'warriors', are not made clear, neither is 'a sense of time that transcends chronology' (Bharucha, 1991:237). The unsatisfactory characterisation of the god Krishna annoys Bharucha and other commentators, both regarding his personality and the rather short coverage in Brook's production of the *Bhagavad-Gita*, frequently considered the key section of the entire *Mahabharata*.

Several traits of major characters in *The Mahabharata* are not included in the production text, although it would have been easy, Bharucha maintains, to do so. Here, the issue is one pertinent to any adaptation of a literary text for the theatre: which elements to choose, which to foreground, and why. Choices have to be made, and they are open to critical discussion. However, these are no longer central only to intercultural theatre. The choice of an international cast for the production of *The Mahabharata* is criticised by Bharucha for its lack of purpose. He asks: 'But what is the point of that if most of the actors' voices, rhythms and performance traditions have been homogenised within a western structure of action, where they have to speak a language unknown to most of them?' (Bharucha, 1991: 245).

Indians assert that the characters of the epic, and the various stories it contains are very familiar to all Indians, independent of their background, social status, etc. This level of familiarity is expressed, for example, by Mallika Sarabhai, who played Draupadi in Brook's adaptation of *The Mahabharata*, when she says:

> [...] if there is one child in a school who is very strong or very large, the other children will compare him with Bhima. In India when you talk of Draupadi or Krishna or Bhima in the middle of a completely contemporary conversation, you still know exactly who you are talking about. And that is the extent of *The Mahabharata's* contemporaneity in India today. (Sarabhai, 1991: 99-100)

Vijay Mishra's argument supports Sarabhai's view: he distinguishes several 'texts' of the epic: first, the edited text, a result of scholarship. Second, the one Sarabhai refers to, which is 'passed on from mother to child'. Third, the text 'as it exists through folk, theatrical and filmic representations'. Finally, *The Mahabharata* in translation, 'both in Indian vernacular and in major world languages' (Mishra, 1991: 200). In India and throughout South-East Asia, David Williams points out, *The Mahabharata* has become 'the common source of the bulk of the dramatic material of dance drama, storytelling, popular folk players, puppet shows, films and even strip cartoons' (Williams, 1991: 19). There has also been an adaptation by the Indian television, in many parts, which was also shown on British TV.

This deep rootedness of Indians in *The Mahabharata* must be accepted as at least one, and perhaps the initial reason that Indian critics have, on the whole, voiced their reservation about Peter Brook's adaptation of *The Mahabharata* for stage, screen and television. Bharucha points out that his own criticism of Brook's work does not imply a fundamentalist attitude: Western theatre artists, Bharucha argues, should not be 'banned from touching our sacred texts'. Instead, Bharucha demands that *The Mahabharata*

> must be seen on as many levels as possible within the Indian context, so that its meaning (or rather, multiple levels of meaning) can have some bearing on the lives of the Indian people for whom *The Mahabharata* was written, and who continue to derive their strength from it. (Bharucha, 1991: 230-1)

A production based on Indian material and directed by a Western director, then, according to Bharucha, has to pay its respect to the source material by leaving the material taken up for the production as much as possible within its cultural context. The aim of this has to be a potential benefit for the audiences in the source culture, who produced the cultural material taken up in the Western performance in the first place, and for whom this cultural material is supposed to have beneficial effects. This demand echoes Bharucha's criticism that none of the intercultural theatre artists in the West have turned 'to India out of the faintest concern for its present socio-cultural tradition. Rather they have been drawn almost exclusively to our "traditional" sources'. (Bharucha, 1993: 4).

In preparation for the production, Brook and his company travelled through India to get a first-hand impression of the country and its culture. A number of the people with whom Brook interacted on this journey later complained about Brook's inappropriate behaviour, such as humiliating his hosts, being insensitive to the conditions they were able to offer, suspicious about moderate fees charged by companies that had been arranged to perform for Brook and his company, promising parts in the production to local people and the forgetting about it, and so on. Such anecdotes serve very well to stir (understandable) resentment against Brook. Some or all of these points of criticism are then usually subsumed under the umbrella of neo-colonialism, neo-imperialism, cultural theft, and orientalism. Thus, Bharucha categoriacally states that Brook's production of *The Mahabharata* 'exemplifies one of the most blatant (and accomplished) appropriations of Indian culture in recent years'. Its neo-colonialist tendencies consist in

> its appropriation and reordering of non-western material within an orientalist framework of thought and action, which as been specifically designed for the inter-national market. (Bharucha, 1991: 229)

The critique of Brook's *Mahabharata*, triggered mainly by Bharucha's essay, is certainly complex and exists on at least the five levels just discussed. The level of discourse adopted (consciously?) by Bharucha and other Indian and Western commentators of Brook's production is clearly set within the confines of the Western mindset with its predominance and superiority of reason, the intellect, concepts, historicity, and understanding, over levels of the mind that in the context of the *Western* mindset are considered inferior, such as intuition, anything that cannot be expressed clearly in words, hunches, myth, archetypes, the spiritual, the universal. It may be expected that Western critics adopt 'their' Western paradigms in critical approaches to Brook's production. Thus, Maria Shevtsova argues that Brook's *Mahabharata* 'obliges performers and spectators alike to review routine assumptions about their own culture through its prism of cultures' (Shevtsova, 1991: 226), and Williams appears puzzled at *The Mahabharata's* 'claim to be a beneficial poem' when he writes: 'all who hear it will be somehow 'better', and he can only interpret 'better' in an political-intellectual way as 'empowered' (Williams, 1996: 70).

What is more striking is that even the arguments 'from India' against Brook's production are clearly located within a Western mindset[1]. Thus, Bharucha considers what Brook could *understand* or not about *The Mahabharata* (Bharucha, 1991: 236); he assumes that an Indian, brought up with *The Mahabharata*, can transform even an unsatisfactory representation of the Epic into 'a deeply spiritual experience' (Bharucha, 1991: 231). Bharucha does not expect such a transformation to take place in Brook or his Western audience, who do not have the *knowledge* of the various *concepts* informing the philosophy of *The Mahabharata*. Bharucha is highly critical of Carrière's decision of entering the deepest places of the characters 'without imposing our concepts, our judgements or our twentieth century analysis, in so far as that is possible' (Carrière, 1991: 64). For Bharucha, Carrière's argument implies that the characters' deepest places can be appreciated without the use of the intellect, without 'a critical consciousness' (Bharucha, 1991: 242). The further implication of this understanding of Carrière's view for Bharucha is that it is as if '*The Mahabharata* lies beyond questioning and that its "story" can be told only through some mystical communion with the work itself' (Bharucha, 1991: 242).

All these examples serve to demonstrate that Bharucha and others clearly favour the aspects of intellect over and above those which go beyond the intellect's capacity. Such a preference is characteristic of the majority of views proposed until very recently in the current Western debate in science and philosophy on the nature of the human mind and consciousness. The emphasis of the debate has been focused on the scientific study of consciousness, fully established in the Western, science-and objectivity-oriented mindset. By definition, this approach has to cancel out subjectivity, precisely those areas of the mind which, in the debate surrounding *The Mahabharata*, have come in for attack or ridicule.

Brook's own comments on his *Mahabharata* have been dismissed as lacking the level of precision required to make it useful in the intellectual debate of the production. He is not interested in politics or historicity. He did not want to imitate India. Rather, most of Brook's comments refer to the experience of *The Mahabharata* on levels of the mind beyond the intellect. Brook expressly insists that we should not come to the production with our 'own set of notions about Hinduism, Christianity, comparative religion, mythology, the relative nature of different types of epic or non-epic storytelling', in order to encounter something 'never encountered anywhere else, which cannot be received on a theoretical basis, which can't be received other than as a direct experience' (quoted in Carlson, 1996: 88). Viewed from the level of the intellect alone, devoid of the experience of subtler levels, especially that of underlying pure consciousness, Brook's statement must seem suspicious at best. The experience aimed at must appear as unmediated, and, as Carlson points out, critical theory has revealed the possibility of unmediated experience as illusory (Carlson, 1996: 88). What Brook is in fact describing as the aim of engaging with *The Mahabharata* is a state of mind in which the mediated (processes on the levels of senses, desire, mind, intellect, intuition and feeling, and ego) and the unmediated (pure consciousness) co-exist. In the context of the *Mahabharata* production, Brook is unable to put into words (Brook, 1991: 52), to name the envisaged experience. All he can say is that the intellect alone (as agent responsible for notions, theories, concepts etc.) is not sufficient as a *means* or *tool* of gaining access to this more comprehensive state of mind, which is *beyond* language. Thus, what *is* illusory, or a 'dangerous, or self-deceptive vision, denying the voice of the Other in an attempt to transcend it' (Carlson, 1996: 91) *only* if considered from the isolated perspective of the intellect, becomes the *potential* of theatre practice at subtler, more comprehensive levels of experience.

How does Brook go about achieving his aims in practice? His *Mahabharata* appeals to all levels of the mind. Many commentators have noted the appeal of Brook's production on the senses, with their display of fireworks, the extraordinary setting in a quarry or in an impressive old theatre. The intellect is stimulated by concepts, by reasoning, by thought experiments. Some of these are found in Carrière and Brook's adaptation, such as the story told by Bhishma on his deathbed, about the significance and implications of death. Indirectly, the debate caused by Brook's production is an indication of the production's effectiveness on the intellectual level. The key method used by Brook to access the subtler levels of the mind, such as intuition and especially pure consciousness, is suggestion. Philosophical concepts, or customs are hinted at, are implied, never didactically presented. Set and costumes create a sense of India without being museum replicas. Brook calls it 'a flavour of India' (Brook, 1991: 44). Similar to the experience of *rasa*, which is at the centre of Indian theatre aesthetics as described in detail in the *Natyashastra*, it is an aesthetic experience that is created within the spectator while watching the performance.

A particularly striking (and controversial!) example of suggestion is Brook's treatment of what many consider to be the most important episode of the entire *Mahabharata*, the *Bhagavad-Gita*. A close look at the actual text of that brief passage in the production reveals, however, that Brook captures its essence: in the course of a long conversation, Krishna in his divinity leads the hero, Arjuna, to the state of full enlightenment. In the structure of the dramatisation chosen by Brook, with its emphasis on action and linear narrative, the spiritual discourse of the *Bhagavad-Gita* does not offer itself for any other rendering: it is in line with the overall concept. A separate production altogether might choose to deal with the *Bhagavad-Gita* only: attempting to fathom its depth in dramatic form is likely to be quite a challenge. Thus, it only appears that Brook did not do full justice to Hindu philosophy and Indian society. He may not have done so on the intellectual level to which the criticism by Bharucha and others is limited. But by taking the Indian epic and adapting it for an audience (irrespective of the audience's culture or nationality), he did make its essence available to all involved, facilitating the development of higher states of consciousness. Not everyone may *understand*, immediately or even after reflection, 'what it is all about'. Deep philosophical concepts may be lost *intellectually* because they have not been mentioned, described, analysed, brought out clearly (enough) in the production. However, all structures, elements, aspects and facets that may be revealed in the text through any means possible (scholarship, intuition, cognition) exist in every part of it, and it is on this level that the efficacy of *The Mahabharata*, and with it, of Brook's *Mahabharata* production lies. Every part contains the whole, which is always active on all levels of the mind.

Thus, Bharucha's argument that Brook's production failed because it did not provide the main audience of the production with sufficient *information* about *The Mahabharata* through the way the epic was dramatised, is again limited to (although accurate on) the level of the intellect: it is not necessary to *know* and *learn about* Indian philosophy to benefit from the deep aspects of that philosophy contained in Brook's production. Those deep aspects are part of the production because the production is based on *The Mahabharata*, and because they are suggested in the specific adaptation created by Carrière and Brook. This Epic was not merely a great literary creation, as, for example, Shakespeare's plays, and it is thus not appropriate to refer to it as an 'artistic product' (Dasgupta, 1991: 263). Rather, *The Mahabharata* was cognised by Vedic *rishis* on the level of the Absolute, Brahman. Thus, each of those units on its own, and taken together, will affect the reader's or spectators' consciousness in line with the general effect ascribed to Veda and Vedic Literature: eliminating blocks from the system, and thereby facilitating the development and permanent experience of higher states of consciousness in all those subjected to it in any possible form of production and reception.

A further aspect of the production's strength relates to the international cast with whom Brook worked both in Paris and on tour on the *Mahabharata*. It is an essential factor in this suggestive approach to the text. The performers bring their own individual cultural backgrounds, languages, etc. to their parts, naturally, unobtrusively, neither emphasising their traditions nor by any means hiding them. Critics have noted the variety of accents and styles of acting: Yoshi Oida, for example, is clearly influenced by his classical Japanese Noh training; Sotigui Kouyate (who played Bhishma and Parashurama) is the 'descendant of a long line of *griots* (the West African storyteller-historian caste preserving and transmitting oral culture)' (Kouyate, 1991: 104). For Italian actor Vittorio Mezzogiorno, the role of Arjuna was his first return to theatre after a major film career. However, despite this diversity, which is all the intellect can perceive, Brook, by integrating the intellect with the subtler levels of the mind, manages to bring out an underlying unity. Ultimate unity exists only on the level of pure consciousness. The aesthetic experience created by Brook's *Mahabharata* is thus one which comprises unity in diversity.

Part of the success of Brook's *Mahabharata* production in affecting all levels of the mind and creating the aesthetic experience of unity in diversity is due to the fact that the source, the *Mahabharata* itself, is 'universal' in a very special sense, which includes but also transcends, intellectual discourse: reading the text, or watching excerpts performed, will produce effects on the whole range of the mind. They are found on the level of the ego when people identify (themselves) with the heroic characters; On the level of the intuition and feelings when even repeated narration of major episodes never fail to move, or when generations of artists in various genres find their artistic inspiration in the epic; On the level of the intellect when generations of scholars come up with new and fascinating interpretations; On the level of the senses, finally, when episodes of *The Mahabharata* are enacted on the stage, or sung about accompanied by music. Most important, *The Mahabharata* has a direct influence on the level of pure consciousness, facilitating its experience in the reader's or spectator's mind. In is important to note that the causes for this multi-level effect of *The Mahabharata* are not restricted to the contents of the epic, or the characteristics of heroes and villains, i.e. to any concept or construct which the intellect could isolate in the text.

The effect of *The Mahabharata* in general, and of Brook's theatre adaptation in particular, on all the levels of the mind may be, statistically, most obvious in India, because the text originates in that country and is alive in its traditions of storytelling, dance, theatre, and folklore. The effect is, however, not *restricted to* India. No matter what may be the background of someone who comes in contact with the epic, its texture is so rich that everyone will benefit on at least one level of the mind. The more of those levels are developed, the richer the resulting experience of the epic will be, the more nuances may be picked up, the more links to one's own previous experience can be established.

An Indian person may resonate more directly with the characters and events, because of the familiarity with them. But who is 'the Indian?' What about the Indian who is not familiar with *The Mahabharata*. Does it make a difference where the Indian was born and lives (i.e. in India or elsewhere?) Will any Indian (familiar or unfamiliar with the epic, born and living in India or elsewhere) be more familiar on some collective unconscious level than any non-Indian, no matter how familiar with the epic the non-Indian may have become through study, life in India, friendship with or marriage to an Indian person ... ? It is quite possible to extend such questions even further, and their purpose in my argument should be clear: the critics' references to the deep-rootedness of *The Mahabharata* in India is poignantly limited to the political discourse, based on the level of the intellect devoid of the experience of pure consciousness. Bharucha's criticism is accurate on that level alone, ignoring (by definition) subtler levels of functioning.

Taking my argument a step further, I want to ask how can drama (and, by implication, theatre) influence the mind of the reader / spectator? I want to start from my observation that many critics have noted that in Peter Brook's *Mahabharata*, philosophical concepts, or customs are hinted at, are implied, hardly ever didactically presented. The key term in this context is *suggestion*. For example, set and costumes suggest India, create a sense of India without being museum replicas. Brook calls it 'a flavour of India' (Brook, 1991: 44). 'Suggestion' is the most common rendering of the Indian aesthetic concept of *dhvani*. This concept was first elaborated by Anandavardana (tenth century CE) in his *Dhvanyaloka*, followed by a commentary by Abhinavagupta (late tenth century CE).

Grammarian Bhartrihari describes several levels of language, *vaikhari, madhyama pashyanti*, and *para. Vaikhari* 'is the most external and differentiated level', on which speech is uttered by the speaker and heard by the hearer (Coward, 1980: 128). Its temporal sequence is fully developed. *Madhyama* represents, in broad terms, the thinking level of the mind.

> It is the idea or series of words as conceived by the mind after hearing or before speaking out. It may be thought of as inward speech. All parts of speech that are linguistically relevant to the sentence are present here in a latent form. (129)

The finest relative level is that of *pashyanti*. At this level 'there is no distinction between the word and the meaning and there is no temporal sequence' (131).

Beyond the very subtly manifest level of *pashyanti*, Bhartrihari locates the fully unmanifest level language, *para* (131). The level of language described by *para* corresponds to the level of pure consciousness in the Vedic Science model of consciousness introduced earlier in this book.

Table 4: Levels of Language and Consciousness

Level of Language according to Bhartrihari	Characteristics	Levels / States of consciousness
Vaikhari	Most external, most differentiated, spoken and heard language	Waking (senses, desire, mind, intellect, feeling, intuition, emotion, ego)
Madhyama	Level of thinking, after hearing and before speaking out	Waking (senses, desire, mind, intellect, feeling, intuition, emotion, ego)
Pashyanti	No distinction between word and meaning; no temporal sequence	Waking, finest levels of the mind
Para	Fully unmanifest level of language	Pure consciousness

Bhartrihari associates the *pashyanti* level of language with the concept of *sphota*. It represents meaning as a whole, existing in the mind of the speaker as a unity. 'When he utters it, he produces a sequence of different sounds so that it appears to have differentiation' (73). The process of differentiation into sounds proceeds from the *sphota* on the *pashyanti* level of language via *madhyama* or inward thought to expressed speech on the *vaikhari* level. For the listener, the process is reversed. Although he first hears a series of sounds, he ultimately perceives the utterance as a unity-'the same *sphota* with which the speaker began' (73). The *sphota* or meaning-whole thus has two sides to it: the word-sound (*dhvani*) and the word-meaning (*artha*) (12). Sound and meaning are two aspects residing within the unitary *sphota*, which, according to Bhartrihari, is eternal and inherent in consciousness (12). Meaning is thus not conveyed 'from the speaker to the hearer, rather, the spoken words serve only as a stimulus to reveal or uncover the meaning which was already present in the mind of the hearer' (12).

Haney points out that the unity of name and form, of sound and meaning on the level of the *sphota* in *pashyanti* applies mainly to the Sanskrit language. In other languages, tradition of usage has led to associating specific sounds with given objects or concepts. Haney argues, however, that

<blockquote>because Sanskrit is considered by orthodox Indians to be the oldest documented language and probably the source of all languages, the same unity of name and form</blockquote>

found in it must exist to some extent in other languages when experienced on sufficiently refined levels of consciousness. (1991: 316)

If subtler levels of language, corresponding to subtler levels of consciousness, are open to individual experience, the identity of name and form should be within experiential reach. For example, in *Ayurveda*, the Vedic system of medicine, ideal treatment is administered when the Vaidya (doctor) tells the patient the name of the herb which is to be used for treatment. Simply experiencing the name of the herb on its most subtle level is expected to have the effect of taking the physical herb, because of the identity of name and form on the subtler levels of language and consciousness. Similarly, if 'red' could be experienced on the level of the *sphota* in *pashyanti*, all aspects of its form (the redness of red) will be available to experience, which in turn could ultimately be processed through the more expressed levels of language.

According to the linguistic theory of Vedic Science, *pashyanti* represents the subtlest manifest level of nature, and must thus be assumed to be closest to nature itself. When we hear words, we do not decode the meaning intended by the speaker. Rather, the speaker's words trigger a recollection of meaning that was already present at the depths of our minds, at the *para* level of pure consciousness. Obviously, different spoken words will trigger different specific recollections, depending on the context. From the stimulation on the *para* level of the mind, the heard word materialises (imperceptibly) via the levels of *pashyanti* and *madhyama* until we consciously become aware of the sounds of the words on the *vaikhari* level. A sufficiently refined awareness should be able to directly experience the subtler levels of language as well (Malekin and Yarrow, 2000). *Dhvani* refers to the various ways to use words in literature to create *rasa* within the reader. If *rasa* is understood predominantly on the level of the emotions, Abhinavagupta's explanation of the process of how *dhvani* 'works'. Pandit summarises as follows:

> Through the semantic *dhvani*-which, again, is not explicitly brought to consciousness-the literary work activates traces in the mind of the reader, but does not bring them into consciousness. Again, these traces may be activated by words, phrases, topics, etc.; thus stories of suffering will activate memories of suffering, stories of romantic love will activate memories of romantic love, and so on, both at a rather general level, and in various specific details (e.g., a wedding day, an estrangement and reconciliation), etc. Once these traces are activated, the associated emotions seep into consciousness (again, not as ideas, but directly as feelings). The experience of the *rasa* of a literary work is precisely the experience of these feelings.

If we take the additional dimension of *rasa*, pure consciousness, into account, then we can argue that *dhvani* in literature is able to not only trigger the recognition of meaning and the appropriate intended emotion, but also the experience of pure consciousness itself, together with expressed contents of consciousness (meaning and emotions).

Spoken or written words thus have an effect on the listener's or reader's mind that goes beyond the apparent surface of the words in question. The process does not operate on the intellectual level. Thus if we attempt to intellectually (as opposed to experientially) understand how *dhvani* works, we end up with the concept of suggestion, which can be suspect, because vague and subjective, to the intellect-dominated Western mindset (see Lingorska and Perry, 1999).

Dhvani encompasses numerous techniques that apply to the use of Sanskrit as a language, where name and form, sound and meaning, are considered as identical. Mishra (*Ulysses*) summarises some of the possible categories of *dhvani*:

1. Laksanamuladhvani : The suggestion arises due to Laksanartha i.e. the implied figurative meaning; here the primary sense is eclipsed/insignificant/not intended. There are two kind of this -
   a) Arthantara Sankramita Vacya Dhvani : - The primary and additional meanings are amalgamated in the final suggested meaning. Some of the literal sense is retained while other meanings are superimposed on this.
   b) Atyantatiraskrta Vacya Dhvani : - The primary significance of the word is totally discarded, only its connotations are intended to be grasped.
2. Abhidhamuladhvani: - Here only literal meaning is taken into account. There is no desire to evoke the secondary meanings. There are again two kinds of this -
   a) Samlaksyakrama Vyangyadhvani: - The primary sense (the Vacyartha) comes before the Vyangyartha and opens the way for the latter to be revealed. There is a time lapse between the comprehension of the two kinds of meaning. The suggested significance follows in the wake of the literal meaning.

There are further three kinds of this -
i) Sabdodbhava: - When word is the source of suggestion of meaning, this Dhvani is known as Sabdodbhava.
ii) Arthasakti-Udbhava: - When suggestion comes from the overall meaning, it is called Arthasakti-Udbhava. Nothing is said overtly, yet we understand a particular sense.
On the level of denotations, the relevant deeper implications are not evident.
iii) Sabdarthodbhava: - When the suggestion of the meaning comes from the word as well as the overall meaning, it is called Sabdarthodbhava category of Samlaksyakrama Vyangyadhvani. In a way it is a mixture of Sabdodbhava and Arthasakti-Udbhava.
   b) Asamlaksyakrama Vyangyadhvani: - This category is applicable when the suggestion is produced by several meanings that are not simultaneously generated even though they enmesh with each other to produce a net significance. In this case, it becomes practically impossible to give priority to one meaning over the other in terms of time lapse between various meanings generated. This Dhvani is also termed as Rasa-Dhvani. It is difficult to translate this term because of its cultural specificity. However, it can be roughly understood as the 'soul of the experience of the poetry'.

I am not proposing that Brook and Carrière intentionally used *dhvani* techniques in creating their play-and screenscripts. That their text uses suggestion rather than explicit explanation of storyline and philosophical concepts is beyond doubt. If we apply the principles behind *dhvani* to Brook's production, the following picture emerges: The text takes up some ideas of Indian philosophy, a flavour, aspects, you may even call it fragments. By using these on all levels of production (spoken text, gestures, facial expression, costume, set design, music, etc.), 'traces', or memories, are activated in the minds of all those exposed to such stimuli (i.e. spectators *and* production team). Such a process, on the *dhvani* theory, applies to any reception process of art. The kind of traces or memories activated through art depend on the nature if art. A horror movie, if we want to call it art, is not likely to trigger much enjoyable material, and one would doubt if it encompassed the experience of pure consciousness. However, in the case of Brook's *Mahabharata*, the source material from the Epic is such that, hologram-like, even fragments of it contain the whole, and thus suggestion of it triggers the emotions appropriate to specific situations, while at the same time enabling the experience of pure consciousness. I propose that on a concrete (in comparison with abstract pure consciousness) not only emotions are triggered, but experiences of aspects that would, intellectually, be described as concepts. For the *Mahabharata*, the most important of those would be *dharma*. I discussed this concept in chapter one. Many books have been written on the subject. Yet *dharma* is not (only) an intellectual concept open to speculation and intellectual discourse and debate. It is considered, in Indian philosophy, an existential, fundamental truth that has its basis not in speculation but in direct *experience*. Whereas drama cannot provide all knowledge about *dharma*, it can provide the *experience* of it by triggering its 'traces' on deep levels of the reader's or spectator's (and the author's, director's, and actor's) consciousness.

One final caveat: Brook's production text is not in Sanskrit, where the *dhvani* theory applies, but in French or English. The effect of dhvani may be more efficient when Sanskrit is used, and this perhaps implies also the use of theatre as described in the *Natyashastra*. However, I would expect that Western drama (text) and theatre (modes of performance) can have the same effect. For me, Brook's production of *The Mahabharata* did, and I have tried to explain why.

Summary

In this chapter, I argued that the *Natyashastra*, understood as a treatise aimed at helping humans regain the state of enlightenment, *moksha*, functions on two levels: it provides a description of what fully developed actors, actors living in higher states of consciousness, will do spontaneously by way of performance to create very specific aesthetic experience in the spectator. In addition, the means of histrionic representation described in the *Natyashastra* serve as a means of development of consciousness for both the actor and the spectator. I have furthermore pointed out that several important twentieth-century theatre artists and theorists took inspiration from the *Natyashastra* and/or other aspects of Indian philosophy. In particular, I discussed such 'points of contact and influence' in relation to Artaud, Grotowski, Barba and Brook. In the course of that discussion, I was able to clarify a number of previously confusing (mis-) understandings, and to add some material to the debate surrounding Peter Brook's production of the *Mahabharata*.

In the section on the *Mahabharata*, I take my own experiences as a spectator (albeit through the medium of the TV version) as point of departure for my argument. In the next chapter, I want to focus entirely on processes of reception and theatre audiences.

Notes

1. This may well be a residue of colonialism itself: Indian intellectuals, whether trained in India or in the West, have (unconsciously?) adopted the paradigm dominating the west. India's education system may be partly responsible, where, for example, at a leading private school in Calcutta students were taught, as late as 1989, to sign business letters with 'Your most obedient servant'...

5: Reception and Audiences

What happens in spectators while they are watching a performance in the theatre? Basically, the reception process consists of three interrelated elements: first the spectators, empirical individuals with their psychological and social backgrounds and positions, which influence how they react to the stimuli of the performance. The second element is the performance, which contains potential stimuli, dramatic and performative means of guiding the spectators. The spectator and the performance merge in the reception process, which takes place within the spectators and constitutes an interaction of spectators and the performance.

Methodologically, probing the nature of empirical spectators may lead to theories that in turn imply empirical research. The Centre de Sociologie du Théâtre in Brussels and the International Committee for Reception and Audience Research, for example, have conducted and published research in this area (Schoenmakers, 1986, 1992; Sauter, 1988). The analysis of the performance and its effects on spectators, has, for a long time, been text-oriented (Bennett, 1990: 7-8), and issues from reader-response criticism in literature have been transferred to studies of theatre. Readers have been described as subjective (Bleich, 1978), in terms of psychoanalysis (Holland, 1968), and 'real' readers have been distinguished from 'virtual' readers who exist in the mind of the authors (Prince, 1973). Iser introduced the concept of the implied reader who

> (...) embodies all those dispositions necessary for a literary work to exercise its effect-predispositions laid down, not by an empirical outside reality, but by the text itself. Consequently, the implied reader has his firm roots planted in the structure of the text, he is a construct and in no way to be identified with the real reader. (1978: 34)

Pfister defines the heuristic construct of an ideal recipient of theatre as able to fully decode all codes employed by the text in a way conditioned solely by the text and not influenced by sociological or psychological dispositions (1977: 66). Such a construct causes a problem: the description of what the ideal recipient decodes in a given text is necessarily based on the limited, and not ideal, view of the critic who describes the ideal. As Suleiman put it: 'I construct images of the implied author and implied reader gradually as I read the work, and then I use images I have constructed to validate my reading.' (1980: 6-7) Fish takes this problem into account by proposing the 'informed reader', that is, the real reader (the interpreter), who does everything in his power to become an informed reader. The intention is to justify, to some extent, that the interpreter projects his own responses on those of 'the reader' (1970).

Theorising of the text/performance with regard to its effects on the reader/spectator is thus far from unified. Susan Bennett tries to get away from the drama-based approach.

Theory from non-literary studies, as diverse as Huizinga's writings on the significance of play, Victor Turner's work on social dramas and ritual, and Jane Goodall's research on the behavioural patterns of chimpanzees-is investigated in an attempt to replace paradigms for dramatic theory that are seen as outmoded. (1990: 10)

In this chapter, I want to deal predominantly with empirical spectators, not reader-response-based hypothetical constructs. My argument is grouped around the senses: I thus begin with a section on the sense of sight in relation to scenography and consciousness. Here I address issues such as mental imagery in relation to the scenographer's craft and art, ways of associating guidelines of Vedic architecture (*Sthapathyaveda*) with potential impact of scenography, and ways in which we can understand how what we see influences our consciousness. Leading on from there I address the relation between scenography as an art of space to scenography as an art of time. A brief section deals with the sense of sound, going back to the model of language proposed by Vedic Science. While stimuli to the sense of hearing and seeing can be switched on and off at will, the sense of smell might be said to function differently as Schechner points out:

> Smell is by chemistry a 'diffusion,' and cannot be 'focused' as can most exactly sight and to some degree sound (volume at least is controllable). Theatre has developed as an eye-driven medium because of the controllability of focus. Sound and sight can be instantly turned on/off: now you see/hear it, now you don't. Smell is not only diffuse it lingers. (2004)

In a section co-written with Dr Martin Mittwede, we address the potential of using smell in theatre specifically to influence the development of consciousness of actors and spectators involved. I finally write about the so-called sixth sense, referring to recent developments in physics in relation to Vedic Science in an attempt at explaining unconventional transfer of information (how do we know if someone is staring at us behind our backs?). In conclusion of the chapter, I provide two examples of unconventional productions or performances that have affected spectators very strongly in a consciousness-altering manner: *Ariadne's Thread*, sometimes referred to as *The Labyrinth*, and Anna and Corrina Bonshek's *Reverie II*.

The Sense of Sight: Scenography

As Pamela Howard points out in her article on *design* in the *Continuum Companion to Twentieth Century Theatre* (2002), design in the theatre has seen major changes in the course of the twentieth century. While it used to be (regarded as) the surface decoration of the stage, it has become an independent and important component in the making of any theatrical event, and with it the designer has gained equal status with the actor and the director. Distinct areas of design are differentiated: set, costume, light and sound. Even among those there is a kind of hierarchy: thus the *Who's Who in Contemporary World Theatre* lists numerous famous designers who specialise in set and costume, much fewer who specialise in lighting, and hardly anyone specialising in sound design. It is striking, though, that quite a number of designers now no longer specialise in one or two conventional forms of design, but combine them all, at times even with directing and devising the productions in question, such as Robert Wilson. The term to capture this combination of formerly distinct areas of design is *scenography*, and the artist becomes the *scenographer*.

Set designer John Gunter, in the *Continuum Companion*, suggests five stages of the creative process: the idea, the drawing, the model, building the set in the workshop, and exploring the set on the stage. Predominantly, the study of scenography deals with the last four stages: developing the ability to critically assess the scenographic work of other artists, which includes aspects of theatre history, and developing practical skills of creating scenography oneself. Thus, a reflection of what happens in the process of scenography from a cognitive perspective in the mind of the scenographer, (the idea and how it transforms to drawing and model and so on) would not (yet) be at the focus of studies. It is this gap I want to begin to address.

Space

Scenography, in most general terms, deals with space. Space is important for us in daily life, regarding, among others, the following issues:

• Where am I, and how are my body parts currently oriented?

• Where are important environmental objects in relation to me?

• Where are these objects in relation to each other?

• What do I need to know about these objects?

• How should I go about doing what should be done?

(Marshall and Fink, 2001: S2)

While moving in space, we always have to take the above points into consideration. This usually happens without us being aware of it at all times-in most cases we realise the level of success, though: if while walking we bump into an object without intending to, or if we loose our way while travelling to a new destination by car, we clearly got it wrong. Human abilities related to space are conceptualised and studied in the discipline of cognitive (neuro-) psychology as spatial awareness, or spatial cognition. Conventionally, the brain area considered in charge of spatial cognition is the right parietal lobe (although research published in *Nature* in 2001 suggests that the superior temporal lobe is in charge, and not the parietal lobe).

I propose that people who create scenography have more highly developed abilities of spatial cognition, and should perform better in tasks devised to test such spatial cognition abilities. Perhaps scenographers recognised as 'great' will perform better than 'average' scenographers. Possibly performance in spatial cognition is correlated with levels of success and recognition. Nader has described that one specific activity will develop one specific region in the brain by developing numerous further connections of neurons. A different activity will develop a second specific area (1995). By implication, the posterior parietal lobe (or the superior temporal lobe) should show more neuronal connections in scenographers than in members of professions that do not engage in activity requiring spatial awareness to the extent that scenographers do.

Spatial cognition is related to mental imagery, which Thomas defines as the 'experience that resembles perceptual experience, but which occurs in the absence of the appropriate stimuli for the relevant perception'. Such experiences may 'seem to anticipate possible, often desired or feared, future experiences' (2001). It would be interesting to collect qualitative data about the creative processes of scenographers, and to compare this with existing research into mental imagery.

Nader proposes that the 36 aspects of Vedic Literature correspond in structure and function to the human anatomy and physiology. The aspects of Vedic Literature that correspond to the parietal lobe are twofold: first, to the third house (*bhava*) in Vedic astrology (*jyotish*), and secondly to the third of four chapters of Patanjali's *yoga sutras*. Nader postulates that reading or listing to the reading, in Sanskrit, of a specific aspect of Vedic Literature would have beneficial effects on the part of anatomy and / or physiology related to that specific aspect. Reading and/or listening to passages in Sanskrit from *jyotish* and *yoga* should improve spatial cognition, and thus the ability for scenography.

In Indian philosophy, the discipline relating most closely to scenography is *Sthapatya Veda*, comprising a range of treatises on architecture and design. Design in the context of *Sthapatya Veda* refers to building on every conceivable scale and in every conceivable context, ranging from a room to a building, a village, a city, and even an entire country. *Sthapatya Veda* also comprises the creation of form in the arts. In each context, and at each point of the scale, the purpose of applying rules of *Sthapatya Veda* is to achieve form that is 'in full alignment with the structuring dynamics of the whole universe' (Bonshek, 2001: 183). Those dynamics are the dynamics of pure consciousness. Thus, *Sthapatya Veda* provides practical knowledge how to create visible form that is in tune with the principles and procedures of invisible pure consciousness at the basis of form. Form created in line with *Sthapatya Veda* will express the laws of nature responsible for that form to their full extent, undiminished and unobstructed.

Why should we wish to achieve such alignment? Because any form that complies with the rules of *Sthapatya Veda* will, in turn, have the impact of enlivening and structuring the laws of nature in the observer of that form that led to its creation in the first place. For example, research suggests that houses built in accordance with *Sthapatya Veda* make their inhabitants think more clearly and creatively, make better decisions, feel happier and healthier, feel more alert and refreshed throughout the day, enjoy more restful and refreshing sleep, enjoy more energy and less fatigue, and experience less stress and greater peace of mind.

What applies for architecture for domestic dwellings should also apply to scenography. Nader discovered that Vedic texts have their direct correspondence in the human physiology. Thus, *Sthapatya Veda* is related to the spinal chord and the nerves emanating from it.

> The spinal chord, with its 35 segments or nerves on either side (...) present two symmetrical parts which total 70 divisions. These 70 divisions correspond to the 70 chapters of *Sthapatya Veda*. (Bonshek, 2001: 180)

The question is whether perceiving form created in line with the rules of *Sthapatya Veda* has the same effect as reading Vedic texts. Thus reading *Sthapatya Veda* should have a measurable impact on the spinal column and the nerves emanating from it. If my hypothesis is true, similar effects should be found when watching a scenography that follows the rules of *Sthapatya Veda*.

How could any impact of scenography on the spectator's consciousness work in neurophysiological terms? Gallese has published his research on mirror neurones (2002), and hypothesises that when we see the movement of another person, specific neurones fire in such a way that we would copy the movement we see if other neurones would not stop this mirror action by firing more intensively at the same time. In some cases, such a yawning, the inhibitory effect seems ineffective or not present. So far, experiments with monkeys have provided some evidence in favour of the hypothesis. Applied to the theatre, when we see the actors' specific movement on the stage, neurones in our brains fire in such a way as to imitate the movement we see, while at the same time other neurones fire in order to prevent the actual movement. However, some neuronal activity in the spectator has been induced by the performance, and it might be possible to theorise further that such neuronal activity may have broader effects, triggering secondary processes short of actual movement. It would also be interesting to establish whether mirror neurones are limited to the sense of sight.

Simultaneity of space and time

All theatre has to take *time* into consideration. On a practical level, the question arises as to how long a performance should last? How many hours can a given audience be expected to pay attention to the theatre event? Originally, *Noh* performances in Japan consisted of several plays in a row, with the comedy form of *kyogen* in between. In India, performances lasting several days were known. In the West today, attention spans are bemoaned to become shorter and shorter, due to television soap operas, and thus plays wishing to be commercially viable have to be adapted and be no more than two to two and a half hours including interval(s). Subsidised companies, such as the Royal Shakespeare Company, or the Royal National Theatre London may exceed this limit, as may occasional experimental productions by acknowledged stars of the theatre, such as Peter Brook's nine-hour *Mahabharata*, or Peter Stein's 21-hour production of Goethe's *Faust*.

Time is of course not limited to the duration of a production and the commercial, socio-cultural and psychological issues associated with it. Time is an important feature of both drama (the literary text) and the performance in the theatre. Plots may progress in a linear fashion, starting at point in time (A) and moving on steadily via points (B) and (C) to the end of the play at point in time (D). The time it takes spectators to watch the play is the time that is suggested to have passed in the fictional reality of the play. Other plays would still fit the category of linear, but some stages in the development are not shown on stage, but occur offstage, and may be reported as past events on stage. Plays may reverse the sequence of events over time, beginning at a chosen point and moving back from it (as in Pinter's *Betrayal*). Some contemporary dramatists have explicitly experimented with time: in *Noises Off*, Michael Frayn juxtaposes events on stage with simultaneous events backstage, presenting us first with the onstage scene (the play within the play), then the backstage events while the scene we had seen before onstage takes place offstage. The same span of time (the presentation of a scene from the play within the play on the fictional stage on the real stage) is shown twice, from different perspectives. In one of Alan Ayckbourn's more recent plays at the Royal National Theatre, London, *House and Garden* (2000), the same fictional time span is presented simultaneously in two of the three theatre spaces in the RNT (Olivier and Lyttleton) by the same cast, presenting indoors and outdoors perspectives.

In all those cases, attempts are made to convey the intricacies of time. However, hard as they try, Frayn or Ayckbourn have not managed to achieve the impression of complete simultaneity. Spectators intellectually *know* that this is a clever device. When they are watching the first part of Ayckbourn's *House and Garden* in the Olivier, they *know* that the situation they have seen is continued next door in the Lyttleton. Once they have seen the first part and now proceed to the Lyttleton, they can match what they see now with their memories of the performance in the Olivier. However, this matching activity is also intellectually mediated, not immediate. In Frayn's *Noises Off*, matching the events of the scene from the play within the play on stage with the events backstage is made easier by hearing at least some of the onstage text while the same scene is repeated from the backstage perspective. However, true simultaneity is not achieved.

A look at Vedic Science can elucidate the specific effect of simultaneity on the stage, and show its psychological significance for the actors and the audience alike. Vedanta philosophy is concerned predominantly with consciousness, which, as subjective monism, is located at the basis of all unmanifest and manifest creation. Time fits in with this approach. The Western mindset, in its aims for scientific objectivity, associates time with a sequential sequence of events, studied in the discipline of history. According to Vedanta, the emphasis of history is on the importance of events, not on chronology, because of the conceptualisation of time as eternal. The following passage provides a rather mind-boggling account of how time is conceptualised in Indian philosophy.

The eternity of the eternal life of absolute Being is conceived in terms of innumerable lives of the Divine Mother, a single one of whose lives encompasses a thousand life spans of Lord Shiva. One life of Lord Shiva covers the time of a thousand life spans of Lord Vishnu. One life of Lord Vishnu equals the duration of a thousand life spans of Brahma, the Creator. A single life span of Brahma is conceived in terms of one hundred years of Brahma; each year of Brahma comprises 12 months of Brahma, and each month comprises thirty days of Brahma. One day of Brahma is called a Kalpa. One Kalpa is equal to the time of fourteen Manus. The time of one Manu is called a Manvantara. One Manvantara equals seventy-one Chaturyugis. One Chaturyugi comprises the totals pan of four Yugas, i.e. Sat-yuga, Treta-yuga, Dvapara-yuga, and Kali-yuga. The span of the Yugas is conceived in terms of the duration of Sat-yuga. Thus the span of Treta-yuga is equal to three quarters of that of Sat-yuga; the span of Dvapara-yuga is half of that of Sat-yuga, and the span of Kali-yuga on quarter that of Sat-yuga. The span of Kali-yuga equals 432,000 years of man's life. (Maharishi Mahesh Yogi, 1969: 253-4)

Clearly, any attempt at chronology, given this conceptualisation of time, would be counterproductive, as would any attempt to grasp this concept of time intellectually. Vedic Science does not expect us to do this. Instead, it argues that human beings may experience the infinity of time (and space) in their own consciousness, in a specific state termed pure consciousness.

Usually plays are directed in such a way that there is always only one scene on the stage. Even Frayn's and Ayckbourn's attempts at simultaneity do not break this rule. The spectator's attention is allowed to focus fully on that scene. In that scene, there will be major characters carrying the scene, while other performers better be in the background physically and emotionally so as not to upstage those at the scene's centre. In contrast, for example, take the production of Mozart's opera *Marriage of Figaro* by David Freeman and the Opera Factory Zurich. Life of the house of Count Almaviva is shown throughout, breaking the boundaries of ordinary opera direction. The traditional rule is to have only the characters on the stage who have to sing something at that time. Not so in Freeman's *Figaro*. Life in the house goes on. The threads of the story come through the house. The focus of the scene is on the singers, but other characters go about their respective business at the same time. A few examples should illustrate this: already during the overture, Don Curzio enters, sits down at a table upstage right, and starts writing. Soon he is joined by Basilio. At the same time, Antonio brings parts of a wooden bed into the small area designated as Figaro's and Susanna's chamber downstage left. After that, Antonio moves to an area centre stage right that represents the garden, indicated by flowers, and starts preparing a beautiful flower bed. Barbarina, Susanna and two maids are busy in Figaro's and Susanna's chamber, cleaning the floor. Cherubino joins them: he enjoys female company. Before the end of the overture, Figaro arrives, makes all others except Susanna leave, so that they are now ready for their opening scene. Meanwhile, Bartolo and Marcelline have also appeared, downstage right, and during Figaro's and Susanna's scene, one of the maids brings hot water for a footbath and a camomile-steam bath against Marcellina's cold. Basilio moves to 'his area', indicated by a music stand, and starts composing. The maids start washing and wringing linen in the background, Basilio eavesdrops on Susanna's and Marcellina's quarrel.

Such a liveliness of parallel action is kept up throughout the production. At the same time, perception habits of the audience are provoked. Whereas the ordinary theatre experience means focusing on one central element on the stage, in Freeman's production of *Figaro*, a flood of visual input reaches the spectator. All elements of input are interesting and make much sense because they are logical elements of the interpretation that Freeman provides. The audience has to learn to focus on the main element, which is provided by the music: they have to focus on the singers, while at the same time allowing the other input not to distract but to enrich the insights gained from focusing.

Freeman carried his use of simultaneity even further in his adaptation of Mallory's *Morte d'Arthur*. The production was presented in two parts. The first half of Part I, and the second half of Part II, were presented in the traditional space of the Lyric Hammersmith, London. For the second half of Part I and the first half of Part II, the audience assembled in nearby Hammersmith Church. The space was empty (the pews had been removed), and the action took place simultaneously around five mobile pageants. Spectators had the choice to follow one storyline, or to shift between the pageants, or to stay somewhere in the space and take in just what happened to make its way towards their perception.

Simultaneity of space and time is a characteristic of pure consciousness. On this level of creation, past, present, and future coexist. If a form of theatre forces the human mind to engage in the experience of simultaneity, it trains it in functioning from that deep level. Repeated exposure to such theatre stimuli may serve in parallel to repeated exposure to pure consciousness in meditative techniques. Theatre, understood and practised in this way, may thus well serve as a means of developing higher states of consciousness.

The Sense of Hearing: Sound, Meaning and the Levels of Language

Regarding spoken language and hearing, reference to Indian linguistics may be useful. As noted in chapter four, Vedic Grammarian Bhartrihari describes several levels of language: *vaikhari, madhyama, pashyanti*, and *para*. According to this model of language, meaning is not conveyed 'from the speaker to the hearer, rather, the spoken words serve only as a stimulus to reveal or uncover the meaning which was already present in the mind of the hearer' (Coward, 1980: 12). Thus, words spoken by the actor in the theatre serve as a reminder of what is already present in the spectator's mind. This perspective adds a new dimension to the possibilities of theatre to develop higher states of consciousness. Other aspects in this context are that voice quality, and accompanying music.

The Sense of Smell: Smell in the Indian Tradition and its Application to Performance (co-written with Martin Mittwede)

In their attempt to counter the deadening of the senses resulting from the impact of realism/naturalism, symbolism, futurism and surrealism had emphasised and made practical use of the sense of smell already at the end of the nineteenth and the beginning of the twentieth centuries. As Sally Banes points out, most of the rest of the twentieth century was dominated by a trend towards deodorisation in Western society as a whole, including the theatre, in line with campaigns to improve hygiene, 'since the spread of disease was linked to foul odours' (2001: 68). Towards the end of the twentieth and the beginning of the twenty-first centuries, however, a new wave of 'olfactory performances' has developed, which even reached the amateur theatre scene. For example, in October 2002, at South Croydon's Emmanuel Church, a show set at a seaside fun fair involved forty young amateurs aged 8 to 18 and used a special ventilation system to bring smells of 'the salty tang of a walk along the sea shore, the sweet smell of freshly-made candy floss and the nutty sweet smell of pop corn' (Van Emst, 2002). This wave of olfactory performance led to the first attempt, by Sally Banes, to critically address the use of smell in performance. The current issue of *Performance Research* further demonstrates the relevance of discussing this new, or at least rediscovered dimension of creating meaning in performance.

Banes uses the terms *olfactory, smell, odour, scent, aroma* and *fragrant*, sometimes synonymously, sometimes with *smell* and *odour* signifying bad smells, while *aroma* and especially *fragrant* suggest pleasant smells. She identifies six representational functions 'the odours in performance are intended to discharge' (2001: 69):

1. To illustrate (words, characters, places, actions). Example: pine needles on the floor of the stage to create the scent of a forest.
2. Related to (1), but more general: to evoke (mood, ambience). Example: perfume is used to create an aura of luxury.
3. To complement or contrast (with aural/visual signs). Example: a wound suggested by stage make-up and crushed berries (together these create an unpleasant visual stimulus, contrasted by the pleasant olfactory stimulus of the berries).
4. To summon specific memories. Example: smells associated with a schoolroom or a child's nursery.
5. Less representational but more to do with framing and contextualisation: to frame the performance as ritual. Example: Incense burning throughout the production of Peter Brook's *The Mahabharata.*
6. Less representational but more to do with framing and contextualisation: to distance (to serve as a distancing device). Example: 'an actor holds a loaf of bread up to a patently fake fireplace, and suddenly, magically, the smell of toast wafts through the theatre (Banes, 2001: 71).

In addition, Banes discusses the use of aroma in performance against the semiotic triad of Peirce, thus allowing further insight.

1. Icon (resembles what it signifies),
2. Index (has a natural relation to what it signifies, such as cause or effect),
3. Symbol (has not natural relation to its signifier but represents it through social convention' (2001: 72).

Banes takes most examples for the six representational functions of the use of the olfactory in performance from the contexts of European and American performance. Her examples for her application of Peirce, taken from less straightforward 'intercultural' performances, lead her to argue that Western productions that 'make use of non-Western themes', often present the West as odourless and 'therefore neutral and the norm', compared and contrasted with the East (or Eastern sub-cultures in the West) which is (are) depicted as 'suffused with aromas, both pleasant and unpleasant'. (2001: 73). Banes concludes her essay on *Olfactory Performance* with two suggestions as to why there has been such an increase in the use of smell in performance at the turn of the twenty-first century: a general reflection of our culture's increased obsession with 'experiencing smells intensely', and / or an attempt of theatre, in its ongoing competition with film and television, to increase its claim on authenticity.

India is indeed a country of smell. The first moment you come out of the plane you can smell India, the hot air that bears a distinct and unique smell of Indian earth. You can find there not only the whole world of spices but also the fragrance of tropical flowers and fruits. According to Indian philosophy, the ability of sense perception is not accidental, but corresponds to the elements that form the cosmos. The *Samkhya* system of classical Indian philosophy provides the details of the specific correlation between individual and cosmic reality. The cosmic mind (*manas*) is connected with the manifest world of objects by the ten senses (*indriyas*), five senses of perception (*gyanendriya*), i.e. hearing, touch, seeing, taste, and *smell*, and five organs of action (*karmendriya*), i.e. language, ability to take hold of, ability to walk, discharge, and procreation. Subtle matter arises in the next stage of development. The *tanmatras* constitute

> the five basic realities, or essences, of the objects of the five senses of perception. They express themselves in the five elements which go to make up the objects of the senses, and which provide the material basis of the entire objective universe. Thus the essence of sound (*shabda tanmatra*) expresses itself in space, the essence of touch (*sparsha tanmatra*) in air, the essence of form (*rupa tanmatra*) in fire, the essence of taste (*rasa tanmatra*) in water, and the essence of smell (*gandha tanmatra*) in earth. (Maharishi Mahesh Yogi, 1969: 482-3)

The elements that constitute material creation are called *mahabhutas*, and they are space (*akasha*), air (*vayu*), fire (*tejas*), water (*apas*) and earth (*prithivi*).

Table 5

Element	Sense(s) related to it
Space	Hearing
Air	hearing and touching
Fire	hearing, touching and seeing
Water	hearing, touching, seeing and tasting
Earth	hearing, touching, seeing, tasting and smelling

To illustrate those relations, we can refer to everyday experience: sounds are formed by different configurations of space. This can be experienced by producing, e.g., the sounds a, ee and u. One can hear the wind, and one can feel the gentle breeze on the skin. But it is impossible to see it. Fire can be heard by its cracking sounds, it can be felt by its heat, and one can see its light and glowing. Water is experienced by four senses, but pure clean water has no smell. Only earth is an object for all the senses. Mainly it is the element of smell. The five elements that constitute the cosmos are direct expressions of all-pervading, pure consciousness. The element of space (akasha) is nearer to the pure consciousness and thus to spiritual values. Air, fire and water are grosser manifestations of absolute consciousness (purusha), and earth is the grossest. Relating the sense of smell to the cosmos allows us to talk about *cosmic smell*.

Conventionally, performances activate the senses of hearing and seeing. These senses function from a distance. Touching, tasting and smelling are close to the subject. All the five senses can affect the spectator's emotions. Hearing and seeing do so at a distance, while the other three senses literally touch the body physically. If a performance really wants to come down to earth, that means if it wants to get a place in the life of the audience (and the performers) it should integrate smell. An aesthetic impression is more holistic if all senses are activated. The activation of all senses means having a connection to virtually the whole cosmos. The result is an integration of the whole of the actor's and the spectator's personality. The same principle is used in the preparation of meals according to the traditional system of Indian medicine. A meal should have all six tastes that are connected to the five elements. If a meal has all these tastes it is really fulfilling. Existing plays can employ smell in new ways. In most cases, such performance will not go beyond the nine categories proposed by Banes, mainly because smell can hardly become a major component, but it will still enrich the experience for performers and spectators alike. In a few cases the use of smell might not only provide the performance with a réligious/ritual *context* or *frame* (those two terms seem to refer to intellectual categories, appropriate to the Western mindset), but take on the role of cosmic smell, leading to a spiritual experience, and experience of a desirable altered (higher) state of consciousness.

New plays-performance events-can be created, based on insights derived from knowledge of Indian philosophy and aesthetics, which give aroma a more central position. The explicit intention of such performances would be to lead to higher states of consciousness through (among other things) cosmic smell. The phrase 'among other things' may well lead to the further thought, inspired by the insight that the senses relate to the cosmos, about *Gesamtkunstwerk* and the role of cosmic smell in it.

Traditional Indian ritual is called *puja*, which means worship. It is performed at home or in a temple. The idea behind it is to be a good host for the adored godhead. Being a host implies to present refreshment, clothes, food, drink, flowers and smell. A *puja* without smell is not imaginable. In fact the offering of incense is a specific feature of Indian and South-East-Asian rituals. Besides the incense we have the smells of fruits, flowers and food that form a part of the ritual. For specific festivals there are cooked special meals with certain spices. Some recipes are connected with godheads, and they are cooked especially for them.

A ritual is a type of performance. Its performance follows specific rules, including preparation and aim. Many rituals are connected with a story: they are like a mythological drama which is performed for uplifting the people, for harmonizing a critical point in the evolution of life and nature, e.g., winter, rainy season, the first taking of earthly food, beginning of school, marriage. The earlier Vedic ritual is very often practiced as a fire ritual. The offerings are given into the fire, the burning of food, etc. produces a smell. Maybe this transformation, which takes place during burning of substances is a root for the importance of incense or camphor flame in the later ritual. Smell in this context is a side product of transformation of matter. The impression of a performance is also a transformational impulse. Another symbolical aspect is the direction. During the process of burning, the smell and the flame go upwards. The earthly smell is going to heaven and is thereby connecting relative existence with spiritual eternity.

Several important twentieth-century theatre artists have been associated with theatre (or aspects of theatre) and ritual. For example, Bates writes that

> Artaud and Grotowski (...) claimed the work of the actor as a ritual testing of the soul, a stretching of the limits of human communication. It is an ambitious, esoteric deeply philosophical view of the actor, which has inspired experimental theatre from creative risk-takers like Peter Brook. (1986: 39)

In his seminal *Holy Theatre: Ritual and the Avant Garde*, Innes argues:

> The attempt to reproduce the effects of ritual theatre helps to explain avant garde elements that might otherwise seem puzzling, such as the apparent incompatibility of stressing emotional authenticity and using stylizes movement or unnatural gesture to express it. (1981: 17)

Schechner devotes an entire book to the future of ritual (1993). The addition of smell to performance may, in appropriate circumstances, re-introduce an additional element of ritual to performance. It is important to note here that smell is an element that is central to performance according to the *Natyashastra*, the classical treatise on drama and theatre in India.

The origins of the *Natyashastra* are probably before Christ, and the traditional text which is preserved can be traced to the first or second century CE. The development of classical Sanskrit drama is closely connected with ritual. Art has emerged out of ritual performances. In the *Natyashastra* itself three types of rituals are described: the foundation of a theatre, the consecration of the theatre, and the introductory ritual (*purvaranga*) before the performance. Since this essay focuses on performance, we will only address the *purvaranga* aspect here. The *purvaranga* has two parts: the first one is performed while the curtain is closed, the second goes on before the audience. In this ritual the technical preparation, e.g., the arrangement of the musical instruments, the tuning, the first singing with accompanying dance, has a ritualistic value. Each action is associated with the adoration of certain demonical or celestial beings. The producer with his two assistants have also a part in this ritual by offering white flowers. The producer is called the *sutradhara*, that means: 'He who draws the strings'. He is responsible for the whole show as the creator is responsible for the cosmic performance. Therefore his first offering is done at the central point of the stage, the Brahma-mandala (the circle of the creator). A performance should not start until the *puja* has been done. The drama on the stage is a microcosmic representation of cosmic life. The introductory ritual brings blessings from all cosmic forces and from the highest absolute ruler of the universe. The smell of incense as a part of the *puja* reminds the actors and the audience that the following drama has a deep existential meaning.

To summarise our argument so far: smell in performance can have any one (or more) of the nine functions explored by Banes. We suggest that locating the concept of smell in Indian philosophy allows us to go beyond those nine functions: smell, together with stimuli for the other senses, may serve to create well-being, beneficial, desirable altered, higher states of consciousness in performer and spectator through performance. Identifying smell as a significant part of ritual further allows us to provide support to endeavours of emphasising the ritual origins and continuing aspects of performance. Now we want to further explore the practical implications of the use of smell in performance for the purpose of affecting such a transformational (lasting, in Schechner's sense of the term) change of consciousness in the spectator (and performer).

What effect can be attributed to a specific smell? The molecules carrying aroma first dissolve in the mucous membrane of the nose. As a result, they are 'noticed' by the nerve cells in charge of smell, and the information is directly transferred to the *hypothalamus*. This is a small but highly important part of the brain which controls bodily function such as temperature, thirst, hunger, waking and sleeping, sexual arousal and feelings of anger or joy. The aroma information is also directly transferred to the *limbic system*, which in turn controls emotions, and to the *hippocampus*, which is in charge of memory (see table 6).

Table 6: Aroma and Brain

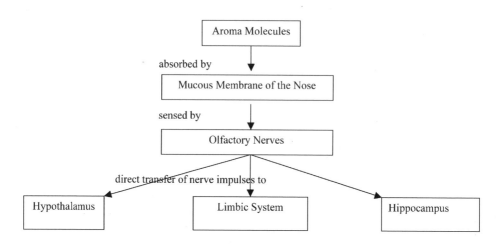

Whereas we have only six categories for taste (sweet, sour, salty, bitter, astringent and hot), there are thousands of aromas we can differentiate (Chopra, 1990: 191). All those aromas will have their effects on the three areas of the brain, *hypothalamus*, *hippocampus*, and *limbic system*, causing a multitude of reactions, different in each individual spectator and performer exposed to aroma during a performance. It is probably safe to assume that the majority of spectators and actors will agree as to which specific aroma they experience as pleasant or unpleasant. The aroma of 'salty tang of a walk along the sea shore' is likely to produce memories of the seaside in the spectators, but it is impossible to predict the precise nature of that memory for each spectator, or even for a group of spectators. Someone may remember walking along the seashore in a blissful, romantic mood, with a loved one, someone else may remember walking alone along the shore in tears, following bereavement. While it is possible to generate a general direction of memory and emotions through the use of aroma in the theatre, precision cannot be achieved.

Let us assume that we want to use smell more systematically in performance to induce (together with other factors) the experience of higher states of consciousness. To achieve this aim, a further look at Indian philosophy proves helpful, in particular at Indian medicine, *Ayurveda*. According to *Ayurveda*, there are three places 'sandwiched between mind and body, where thought turns into matter; it is occupied by three operating principles called *doshas*' (Chopra, 1990: 25). The three *doshas* are *vata*, in control of movement; *pitta*, in control of metabolism; and *kapha*, in control of structure. *Vata* arises from the combination of space and air. *Pitta* is associated with fire and water, and *kapha* has its origin in water and earth (see table 7).

Table 7: The Elements, Doshas, and related Senses according to Ayurveda

Elements leading to	Dosha	Related sense(s)
Space and Air	Vata	Hearing and Touching
Fire and Water	Pitta	Sight
Water and Earth	Kapha	Taste and **Smell**

Since *Ayurveda* argues that any imbalance of the three *doshas* is the root cause of any symptom of physical or mental illness or lack of well-being, the aim of ayurvedic treatment is to achieve a balance of the *doshas*. Aromatherapy is one of the numerous approaches in *Ayurveda*. Table (8) shows aromas that are known to balance specific doshas:

Table 8: Balancing the Doshas through Aromatherapy

Dosha	Balanced by the Aroma of
Vata	Mixture of sweet and sour aromas: basil, orange, geranium, clove, and other spices
Pitta	Mixture of fresh, sweet aromas: sandalwood, rose, mint, cinnamon, jasmine
Kapha	Mixture of stronger aromas: eucalyptus, camphor, clove, marjoram

It should be possible to either find passages in the textbooks of *Ayurveda* to identify the impact of many more aromas, or to experimentally test which (if any) of the doshas a given single aroma, or mixture of aromas will balance. Let us assume that a detailed table matching aroma and effect could be developed. The challenge in preparing a production would then be to match the desired effect of any aroma or mixture of aromas on the emotions and memories of the spectator with the equally desired effect on balancing the doshas.

We also need to address whether the substances used in the performance space should be taken directly from nature, as in the essential oils dispersed though the steam of hot water usually used in Ayurveda, or whether one should use chemical compounds created in laboratories said to lead to aromas that are like the aromas we can smell in nature. It is the latter that are used to a large extent in the fragrance industry, especially those branches that seek to establish themselves in the entertainment sector. Would synthetic aromas have the same effect on the brain as natural ones, and would they have the same holistic effect on consciousness, grounding the experience in the theatre and enhancing the chances of transformational impact on consciousness? There are clearly ethical implications to the use of aroma in performance.

How to distribute aroma in performance? An 1891 production of *Song of Songs*, by Paul-Napoléon Roinard 'featured scents pumped into the auditorium on cue by young symbolist poets stationed in the far edges of the proscenium and in the balcony and using hand-held vaporizers' (Shepherd-Barr, 1999: 152). Apparently, some members of the audience were too far away to smell the aromas used, others were subjected to too much and the performance was accompanied by a lot of coughing. Technology has advanced since then. UK-based Aroma Company Europe offers aromabox or aromacube, covering 200 or 100 square metres respectively, and operates with tailor-made aromas in cartridges that insert into the box or cube. The Royal National Theatre, for example, owns a number of the boxes and used them for distributing the smell of peat in their production of Synge's *Playboy of the Western World*. The box costs £550, and a cartridge contains 30ml of aroma, lasting for 189 hours, at £15-25, depending on the fragrance. Several questions arise: how long will the aromas stay in the air, how quickly can they be made to stop, or changed from one to the next. Germany-based Aerome does not work on the principle of distributing a specific aroma over a whole space. Instead, each spectator is issued with a scent nozzle that issues specific aromas with to-the-second accuracy. To quote from the company's product datasheet: 'Sophisticated scent management within the device reliably avoids any overlapping of different scents'. As a result, users can decide whether they want to expose themselves to the smell or not.

To summarise: looking at the use of smell in performance from the perspective of Indian philosophy suggests that

- The more of the five senses are stimulated during performance, the more cosmic the performance, and the more likely to be conducive to the experience of higher states of consciousness.
- Different smells will have different effects. If aim is to shock, the use of smell is likely to add to the potential of achieving that effect. If the aim is to induce transformative change of consciousness, then the choice of smells used will be different. Concepts of aromatherapy in Ayurveda might prove valuable in making that choice.
- Questions arise regarding the possible differences in impact depending on whether the substances used are natural or nature-identical, and how they are being distributed.

We conclude that there is a rich potential here for exploring the realm of smells in the context of performance further, combining a range of methodological approaches:

1. Further study of the textbooks of Indian philosophy to elaborate on the material explored in this essay;
2. Further research in India, where material to date not known in the West may be uncovered;
3. Discussion of that material with experts from India, who are likely to shed further light on the details;
4. Empirical exploration of smell in performance based on the insights derived from this essay and from further research outlined in (1-3) above, including
   • Developing the use of specific smells in a specific performance and, through the use of questionnaires, establishing the impact of the smells on the audience. Psychological measures could assess impact on emotions, well-being, happiness, and aspects related to transformation of consciousness.
   • Studies to assess any difference between natural and nature-identical substances used to produce smell.

The Sixth Sense: new forms of matter

American director Peter Sellars made an experiment: actors in one his productions were on stage and played a scene, as rehearsed, which contained by nature a number of specific emotions. Neither those onstage actors nor the audience knew that, backstage, a further group of actors were engaged in getting involved in, and thus *radiating*, emotions that were either exactly the same emotions portrayed by the actors onstage, or exactly the opposite ones. Both onstage actors and spectators noticed a difference in *atmosphere*. I would like to postulate that this effect of emotions, this change in atmosphere, is due to effects relating to what is commonly called the sixth sense, similar to us noticing if someone is staring at us behind our backs. It is possible to study such phenomena in terms of transpersonal psychology. Even more exciting, though, is the research by Volkamer and colleagues (1999), who have published quantitative experimental evidence of a new type of matter. This 'new' form of matter is not visible, thus called *dark matter*, but weighable. It has a low energy level, thus called *cold*, and a low density, thus called *soft matter*. It has field-like qualities, i.e. it builds spatially extended fields around ordinary matter. This cold, dark, soft matter is a form of *ether* as initially theorised at the beginning of this century, among others by Einstein. For the theatre, the picture might be this: actors produce stimuli on all levels of the mind. Such stimuli affect the spectators on all those levels. Current empirical research tries to establish the immediate physiological impact of such stimuli, and is thus clearly located on the level of traditional matter. The implications for the theatre of Gallese's description of mirror neurones represent a recent development of this approach. The discovery of the existence of cold, dark, soft matter adds a further dimension to the understanding of the reception process: reception is not restricted to the physical, geographical proximity of the stimuli. Sheldrake's morphogenetic fields come to mind, or, in the theatre, Peters Sellar's experiment, which I propose to explain as an interaction of dark, cold, soft matter with conventional matter. If this hypothesis can be confirmed, it should be possible to understand and use terms such as *atmosphere* or *presence*, which have some element of vagueness attached to them, more clearly and comprehensively.

The question arises whether all action always, and to the same degree, functions on the level of cold, dark, soft matter. Perhaps *presence* is dependent on the actor's ability to impact on the level of cold, dark, soft matter, which may, in turn, be dependent on the state of consciousness the actor is in at any given time: the higher the state of consciousness, the stronger the impact on the level of cold, dark, soft matter.

Examples of Performance Practice

In the previous sections of this chapter, I have discussed the relation of the senses of sight, hearing, smell, and the sixth sense, in relation to theatre and consciousness. I want to conclude the chapter with a descriptive analysis of two theatre/performance events that stood out, besides Brook's *Mahabharata*, for me in their consciousness-raising impact.

Ariadne's Thread

When I asked recent final-year students about their most impressive experience while studying drama at the University of Wales Aberystwyth, the almost unanimous response was: *The Labyrinth*, also known as *Ariadne's Thread*. This was a non-traditional, non-mainstream event, presented by a group of Colombian performers, Taller Investigacion de la Imagen Theatral. They created a labyrinth of pathways within the theatre space, leading to individual defined spaces, such as a children's nursery, a schoolroom, a space covered with sand where a performer dressed as a gypsy would sit by a real fire and perform magic spells and manipulate the fire. Spectators went through the labyrinth on their own, groping their way along the black cloths in total darkness, sometimes guided by performers' touch or sound, encountering various 'characters' in the defined spaces, and experiencing a wide range of smells, sounds and touches without being able, in many cases, to *see* the origin of the sensory impression. In one installation, spectators had to crawl though a well-lit, comfortably padded 'umbilical cord', leading to a pitch-dark end where they had to slide downwards into the unknown. Some were initially too afraid to take the risk, but returning was impossible. At the end of the slope, they ended up in a large mass of unroasted coffee beans, stroked and comforted by a performer. The reaction of individual spectators was different to each and every of the defined spaces, the installations and whatever went on in them, but all agreed that the experience had remained vividly in their minds, unlikely to be forgotten ever, and the non-visual impressions, especially the unfamiliar but generally pleasant smells, had stayed with them for days.

Reverie II

Reverie II is a video installation project by Anna and Corrina Bonshek; Anna Bonshek is the author of *Mirror of Consciousness* (2001), which looks closely at fine art from the perspective of Vedic Science. *Reverie II* it is expressly based on the principles of consciousness proposed by Vedic Science, and wishes to express them through its chosen media.

My first encounter with conceptual art came as a teenager: in the conservative, strongly Catholic town I was living in at the time, the local museum held a one-off exhibition of modern art. One piece caught my attention in particular, and I still recall my reaction to it some 30 years later. The piece consisted of a nice, plain, grey wooden frame around a surface of Styrofoam painted grey. Into the Styrofoam the artist had placed ten plastic spoons, five neatly pointing with their scoop down, and the others neatly pointing with their scoop up. The piece had a fancy name (which I forgot), and was on sale for DM 100 (today's equivalents would be €50, £35, or US$40). I remember feeling that I could do this kind of art; the feeling recurs when I see, for example, an unmade bed as a highly praised work of art, or a blotch of rancid butter in the corner of an exhibition room ceiling. Although I believe I could easily produce (note that I am not saying *create*) such art, I would not have the sheer cheek; I would not be shameless enough to put my name to it.

In the course of my training and career as a theatre academic (and to some extent theatre maker), I came across, naturally, performance art. In my department, a new degree scheme in performance studies was recently introduced, alongside theatre studies, and for some time the common denominator for distinguishing between what is done in theatre studies and performance studies became: theatre studies deals with text-based performance, while performance studies deals with performance that is not text-based. A dictionary definition of performance art will indeed tell you that performance art grew out of mainstream theatre, in explicit and intentional opposition to it, and indeed generally in opposition to the values traditionally attached to art (Meyer-Dinkgräfe 2002: 590). I was struck, however, by a parallel in the developments both in theatre and performance art. In British theatre, there was a wave of politically motivated theatre following the abolition of censorship in 1968. When the dramatists became disillusioned because they were unable to change society through their politically involved theatre to the extent they had hoped for and expected; they turned to more individual subjects, to themselves as artists, amongst others. A similar development, albeit against a culturally and nationally different historical background, can be observed in German theatre of the same time. What those plays focusing on the individual have in common is their attention to individual suffering, in all possible facets and shapes and shades. Drama and theatre work well with suffering, because suffering is conflict and drama is built around conflict. Plays can have strong storylines, can be moving, can strongly affect audiences through the appropriate dramatisation of suffering, and many an actor has excelled in their portrayal of suffering. Often, suffering in theatre tended to become an end in itself, gratuitous revelling in other people's misery, and yet another foray into psychopathology. At first glance, much of British 1990s 'In-Yer-Face' theatre (Sierz 2001) would fall into that category. It is of course much more challenging to write happiness, because of the assumed lack of conflict in it. It is easy, wrote German director Gustaf Gründgens, to direct a production in such a way that it will turn into a public scandal, but much more difficult to direct in such a way as he considered most appropriate: as far as possible in line with the intentions of the author and the play. In the last quarter of the twentieth century, some new plays have emerged that manage to use conflict in the form of suffering to bring out a development of the characters: they overcome suffering, and suffering does not remain a gratuitous end in itself.

Although performance art arose in opposition to conventional theatre and conventional art, it seems to me that performance art follows the same pattern. The kind of performance art that attracts the most publicity is that which focuses on, broadly speaking, suffering, the negative, the ugly, while the artists, and critics alike, at the same time do not own up to those descriptors, but deny them, sometimes quite vehemently. In extreme cases, behaviour is carried out, is watched, is critically discussed, is at times admired and is sold as performance art that, in different circumstances, would lead its performer(s) to be investigated with quite genuine alarm for their mental stability. There are, however, occasional instances of performance art, thankfully, in my opinion, growing in number, which defy the current *negative* dominant mode of performance art and thus contribute seminally to its further development. *Reverie II*, by Anna and Corrina Bonshek, is a shining light among those few instances of *positive* performance art.

By *positive* I do not mean some shallow mood-making which somehow seems to make us feel better for a brief span of time only for reality to hit us over the head and make us feel even more miserable when we wake up from such artificially induced moods. What I have in mind is genuine change of consciousness, enabled through performance art. *Reverie II*, I suggest, aims to, and does achieve, change of consciousness. It is thus clearly positioned within the current debates of consciousness studies.

Reverie II is seminal not only as leading the move towards *positive* performance art. It is seminal also, in combination with Anna and Corrina Bonshek's critical essays about their own work, in showing us the potential for the *reflexive artist*. For some time now, attempts have been made across disciplines in literatures and the arts of enhancing the dialogue between academics and practitioners; the latest phase in this development is the merging of the two in one and the same person: the academic who is an active artist, and artists who reflect on their own artistic creation. The academic element in this merger is usually related to theory, while the artist's aspect is practice. Theory is predominantly on the level of discourse, of speaking and/or writing, and practice is doing. Prior to the attempts at merging theory and practice in this way, artists were free (?) to create independently of any theoretical restrictions. If academics wanted to read theory into their works of art, so be it. Academics were equally free (?) to approach any work of art of their choice and subject it to the theory of their choice. The merger of theorist/academic and practitioner/artist changes this picture. Academic ideas might now serve as 'inspiration' for artistic activity, and artists (are expected to) reflect their creation in academic discourse. The question arises whether either theory or art will be the same as before. Theory is likely to thrive, because with artists becoming fellow producers of theory, more theory is certainly in the process of being written even now. There is thus a statistical chance that with more theory, more useful theory might result. It will be interesting to check, with hindsight, whether this statistical potential is met. Equally, hindsight will establish whether the kind of art created by reflexive artists, artists who not only continue producing works of art, but who write theoretically about them, is different from the art possibly still produced by artists who either never had the idea of turning reflexive, or who make a clear and conscious decision not to join the reflexive artist bandwagon. If there are differences, what could those differences be? I propose that reflexive art is likely to be different: I expect that it involves more of the artist's intellect, and less of other levels of the mind, such as emotions, intuition, feeling, ego, etc. and that, in consequence, it will appeal more to the recipient's intellect. The intellectuals among recipients are likely to be able to write about the works of art created by reflexive artists more readily, and further reams of theory will ensue. Less intellectually inclined recipients are likely to get less from those reflexive works of art. Reflexive art, on this argument, is potentially less inclusive than non-reflexive art, and its impact on recipients potentially less comprehensive than non-reflexive art. Clearly, such potential loss in inclusiveness and comprehensiveness has implications for any discussion of the value, worth, merit, or quality of the work(s) of art in question, no matter how despised such concepts may be in the present climate of political correctness.

In the case of Anna and Corrina Bonshek's *Reverie II*, I do not see the problems inherent in the concept of the reflexive artist, quite the contrary. Anna Bonshek's *Mirror or Consciousness* describes, with all necessary detail and depth, the relation between the arts and consciousness from the perspective of Vedic Science, Maharishi Mahesh Yogi's reassessment of the entire body of Vedic literature of India. Her, and Corrina Bonshek's art, are informed, saturated by this knowledge. In their work, as exemplified by *Reverie II*, theory and practice are no longer separate entities: they become two aspects of the same phenomenon. Anna Bonshek does not only write about consciousness and the arts (theory), but expresses what she writes about in her art (practice). Knowledge is no longer theoretical and hypothetical, and practice is no longer somehow devoid of any conceptual background or basis. Theory and practice, in their performance art, become one, self-referral, enriching each other rather then presenting seemingly insurmountable tension, conflict and incongruity.

Reverie II, and indeed any (performance) art created in this integrated way, has not only the intention, but also the very impact of affecting the spectators' consciousness (and indeed the creation process itself will have had an impact on the production team's consciousness). What does that mean precisely, what are (some of) the processes involved, and how can we be sure? The model of consciousness behind *Reverie II* is that proposed by Maharishi Mahesh Yogi's Vedic Science. Vedic Science distinguishes, initially, between three basic states of consciousness: waking, dreaming and sleeping. During the waking state of consciousness, several *functions* of consciousness can be differentiated, including decision-making, thinking, emotions, and intuition. Vedic Science postulates a fourth state of consciousness which serves as the basis of the states of waking, dreaming and sleeping, and their related functions. The fourth state is without contents, but fully awake. It is referred to as *pure consciousness*, or *samadhi* in Sanskrit. It has been described, albeit in different terms, across cultures. W. T.

Stace, for example, writes about *pure unitary consciousness* in the context of Christian mystic experiences (1960). If pure consciousness is not experienced only briefly, and 'just' on its own, but together with waking or dreaming or sleeping, according to Vedanta, higher states of consciousness have been achieved.

Different aspects, features, elements or modes of *Reverie II* function on their own or in combination to serve as means enabling the spectators' minds to reach the state of pure consciousness. Spectators, however, do not engage in meditation, with eyes closed, while watching *Reverie II*. This is the reason why they will experience pure consciousness together with the artistic stimuli of *Reverie II* that led them to the experience of pure consciousness in the first place. *Reverie II* thus enables spectators to experience a higher state of consciousness (i.e. pure consciousness together with waking) as defined by Vedic Science. Development of higher states of consciousness is the aim, and the outcome, of *positive* works of art.

What are some of those aspects, features, elements or stimuli of *Reverie II* that may enable the experience of higher states of consciousness? According to Maharishi Mahesh Yogi's Vedic Science, pure consciousness is the basis of the entire world, the universe, including the earth, including matter, including human beings, including just everything there is and there ever can be. Pure consciousness follows precise processes in creating everything out of itself, processes both intricately complex and beautifully simple. Anna Bonshek has researched Maharishi Mahesh Yogi's cognition of those principles of creation, and her *Mirror of Consciousness* represents their most comprehensive description to date. As the essays by Anna and Corrina Bonshek in this catalogue will demonstrate in much more detail, the images and sounds of *Reverie II* are intended to represent, or to mirror, and ultimately *to be*, patters of pure consciousness. I propose that when the spectators are exposed to visual and auditive representations of the patterns of pure consciousness creating from within itself, their own waking consciousness is led towards the experience of pure consciousness together with the experiences of the visual and auditive stimuli. Thus exposure to *Reverie II* leads to the experience of a higher state of consciousness: pure consciousness together with the aesthetic stimulus perceived in the waking state. It is important to remember that some spectators may react more or less to specific stimuli than to others.

What could the experience of higher states of consciousness, naturally induced by *Reverie II*, be *like* for those who watch *Reverie II*? The impact of any *positive* work of art, including performance art (and thus *Reverie II*), the development of higher states of consciousness, will be experienced by the observer or spectator as an increase of well-being. For different individual spectators or observers, well-being may mean something different: different aspects of *Reverie II* may register with different spectators, and thus impact on them. Such impact may be conscious, i.e. the spectator realises something like: 'Oh, I like those golden waves, they give me a warm feeling and send pleasant shivers down my spine when they shift shape to become those spiralling lines'. The impact may be unconscious as well, in three ways: the spectator may notice an increase of well-being without being able to pinpoint where in the body this well-being is located, and/or without being able to associate specific experiences while watching *Reverie II* with specific phases, images or sound impressions of the installation. Finally, some spectators may not even be aware of any change in themselves while watching, or after having watched *Reverie II*, but I would still maintain that such a change will have occurred, although it remained unnoticed.

How can we be sure that a change does take place, that *Reverie II* does cause the experience of a higher state of consciousness in the spectators, independent of whether they notice or not, and if they notice, independent of what that experience *is like* for them. The practical aspect of Maharishi Mahesh Yogi's Vedic Science has been subjected to rigorous empirical research. Those studies suggest that the Transcendental Meditation (TM) technique and the TM Sidhi programme effect significant improvement of physical and mental well-being, and equally significant decrease of any aspect of life that might adversely affect well-being. In particular, electrophysiological studies have yielded clear information about brain wave patterns characteristic of pure consciousness and higher states of consciousness. Based on the knowledge and experience gained from those studies, it should be possible to predict, in the mode of scientific enquiry, the kinds of physiological and psychological changes you expect *Reverie II* to cause in spectators. In the second stage of the experiment, you would expose a group of people to *Reverie II* and to take measures of those parameters that you initially predicted to change. If the hypothesis (*Reverie II* leads to the experience of pure consciousness and higher states of consciousness) is correct, the results of the measurements should confirm your prediction.

Reverie II, to conclude, is not just another of the thousands of performance art installations created over the years. It is not just nice to watch and pleasant to listen to (which in itself is rare for much performance art!) It is a groundbreaking work of art, pioneering theory-informed art practice that takes seriously the enormous potential of art in changing human consciousness for the better.

Summary

In this chapter, I argued that theatre affects human consciousness by impacting directly on the senses, predominantly sight and sound, but potentially also smell. In those contexts I discussed scenography, aspects of sound (the words that are said, and the voice qualities that says them), the potential of smell and implications of the sixth sense. I concluded the chapter with two examples of striking performances capable of inducing profound change of consciousness in the spectator. I will take the opportunity in the conclusion of the book to come back to a number of the points of my argument in this chapter when I draw attention to future research into the relation between theatre and consciousness.

6: Concepts of Theatre Studies

In the introduction to this book, I set two clear questions at its centre: to see whether we can better understand theatre as a result of such an analysis, and to think through the implications of the *Natyashastra's* claim that theatre may serve as a tool to the development of moksha, enlightenment, higher states of consciousness. So far, I have discussed those two questions in relation to the inspiration and creative process in the dramatist, consciousness reflected in drama, aspects of acting, Indian theatre aesthetics and spectators' reception processes. In this chapter, I want to complete the picture by addressing a number of issues that have come to prominence in their own times in the course of theatre history. Since they are frequently quoted in academic contexts even today, I take for granted that they are still considered important to our understanding of theatre, and that they, therefore, merit reconsideration in the context of consciousness studies. The first two sections relate to the *language* of theatre: Artaud's conceptualisation of a language of nature, and attempts, by Peter Brook, for example, to arrive at a universal language of the theatre. In the third section, I address the question of how theatre relates to ritual-in view of the fact that ritual is often quoted as a source for the development of theatre, a view recently refuted by Rozik (2000). I explain how ritual is understood in Vedic Science, and how theatre that follows the aesthetics of the *Natyashastra* can be understood in terms of Vedic ritual. The fourth section deals with the phenomenon of *postmodernism* in the context of theatre. With reference to key critics in this area, I argue that many theatre artists' search for access to pure consciousness can be understood as the search for an overarching structure so vehemently rejected by postmodernism. Finally, I discuss the concept of *utopian performative*, recently introduced by Jill Dolan, in the context of Vedic Science.

Language of nature (Artaud)

Theatre of Cruelty
Artaud insisted on the necessity of a revolution of traditional theatre. In his scathing cultural critique, Artaud regarded the theatre of his day as only one aspect of art that is generally inert and disinterested (1974: 4). In contrast, 'true culture acts through power and exaltation while the European ideal of art aims to cast us into a frame of mind distinct from the power present in its exaltation' (4).

In response to the need for a magic culture, Artaud wished to create a form of theatre that could do justice to the demands of a genuine culture: theatre should be 'magical and violently egoistical, that is, self-interested' (4). He developed the *Theatre of Cruelty*, a frequently misinterpreted concept (Innes, 1981: 110). Artaud took great pains to point out that *cruelty* was not synonymous with bloodshed; he regarded any variety of physical violence as merely one minor aspect of *cruelty*. Nevertheless, Artaud's own plays, later productions of those plays, and in general theatre (both plays and productions) that lays claim to being in the spirit of Artaud is characterised mainly by its shock values, achieved through various forms and expressions of violence and ugliness. 1990s British 'in-yer-face theatre' is a good example (Saunders, 2002, Sierz, 2001)

In view of such an apparent contradiction, it is vital to investigate further how Artaud himself understood the term *cruelty*, if it was not predominantly bloodshed and violence. He understood the term from a 'mental viewpoint', implying 'strictness, diligence, unrelenting decisiveness, irreversible and absolute determination' (1974: 77). He emphasised that *cruelty* is 'very lucid, a kind of strict control and submission to necessity' (78).

The mental viewpoint that Artaud adopts to regard cruelty implies, I suggest, that an experience is involved on his part. He does not merely conjecture, hypothesise, theorise, intellectually juggle ideas, devoid of subjective experience, to arrive at those descriptions and definitions. Rather, he intuits general characteristics, the essence, as it were, of the theatre he wished to establish as the alternative to the theatre he rejects. It is striking that the characteristics he attributes to the essence of that alternative theatre correspond very closely to specific qualities proposed in Vedic Science for the field of pure consciousness.

Table 9: Artaud's Concept of Cruelty and Qualities of Pure Consciousness

Concept of *Cruelty*	Quality of Pure Consciousness
Strictness	Differentiating
Diligence	Establishing
Unrelenting decisiveness	Measuring and quantifying
Irreversibility	Self-referral
Absolute determination	Distinguishing and deciding
Lucidity	Unfolding
Strict control	Structuring
Submission to necessity	Invincible and progressive

Anything emerging from the field of pure consciousness carries its qualities. Thus, theatre emerging from the field of pure consciousness, i.e. written and/or performed while the dramatist and/or performer experiences pure consciousness carries the qualities of pure consciousness. In defining *theatre of cruelty*, Artaud thus conceptualises theatre that includes pure consciousness. Vedic Science proposes that there are altogether 40 qualities; Artaud managed to intuit only a few of those, not all.

Of course, Artaud was not aware of Vedic Science. He tried to understand and conceptualise his intuition, in this case about the nature of what he came to term *cruelty*. He used the bodies of knowledge available to him to make sense of his ideas, and concluded, that cruelty is a

> hungering after life, cosmic strictness, relentless necessity, in the gnostic sense of a living vortex engulfing darkness, in the sense of the inescapably necessary pain without which life could not continue. (78)

It is precisely this, Artaud's own *intellectual interpretation* of his experience, which gives rise to the dark aspects of the concept of *cruelty*. Artaud argues that cruelty does not predominantly equal violence. He is right here, in so far as his experience of some qualities of pure consciousness (strictness, etc.) does indeed, understood in the context of Vedic Science, not imply violence at all. But when he tries to make sense of his experience in terms of the bodies of knowledge at his disposal, violence, darkness, pain are foregrounded; those concepts take hold of his own imagination, fuelling his attempts of putting the theory derived from his experience into practice. Both this theory (in the form of the concept of *theatre of cruelty*) and his practice influenced later theatre artists to ignore Artaud's experience (related to pure consciousness), which implies that cruelty is not predominantly violence, and base their own Artaudian practice exclusively on Artaud's rationalisation (with a dominance of cruelty as violence).

Language of Nature

Artaud calls the language beyond speech, which he intuits, the language of nature. I want to introduce a particular view on language as proposed in Indian linguistics, which is clearly related to the Vedic Science model of consciousness outlined earlier in this book. The grammar of this language, Artaud argues, has not yet been discovered. However, in the context of Indian linguistics, experience of sufficiently refined states of consciousness, i.e. direct experience of the *pashyanti* level of language, should be able to reveal that grammar. Artaud assigns an 'ancient magic effectiveness to the language beyond speech'. In parallel, Abhinavagupta, the main classic commentator on Bharata's *Natyashastra*, states that it is the poetic experience of *dhvani*, the sound aspect of speech, that brings about the experience of *rasa*

> as a transcendental function of suggestion removes the primordial veil of ignorance from our minds and thereby allows the bliss associated with the discovery of true meaning to be experienced. (Coward, 1980: 76)

Artaud may well have sensed levels of language beyond speech. The following passage, from a letter to his doctor from 1932, suggests as much: here Artaud describes a characteristic of thought in relation to spoken language:

> the brain sees the whole thought at once, with all its circumstances, and it also sees all the points of view it could take and all the forms with which it could invest them ... which all the complexities of syntax would never suffice to express and expound (293).

Artaud proceeds to analyse the experience of different levels of language in terms of knowledge available to him. He concludes that the experience that it is impossible to clearly express the density language on the level of thought in spoken or written words, is not due to the complexity of thought language, but due to an inability to formulate a precise thought (293). In the context of theatre, Artaud associated the levels of the mind gained by the spectator through watching such performances with the intellect rather than with the emotions, let alone the even subtler level of *pashyanti*: 'Thus we are led *along intellectual paths* [my emphasis] towards reconquering the signs of existence' (Artaud, 1974: 45). Artaud here shows influence by contemporary science, which places the intellect above the emotions and has no place for a level of the mind beyond speech. The lack in Western psychology of a model of the mind that takes levels of language beyond speech, as the *pashyanti*-level described by Bhartrihari, into account, leads to the vagueness and confusion of terminology in Artaud's argumentation. Vedic Science clearly associates *para* with the level of pure consciousness. Appendix (2) describes how Vedic Science conceptualises the processes involved in creation, taking their origin in the level of pure consciousness. Those processes represent a grammar of the language of nature. Artaud sought to discover and use the language of nature in the context of theatre, hoping to one day discover its grammar. Vedic Science provides a clear intellectual understanding of the language of nature, the processes of creation, and thus the grammar of that language of nature, and implies that this level of consciousness is common to all human beings. Thus, all human beings have the potential of not only theoretically discussing, but also directly experiencing that level of consciousness, the grammar of the language of nature that is lively at the level of *para* in human consciousness. Future theatre could benefit much from exploring ways and implications of applying nature's language as intuited by Artaud, and as detailed in Vedic Science.

Universal Language of Theatre (Brook)

In our discussion of concepts of theatre that can be clarified by reassessing them from the perspective of consciousness studies, we now come to the theatre of Peter Brook. From the perspective of consciousness studies, several aspects of Brook's work are worth discussing in further detail:

1. his concepts of *holy theatre* and *total theatre*,

2. his aims to achieve a universal language of the theatre.

Total and Holy Theatre

Brook's main interest in the theatre is concerned with the 'possibility of arriving (...) at a ritual expression of the true driving forces of our time' (1987: 31). Whereas Grotowski tried to turn theatre back into ritual, Brook turns ritual into theatre (Kott, 1990: 203). Brook's ultimate aim is a 'totality of theatrical expression' (Bradby and Williams, 1988: 31), a theatre that transcends 'the surface of reality' (Brook, 1987: 30). This may be achieved by shocking the audience, as in Brook's experiments with Artaudian *theatre of cruelty*, by working with an international cast, by forays into anthropology (*Conference of the Birds*), by creating (or re-creating?) a new (ancient) language (*Orghast*), by making the elitist genre of opera accessible again (*The Tragedy of Carmen*, seen, worldwide, by at least 200,000 people), by bridging the gap between theatre and storytelling (*The Mahabharata*), or the gap between theatre and science (*The Man Who*) and scaling down canonical plays to their essentials (*Hamlet*).

Brook argues that specific conditions have to be met for the *invisible* to become *visible*, characteristic of *holy theatre*. Those conditions are either a mental state or a certain understanding. It is possible to understand *invisible* and *visible* either literally, as objects of sensory perception, or as insights of a nature that reach beyond the sensory experience (although a non-ordinary sensory aspect may be part of that experience), intangible, and difficult to communicate other than in poetic terms such as the ones chosen by Brook. No matter which meaning is applied, *holy theatre* may be taken to refer to an experience of refined cosmic consciousness as proposed by Vedic Science: a 'mental state' characterised by refined perception, allowing the eye to see layers of creation not available to perception in the ordinary waking state of consciousness. To the intellect in waking consciousness, such experiences are well beyond its scope. The intellect devoid of permanent experience of pure consciousness can understand experiences only on its own level and on more expressed levels of the mind (mind, desire, senses). Such a restricted intellect will have difficulties *understanding* any temporary experience of refined cosmic consciousness once the experience has disappeared and consciousness has returned to the ordinary waking state of consciousness. Full understanding (as an intellectual function) of a higher state of consciousness is possible only on the level of that higher state.

When Brook says that the conditions for *holy theatre* to take place are either a mental state of a certain understanding, he implicitly refers to a higher state of consciousness in both cases: a mental state of refined cosmic consciousness, in which the *invisible* becomes *visible* quite literally; and an understanding of that higher state, which is possible only from the level of that higher state itself. *Holy theatre* presents the *invisible* on the stage, i.e. facilitates the experience of a higher state of consciousness; at the same time, it makes the perception of that *invisible* possible to the spectators in the first place. What *and* how together make theatre holy. *Holy theatre* thus takes account of all levels of theatre: the subject matter of the production (i.e. written text, or material resulting from improvisations /collaborative work, etc.), the direction, the various areas of design, the performers, and the reception by the spectators.

Total theatre is still further advanced than *holy theatre*, even more powerful in effect, and for that reason even more desirable; at the same time, its achievement is even more rare. From Brook's description of *total theatre* as unifying the previously existing division of deadly, rough and holy theatre, as merging theatres of joy, catharsis, celebration, exploration and shared meaning, as establishing a unity of play, actors and spectators, I conclude that he is in fact describing theatre on the level of unity consciousness.

The quest for a universal language of the theatre

Fischer-Lichte considers Brook's work in the context of three categories of intercultural theatre she proposes. The first category comprises productions in which reference to the foreign (theatre, culture) dominates. They regard the foreign components as ideal or model for their own theatre, placing the foreign next to the existing forms of theatre. In the second category, reference to the production's own theatre and culture dominates. Foreign elements enlarge the range of possibilities for expression, aiming at further development or relativation of one's own forms of theatre (1989: 115). The aim of the third category is the development of a universal language of theatre. As Peter Brook put it in relation to his production of *Orghast*:

> There are rare things-pieces of music, gestures-that can communicate to anyone anywhere. What we are looking for in Orghast and Greek is whether there are rhythms, forms of truth and emotional involvement which can be communicated without going through the normal channels. (Smith, 1972: 159-60)

Fischer-Lichte considers not only Peter Brook's *Orghast*, but also Tadashi Suzuki's *The Trojan Women* as examples of productions striving for a universal language of the theatre. In *Orghast*, Brook had the poet Ted Hughes develop a new language, also called *Orghast*. The language was based on the concept of total identity between sound and meaning (Pronko, 1988: 110). The intention, according to Innes, was

> not only (...) to reflect the sensation of a half- barbaric world, but to affect 'magi-cally' the mental state of the listener on an instinctive level in the same way as a sound can affect the growth of plants or the patterning of iron filings. (Innes, 1981: 139)

Innes points out, however, that *Orghast* worked only with intellectually sophisticated spectators, whereas a 'supposedly more primitive (and therefore in theory more receptive, even more susceptible) audience on Brook's African tour, apparently found those dark primordial cries hilariously funny' (142).

Brook's production of *The Mahabharata*, both for the theatre and for film/television, has been called the apotheosis of Brook's research into theatre (Shevtsova, 1991: 210). The title of the Indian epic implies 'the great history of mankind', and the 'great poem of the world' (Pronko, 1988: 220-1). Whereas Brook attempted to arrive at universality through language in *Orghast*, he strove for the same aim in the *Mahabharata* project through the concept of *dharma* (duty) which he located at the centre of the philosophy expounded in the Epic. In his view, the *Mahabharata* does not 'explain the secret of *dharma*, but lets it become a living reality. It does this through dramatic fictions, situations that force *dharma* into the open' (Brook, 1987: 164).

Suzuki, Fischer-Lichte points out, assumes that language and body are initially universals of human expression, a quality that they have lost in the course of history. Suzuki seeks to restore them as universals through his theatre. Since language has developed furthest in Western theatre, while the body has developed comparatively much further in the Japanese art of acting, Suzuki's method of achieving universality of combining Western text (Euripides *The Trojan Women*) and a Japanese style of acting that combines elements of Shinto ritual, No and kabuki. (Fischer-Lichte, 1989: 116)

Both Brook and Suzuki, then, are searching for a universal language of the theatre. Their approaches of achieving this common goal are different. Fischer-Lichte shows that Brook's (and Suzuki's) reasoning in favour of the possibility of a universal language of the theatre are based on two arguments: one archetypal and the other biological. Explicitly referring to Levi-Strauss, Brook hopes to emphasize the dehistoricising function of myth by taking recourse to a montage of different myths, leading to a collage of archetypal constellations and situations. The biological argument views the human body as a common human basis, beyond race or culture (Fischer-Lichte, 1989: 117). Brook explains:

> Our work is based on the fact that some of the deepest aspects of human experience can reveal themselves through the sounds and movements of the human body in a way that strikes an identical chord in any observer, whatever his cultural and racial conditioning. And therefore one can work without roots, because the body, as such, becomes a working source. (1973: 47)

Fischer-Lichte points out, however, that both arguments, archetypal and biological, are quite controversial. Recent research into myths, she argues, deny the archetypal aspect of myths. Research also suggests that although humans all over the world share the same basic needs, and behaviours, such as eating, sleeping, walking and standing, the ways in which those activities are carried out are culturally determined (118).

As Fischer-Lichte indicates, the case for a universal language of the theatre is not lost because Brook or Suzuki have not been able to provide a cogent explanation. In order to test in principle the possibility of a universal language of the theatre Fischer-Lichte suggests several levels of theoretical discourse. The first implies the question as to what could be communicated in such a universal language of the theatre. Modern semiotics could provide answers, as could recourse to old treatises on drama, i.e. Aristotle, *Poetics*, the Indian *Natyashastra*, or Zeami Motokiyo's poetics of the Japanese Noh. Although different, they agree in pointing not towards a cognitive, but psychological-emotional aspect of the reception process. Could this psychological-emotional level be the aim and contents of a universal language of the theatre?

The second level deals with the specific conditions that would enable a universal language of the theatre. It has to be established whether cultural determination of everyday use of the body can be transferred to aesthetic use of the body. If not, universal language of theatre need not be dependent on intercultural performances but every culture could develop a universal language of the theatre.

Finally, Fischer-Lichte argues, the function of such a universal language of the theatre should be discussed. In Third World countries, only intercultural theatre of categories one and two can be found, category two clearly dominating. With its major reference to the culture's own theatre, it is related to the countries' attempts to establish their own cultures. Collage techniques, merging different cultures, is in opposition to such an attempt, and might have to be discussed in the context of postmodernism and cultural imperialism (1989: 117-21).

I introduced the Vedic model of language, with its four levels, *para*, *pashyanti*, *madhyama* and *vaikhari*, to explain Artaud's intuition of a language beyond speech, of the language of nature (*pashyanti* and *para*). Reference to this model of language equally addresses all three levels raised by Fischer-Lichte, i.e. contents, conditions and function of a universal language of the theatre. It helps to understand Brook's quest for a universal language of the theatre.

Hogan defines literary universals as

> For any given domain (e.g., narrative), universals are features (properties, relations, structures) of works in that domain that recur across genetically and areally unre-lated traditions with greater frequency than would be predicted by chance (2003)

Language is universal only on the level of pure consciousness. Traditionally, that level of consciousness, because it is beyond activity, is regarded of little use to an active life, especially because pure consciousness, being 'pure', contentless, can only be described in very subjective, individual terms of expressed language. If theatre is able to reach beyond the performer's and the spectator's intellect, even beyond their emotions, if theatre is able stimulate the co-existence of pure consciousness with the waking state of consciousness, i.e. higher states of consciousness, then theatre will have reached the level of language which is universal.

If we assume that theatre can allow actors and spectators to access the universal level of pure consciousness, it has to be asked whether in addition to universality as the goal of theatre, the relative, expressed languages of the theatre, verbal, gestural, costume, make-up, etc., and their combination, can also be universal, i.e. independent of culture and history. Here Fischer-Lichte's question is relevant whether aesthetic activity, as opposed to everyday activity, could be independent of cultural determination. Vedic theory of music, *Gandharvaveda*, proposes that the primordial sound, *nada*, is at the basis of all creation, including consciousness, and that the dancer's/actor's body starts moving in the rhythms and movements of nature when all cells of his/her body begin to resonate with that primordial sound

(Hartmann, 1992). Thus sound is directly transformed into movement of the body. It could well be argued-as a working hypothesis for further studies-that if the composer composes, (or the choreographer choreographs, the dancer dances, the actor acts) in a higher state of consciousness, the result (the composition, choreography, dancing or acting activity) will be fuelled by impulses emanating directly from the universal level of pure consciousness, unmediated by culture or history. Such impulses will then reach the spectator and enable his mind to reach the same underlying, universal level of consciousness from which the aesthetic impulses originated. Creative activity will be culturally and historically mediated when such activity does not originate from higher states of consciousness characterized by a simultaneity of pure consciousness and activity, but if it originates from ordinary waking state of consciousness which has no systematic, only ephemeral, 'coincidental' experience of pure consciousness (e.g., Grotowski's *translumination*, or Brook's *total theatre*).

Coming back to the three levels of enquiry proposed by Fischer-Lichte: what would be communicated is the experience of pure consciousness together with aesthetic stimuli of the theatre. A universal language of the theatre would be enabled by techniques of using expressed language of the theatre to lead the actor's and spectator's mind to pure consciousness. The function of a universal language of the theatre aims at a level of consciousness beyond history and culture, and thus, perhaps, beyond postmodern fragmentation or cultural imperialism.

Why did the attempt of achieving an effect on the mental state of the listener fail in Brook's case (if we are to believe critical voices such as Innes)? In the case of *Orghast*, a *new* language was created, and it can only be assumed that the result was not of such a kind that it *did* facilitate the experience of subtler levels of language. This failure does, therefore, not rule out the principle. In *Orghast*, Brook experimented with language, more specifically, with the idea that sound and meaning are identical. Such an identity has been claimed for Sanskrit. In theory, this approach should work. Recent research has shown that accurately reciting Sanskrit texts without intellectual knowledge of the contents of the text read, will produce effects closely resembling those observed during meditation, whereas the reading of texts in any other language does not produce any such effects at all (Travis, 2001). Travis' empirical approach can be modified to fit the universal language of the theatre paradigm. Take a production that lays claim to achieving universality (defined as including the experience of pure consciousness), and predict a specific impact of such a production on specific psycho-physiological parameters in performers and spectators, then carry out a series of appropriate tests to see whether the predictions come true.

Theatre and Ritual: Yagya

Is theatre really as ephemeral as many critics suggest? Or can it have truly lasting impact on those who make it and those who watch it? Richard Schechner distinguishes between *transformation* and *transportation*, defining *transportation* as performances during which performers are 'taken somewhere', but after which they 're-enter ordinary life just about where they went in' (1985: 125) to the performance mode:

> The performer goes from the 'ordinary world' to the 'performance world', from one time/space reference to another, from one personality to one or more others. He plays a character, battles demons, goes into trance, travels to the sky or under the sea or earth: he is transformed, able to do things 'in performance' he cannot do ordinarily. But when the performance is over, or even as a final phase of the performance, he returns to where he started. (1985: 125)

A long series of transportations, experienced over a large number of individual performances, may lead to *transformation* for the performer: the performers are changed without returning almost unchanged to their starting point (as in *transportation*). Originally, and still in many cases today, transformation occurs in ritual, where

> the attention of the transported [performers] and that of the spectators converge on the transformed. This convergence of attention-and the direct stakes spectators have in the performance-is why so many transformation performances use audience participation. (1985: 131)

The *change* referred to by Schechner may be of a significant dimension during performance for both *transformation* and *transportation*. In *transformation*, change is noticeable, immediate and lasting. In *transportation*, change is noticeable, immediate, but lasting only as long as the performance itself: only traces of such change are left in daily life outside performance; those traces, however, accumulate to reach the status of *transformation*.

In Indian philosophy, ritual, one of the ways of achieving *transformation* in daily life, is associated with the concept of *yagya*, sacrifice, religious performance, or holy ritual, in which gifts are offered to the presiding deity and consumed in fire. In this section I want to discuss the implications for the theatre of Maharishi Mahesh Yogi's recent reassessment of the concept of *yagya*. He published a detailed commentary on the first six chapters of the *Bhagavad-Gita*, an important section of the major epic in Indian literature, *The Mahabharata*, and this commentary in turn contains his reassessment of the concept of *yagya*.

In very general terms, *yagya*, according to Maharishi Mahesh Yogi, comprises all kinds of means, or practical tools, for an individual to achieve the ideal state of human spiritual development, *moksha*, or enlightenment. This aim, enlightenment, is also the states aim of theatre, according to the *Natyashastra*. The function of the art of theatre, described in the *Natyashastra* is to restore full human potential, life in enlightenment. This function gives all actions described or prescribed in the *Natyashastra* the status of *yagya*.

Maharishi Mahesh Yogi's commentary of *yagya* provides more detail, which in turn allows further elaboration of theatre as *yagya*. He relates the concept of *yagya* to the concepts of the mind as proposed by Vedic Science. I have summarised the main features in tables 1 and 2 in chapter one. Seen in the context of Vedanta philosophy, the concept of *yagya* takes on a much wider range. Not limited to particular ceremonies, *yagya* becomes 'a way of life' which furthers spiritual development towards unity consciousness (Maharishi Mahesh Yogi, 1969: 194). Maharishi further elaborates on the meaning of *yagya*: Vedic literature, he explains, is divided into various branches, called *shakhas*. Each *shakha*, in turn, has three sections, dealing with the gross, subtle, and transcendent aspects of *yagya*, understood in the wide sense of means to enhance evolution. *Karma Kanda* (Chapter of Action) deals with the gross aspect of *yagya*, relating mainly to the human body:

> [It] establishes the duties of men belonging to different levels of evolution, living in different times, in different places, and under different circumstances, so that they do not act against the laws of nature. (Maharishi Mahesh Yogi, 1969: 195)

The second section of each *shakha* is called *Upasana Kanda* (Chapter of Worship). It provides information and guidance of how to gain support and blessings from higher powers of nature, Vedic gods. Such guidance is provided on two levels: on a gross level, rituals are described, and on a subtle level, the mind is trained 'to contact higher powers and receive their blessings upon all achievements in life' (Maharishi Mahesh Yogi, 1969: 195). The third section in each *shakha*, called *Gyana Kanda* (Chapter of Knowledge), contains 'wisdom of eternal life', describing techniques that allow the mind to transcend its own relative aspects (senses, desire, mind, intellect, emotion, intuition, feeling, and the individual ego, see table 1 to reach pure consciousness and 'thereby infuse the divine nature into all spheres of human existence' (Maharishi Mahesh Yogi, 1969: 195). Each level of action is thus guided by *yagya*, and the ultimate aim of *yagya* is the evolution of human beings who have fully developed their mind to the level of unity consciousness (state 7 in table 2).

On the gross levels of *yagya*, various objects may be sacrificed. On the subtler levels, described in *Gyana Kanda*, offering takes on a less material and, at the same time, a much more general and encompassing shape. According to Maharishi, the gods preside over relative life, represented by states (1-3) in table 2, waking, dreaming and sleeping. Once pure consciousness has been established as a permanent experience together with waking, dreaming or sleeping, characteristic of higher states of consciousness (states 5, 6, 7 in table 2), pure consciousness, 'remains in the freedom of the Absolute' (Maharishi Mahesh Yogi, 1969: 196). In higher states of consciousness, all of human activity becomes an offering to the gods, and thus a *yagya*, maintaining the state that has been achieved, and allowing for further progress. It is important to note here that this manner of offering to the gods does not 'imply surrender to them or coming under their subjugation', because pure consciousness is completely free 'from all the influences of relative life, including the gods' (Maharishi Mahesh Yogi, 1969: 196).

Table 10: Levels of yagya

Kanda (chapter)	Aspect of yagya	Contents
Karma kanda	Action (gross)	Human duties according to the laws of nature active at the time of their lives
Upasana kanda	Workship (subtle)	Rituals; guidance of how to gain support from the gods
Gyana kanda	Knowledge (transcendent)	Techniques that allow the mind to reach pure consciousness

Maharishi expressly warns against confusing genuine *yagya* as offering on the one hand, and mood-making and imagination. He explains that 'the fruit of every action is the response of nature to that action and is therefore nothing but the gift of the powers of nature, the gods' (1969: 199). Genuine offering is possible only when pure consciousness has been established in daily experience as separate from action. Direct experience of pure consciousness, as the basis of all manifest levels (see table 1) is quite different from some vague assumption of what such separation may feel like if one has heard about it, and any intellectual attempt to create such an assumed feeling would be futile and would not help in achieving genuine offering.

So far I have established that theatre as defined by the *Natyashastra* can serve as a *yagya* in that its aim is the development of enlightenment, unity consciousness, in performers and spectators. Now I want to explore parallels between the levels of *yagya* just introduced to aspects of theatre that follows the aesthetics of the *Natyashastra*.

The second chapter of the *Natyashastra* deals with the theatre building. Following sections on suitable sizes and shapes, instructions are given for measuring the building site. They include suggestions that the date and time for the measuring should be auspicious according to calculations of Vedic astrology, *Jyotish*. The planets are regarded as divine in nature, and their blessing, as it were, are sought in this way. The laying of the foundation of the theatre building is accompanied by a specific ceremony which involves making offerings of 'sweet scent, flowers, fruits and eatables of various other kinds' in all the ten directions 'to various gods guarding them' (Ghosh, 1950: 23). Each phase of the actual building process should be carried out at auspicious times in accordance with calculations by *Jyotish*, and the people involved may have to undergo special, individual preparations such as fasting. Jewels and precious stones have to be placed under the stage, with diamond in the east, lapis lazuli in the south, quartz in the west, coral in the north, and gold at the centre. Precise instructions are also given as to the shape and measure of various parts of the theatre building, including number and position of doors. Once the theatre has been built, it is consecrated in a sophisticated series of *yagyas* carried out by the stage manager after specific preparation.

Before the play proper begins, a number of preliminaries have to be carried out. They range from quite practical actions such as tuning instruments and establishing basic harmonies of playing together, to specific *yagyas* invoking various deities for their blessing of the ensuing performance. The director has to walk around the stage praising the guardian deities of different worlds, and invokes Indra's divine protecting weapon, the *Jarjara*. The director also intones a benediction in four verses:

> Salutation to all the gods. Blessed be the twice born class. May Soma the king attain victory as well as healthy life and [earthly] enjoyment.

> Let there be an advancement of the cause of the Brahmins, and let their enemies be killed, and let the great king rule this earth together with all the seas.

> Let this state prosper, and this theatre flourish and let the producer of the theatrical show attain virtues proceeding from the Vedic knowledge.

> Let the playwright attain fame and let his virtue increase, and by this kind of sacrifice (*yagya*), let the gods be always pleased with him. (Ghosh, 1950: 90-91).

The processes involved in building the theatre, and the preliminaries before the performance are thus clearly associated with *yagya*, in the broad sense of furthering spiritual development. They are related to *Karma Kanda* (assisting people 'not to act against the laws of nature') and the gross level of *Upasana Kanda*, to 'gain support and blessings from higher powers of nature, Vedic gods' (Maharishi Mahesh Yogi, 1969: 195). Together, they represent important elements of the declared task of the *Natyashastra*: to lead humans back to enlightenment. The next chapters of the *Natyashastra* deal with the aesthetics of the performance itself, which represents *Gyana Kanda*.

In chapter four, I re-defined *rasa* from the spectator's perspective as a combination of blissful pure consciousness and the specific impressions on the mind provided by a theatrical performance. In this sense, theatre can be understood as *yagya* on the level of *Gyana Kanda*, 'the act of going to Transcendental being' (Maharishi Mahesh Yogi, 1969: 194).

To summarise: if theatre follows the aesthetic principles of the *Natyashastra*, it serves as *yagya*, because it enables the actors and spectators to experience pure consciousness (together with the performance-specific contents). This kind of theatre is a means, a tool, of developing higher states of consciousness, while being entertaining at the same time. The amount of pure consciousness that each actor and each spectator will be able to experience during any one performance depends on how far they have developed towards liberation, *moksha*, enlightenment: the further advanced that development, the more frequent, and the longer in duration, those theatre-induced experiences of higher states of consciousness. More mundane issues are relevant, too, such as: have they slept well the night before, have they eaten well, or too much, or too little, and so on.

Performance as described in the *Natyashastra*, functions as a *yagya* on several levels (see table 11).

• On the level of *Karma Kanda* and *Upasana Kanda*, ceremonies are described in relation to the process of building a theatre, its consecration, and preliminaries preceding every performance.

• On the level of *Gyana Kanda*, the aesthetics of performance suggests that performers (ideally) experience a higher state of consciousness characterised by simultaneity of pure consciousness and impressions of the senses, desire, mind, intellect, emotion, intuition, feeling, and the individual ego. Through performance, the performers transmit this state to their audience. Repeated exposure to the higher state of consciousness during performance trains both performers' and spectators' minds to retain this higher state of consciousness for longer periods of time during performance, and ultimately at all times throughout any activity, no longer limited to theatre.

Table 11: Yagya and Natyashastra

Kanda (chapter)	Contents	Natyashastra
Karma kanda	Human duties according to the laws of nature active at the time of their lives	Ceremonies are described in relation to the process of building a theatre, its consecration, and preliminaries preceding every performance
Upasana kanda	Rituals; guidance of how to gain support from the gods	Ceremonies are described in relation to the process of building a theatre, its consecration, and preliminaries preceding every performance
Gyana kanda	Techniques that allow the mind to reach pure consciousness	Performers (ideally) experience a higher state of consciousness, which they transmit to their audience in performance

Performance functioning in accordance with the *Natyashastra* thus fulfils its aim of restoring fully developed individuals. This action of restoration was the initial reason for the creation of *Natya*, theatre.

Is the relationship of ritual in the connotations of *yagya* and performance, as discussed above with regard to the aesthetics of the *Natyashastra*, only of historical interest because it is far removed in space, time and conceptualisation from contemporary Western theatre practice? The main questions for us today are:

1. Can performance lead to transformative rather than transportative changes of performers' and spectators' consciousness?

2. Is it possible to confirm, and practically apply, the proposed *Natyashastra*-based tools of effecting transformative changes?

3. Can theatre following Western aesthetics achieve effects similar to those *Natyashastra*-based theatre claims for itself?

Such questions are especially relevant in view of the growing practice and debate of intercultural theatre, in which materials from various cultures merge. Further theoretical elaboration is needed, leading eventually to practical, empirical testing of relevant cogent hypotheses.

Postmodernism

Writng in 1981, Innes notes a growing emphasis of the theatre artists on 'myth, ritual, and what might be called the spiritual side of human nature-the subconscious, instinctive and irrational' (Innes, 1981: 255). Such an emphasis also features among 'the leading characteristics of Postmodern theatre' (Martin, 1991: 119).

However, the concept of postmodernism is ambiguous in at least four main areas: some critics put the legitimacy of the concept in question, arguing that there are no new phenomena that might justify the introduction of a new term (Welsch, 1988, 9). The next issue is the field of the term's application. According to Welsch, the term originated in the North American literature debate, then spread to architecture and painting, sociology and philosophy, and by now there is hardly an area 'not infected by this virus' (9). As far as the time of origin is concerned, the debate originated in the USA in 1959, referring to phenomena of the 1950s; in 1975, when Europe had caught up with the development, the *New Yorker* wrote that postmodernism was out and there was demand for a post-postmodernism (10). In the same line of argument, Welsch quotes Umberto Eco's worries that before long even Homer would be considered postmodern (10). Finally, the contexts of postmodernism are ambiguous: the age of SDI technology versus a green, ecological, alternative movement; a new integration of a fragmented society versus increased intentional fragmentation and pluralisation (10).

Welsch attempts to define a common denominator for different approaches to postmodernism:

> We can talk about postmodernism where a fundamental pluralism of languages, models, and procedures is practised, not just side by side in separate works, but in one and the same work, i.e. interferentially. (15)

Postmodernism is often associated with Derrida's criticism of Western dualism. Indeed, the paradoxes resulting when Western dualism in the mind-body relationship is applied to theories of acting could be discussed in a Derridian discourse. However, this would be more of a philosophical inquiry, which is possible, perhaps even more efficient, without reference to the theatre, as Coward's comparison of Derrida and Indian philosophy shows (Coward, 1990).

According to Birringer, 'there is very little discussion about what '[p]ostmodern theatre' might be among 'actors, directors, and writers' (1991: xi), and he notices the same reluctance 'among drama critics and scholars who continue to write about a world of texts and performances that seems largely untouched by the debates on the politics of postmodernism or on the technological transformation of late modern culture' (xi).

From among the few critics who do discuss postmodernism in the context of theatre, Fischer-Lichte points to Brook's collage technique as relevant for discussion of his theatre under the heading of postmodernism. Bharucha discusses Schechner's wish to celebrate his own 'fragmentation', evident in Schechner's 'eclectic interests and modes of perception', the 'seeming randomness' of Schechner's thoughts, and regards that attitude as characteristic of 'post-modern consciousness' (Bharucha, 1993: 16-18). Indeed, more and more theatre artists draw their inspiration from an increasing number of intercultural sources, and they put their source material to practice in different ways. If interpreted as fragmentation, as an active endorsement of intended and precise pluralism, then it is a postmodern aspect of theatre.

Drawing on a wide, intercultural range of source material can be considered postmodern also because it is a strikingly postmodern intertextual activity. Intertextuality can be regarded as a superimposed concept for methods of more or less conscious, and to some extent concrete references in the text (including the performance text) to individual pre-texts, groups of pre-texts, or underlying codes and complexes of meaning (Broich and Pfister, 1985: 15). These methods are already established individually in literary criticism under such terms as source study, influence, quotation, allusion, parody, travesty, imitation, translation, and adaptation (15). Two extreme concepts of intertextuality with different points of departure can be differentiated: the global model of post-structuralism regards every text as part of a global intertext. In contrast, structuralist and hermeneutic models argue in favour of a more conscious, intended, and marked reference between a text and a pre-text or groups of pre-texts (25). Broich and Pfister propose a model if intertextuality that mediates between the two positions: specific criteria for intertextuality can be defined and their intensity evaluated in quality and quantity from case to case. Those criteria are: referentiality, communicativity, autoreflexivity, structure, selectivity, dialogue, density and number of intertextual references, and number and range of pre-texts (25). Detailed analyses of intercultural performances on the basis of those criteria are likely to yield high levels of intertextuality.

George highlights *ambiguity* as a postmodern characteristic of performance. He argues that postmodernism 'finds the world hyphenated, elliptical; reversing all established hierarchies and questioning the reduction behind them, deconstruction finds the world doubled, ironic, decentered' (1989a: 71). George then asks: 'Beyond roles, masks and other "duplicities", was it not always this which performance already proclaimed: "I am-biguous"?' (71). George extends this argument to the reception process: all spectators (as, indeed, performers) 'are always negotiating between at least two worlds' (75), i.e. the real world of the spectator's life as a spectator in the audience, and the fictional world presented on the stage. Such negotiation leads to doubts. In a non-theatrical context, such doubts would in turn lead to 'existential anguish'. In the theatre, however, the doubts are 'restricted to the realm of the possible', and therefore, they can be 'enjoyed, relished' (75). This pleasure, an ambiguous phenomenon, has been analysed in Western culture in terms of psycho-analysis, conceptualised as a 'form of retarded climax and therefore ascribed, like all ambiguous phenomena, to the realm of the abnormal' (75). Because postmodernism does not fear contradiction, because it recognises contradiction as the existential base, ambiguity of performance, in the performative and the receptive aspects, could be an essential feature of a postmodern performance theory. George concludes as follows:

> The predominance in post-modern and deconstructionist discourse of terms such as play, game, contradiction, process, performance, suggests that we may be entering an age in which there *are only* media (semiosis, assumptions, paradigms, models) and no ontology, only experiences (and no Self except the one like an actor's career made up of the parts we enact and rewrite), a world in which difference is primordial (no ur-whole) and time endless. For such an age, performance is the ideal medium and model and ambiguity is its life. (83)

In describing postmodernism, George uses the term 'decentered', a reference to Jacques Lacan's theory. Lacan holds that psychoanalysis reveals a split between 'the self, the innermost part of the psyche, and the subject of conscious discourse, behaviour and culture' (Lemaire, 1977: 67). This division creates a hidden structure inside the subject-the unconscious. The conditions of human existence, according to Lacan, imply that man is 'essentially a being by and for the other' (67). The common ground on which individuals 'assert themselves, oppose each other and find themselves again' (67) is the symbolic. To become an individual, accession to the symbolic is necessary. However, such accession is balanced with 'the division of the subject'; in the symbolic, 'the subject can be no more than represented or translated' (48).

Proposing a decentered self, a split between the self and the subject of discourse, is a postmodern phenomenon. If performances represent the fragmentary, in opposition to 'unitary ambitions' (George, 1989a: 74), they thus represent what

Lacan's postmodern discourse has discovered: the decentered self, the split between self and subject of behaviour and culture.

Regarding performances as postmodern when they show fragmentation of sources and ambiguity together with a high degree of intertextuality is in line with critics like Crohn-Schmitt, or George (George, 1989b), who research the parallels of contemporary quantum mechanics and the theatre. Crohn-Schmitt distinguishes between Aristotelian theatre and the 'important segment of contemporary theater variously referred to as antitheater, post-modern theater, or simply, new theater' (1990: 1), maintaining that new theatre violates 'not only Aristotelian aesthetic principles but also the view of reality that they imply, thus profoundly disturbing many audience members' (2). From twentieth-century quantum physics, Crohn-Schmitt infers that 'the idea of a single true account of reality is challenged' (9), and together with it the role of the individual:

> Because there is no correspondence between mind and nature, human beings cannot find their unique, essential purpose and pleasure in knowing; like the rest of nature, they have no ulterior purpose. They have no more importance in nature than any other part. (14)

Crohn-Schmitt quotes John Cage's view that art must teach us 'to accept our purposelessness' (28). In her opinion, contemporary artists do not feel depressed by the fact that neither the self nor the perceived world are 'discrete, inviolable, and constant' (130). Their excitement with the exploration of this newly discovered world view mirrors the optimistic, even euphoric mode of postmodernism.

Birringer, however, has quite a different view of postmodernism. He links postmodernism strongly with technological advances and deplores that in 'today's mass market of overproduced images and ubiquitous information circuitries, the imaginary has trouble surviving, since reality seems already always replaced by its simulations' (1991: 79). Rather than accept the fragmented impression of reality conveyed by our senses, especially sight, Birringer argues, theatre should enable a 'radical and unfashionable vision' (31); without forgetting 'the limits and frames of the conditions of its theatricality', performance practices should be developed that 'think of themselves as "acts from under and above" (...)-acts that need the limits of the theatre in order to be able to imagine different realities, under and above our normal ways of seeing' (100).

Birringer's quest for 'acts from above and under', non-ordinary modes of perception, fits in with the insight that many contemporary theatre artists share a common interest in Eastern, especially Indian, theatre practices, mixed with religion and philosophy. What inspires their 'turn to the East' are Eastern assumptions about states of consciousness beyond the intellect, beyond the emotions, parallel to Birringer's 'under and above our normal ways of seeing' (100).

Such states of consciousness are experienced by the theatre artists, induced by all kinds of techniques, both Western and Eastern. Their attempts, however, to understand or even systematically reproduce those experiences are often enough frustrated: altered states of consciousness are met with scepticism in Western psychology, and the few attempts in the West to account for ASC are limited in scope and explanatory value. Although altered states of consciousness feature prominently in Indian philosophy, their understanding is far from clear. This makes it difficult for some Western theatre artists like Grotowski to use Eastern theatre techniques efficiently.

The search for states of consciousness beyond the intellect, beyond the emotions, ultimately, then, the search for 'pure consciousness' together with all aspects of the waking state of consciousness, is where theatre artists, postmodern in their intercultural, intertextual activities, part with postmodernism: Crohn-Schmitt points out that 'at the most elemental level, the description of nature necessarily becomes the description of experienced phenomena, not a representation of something more fundamental, an independent physical reality' (1990: 8).

There is, thus, no overarching universality underlying all phenomena of the world. The denial of a universal basis for creation, arrived at by application of quantum physics to human life, is the basis for pluralism. Crohn-Schmitt's argument is thus in line with postmodernism's critique of any position that opposes in principle the pluralism characteristic of postmodernism. The emphasis of postmodern philosophers on pluralism arose as a countermovement against metanarratives, grand narratives, such as 'dialectics of the Spirit, the hermeneutics of meaning, the emancipation of the rational and working subject or the creation of wealth' (Sarup, 1988: 131): according to postmodernist philosopher Lyotard, the postmodern condition is one in which the grand narratives of modernity formulated in the eighteenth century by philosophers of the Enlightenment 'have lost all their credibility' (132).

From the perspective of Maharishi Mahesh Yogi's Vedic Science, the theatre artists' search for pure consciousness is, however, nothing but a search for a new grand narrative. In this sense, theatre artists, whose endorsement of pluralism is a postmodern aspect of their work, ultimately do not share the distrust of grand narratives. However, they follow different grand narratives than Hegel or Marx: as shown by the fact that the more the artists are influenced by Western, and especially Eastern aesthetics and psychology, the more they aim for experiences in both actors and spectators that go beyond the senses, beyond the intellect, and even beyond the emotions, although the latter are mainly used to reach for the area of the mind called, with reference to Freud, Jung and other Western psychologists, the subconscious or unconscious. Through activation of the unconscious level of the mind, they hope to stimulate the experiences of communitas, of flow, of unification of binary opposites. They are, in other words, searching for an overarching totality, but not in the expressed fields of science, art, morality, or law, as the eighteenth-century philosophers of the Enlightenment, but in a field beyond expression, in the field of consciousness.

In aiming at experiences of *rasa, language beyond speech, translumination, total theatre, the invisible made visible*, or *tradition of traditions*, twentieth-century theatre artists are in search for experiences of pure consciousness together with the ordinary waking state of consciousness. They try to express, explain and recapture this experience through the various bodies of knowledge available to them, including Western psychology, Cabbala, and non-Western concepts. In looking for a level of consciousness which is beyond the intellect, beyond the emotions, which is a field of consciousness underlying every individual, and which is universal, the theatre artists are indeed striving for an overarching hierarchy, one of the focal points of postmodern criticism.

Against the background of this overarching characteristic of pure consciousness, the interpretation of one of the key elements of the postmodern condition, *fragmentation*, is subjected to a striking shift of emphasis. Without a universal background in pure consciousness, fragmentation is frightening, prone to ambiguity, and art may acquire the function of helping the audiences to overcome such anxieties, helping the spectators to come to terms with the purposelessness of life, a view which is supported by a certain interpretation of quantum physics (Crohn-Schmitt, 1990: 28). If pure consciousness is accepted as an underlying level of human existence, then the Vedantic principle of *unity in diversity* applies. Diversity is seen as manifestations of unity, in the sense of a playful expression (Sanskrit concept of *lila*). In this view, Intertextuality becomes a playful, conscious activity. Vedic Science's model of creation, i.e. all creation emanating from the various directions of interaction of *rishi, devata* and *chhandas* within *samhita*, and in relation to wholeness of *samhita*, makes further sense of the principle of unity in diversity by explaining that diversity is an inherent aspect of unity.

It is thus possible to make sense of the apparent paradox of unity in diversity. How does this interpretation fare in view of apparently contradictory views of quantum mechanics which has been used to highlight the fragmentary nature of life? The fragmentary aspect is accurate when expressed levels of matter are concerned. The ground state theorised in quantum physics is the unified field, which, in turn, has been proposed to be identical to the field of pure consciousness as experienced by the human mind (Hagelin, 1987).

The postmodern concept of the *decentered self*, theorised by Lacan, also undergoes a shift when viewed from the perspective of Vedic Science. According to Lacan, the self is the innermost part of the psyche (Lemaire, 1977: 67). But this self cannot be expressed directly: it is decentered because it can only be represented or translated to function on the level of symbolic discourse. Vedic Science's model of the mind is different. The innermost part of human psyche, according to Vedic Science, is pure consciousness. As long as someone has not reached the higher stage of development, cosmic consciousness, pure consciousness is overshadowed by the impressions of the senses, and in this sense the term 'decentered' might be used. However, in cosmic consciousness, pure consciousness is independent of the sensory impressions, witnessing mental and physical activity. All the more expressed levels of the mind, i.e. ego, intuition and feeling, intellect, mind, desire, and senses, are fully developed, and thus fully able to express whatever is latently available on the level of pure consciousness. There is, therefore, no longer a split between pure consciousness (*self* in Lacan) and (symbolic) expressions of it in conscious discourse, behaviour and culture. Pure consciousness, which contains, in seed form, as it were, all forms of expression, can express itself fully without mediation, representation or translation.

Previous overarching hierarchies which are at the centre of postmodern criticism lack the possibility of being directly experienced: they are limited to the intellectual discourse of philosophers. (Some critics argue that even most of Western philosophy is based on direct experience of the philosophers concerned. They described their experiences, but did not have technique to facilitate the same experience to recur systematically in themselves or in others. For that reason, their philosophy was taken as intellectual speculation by critics unable to fathom with their limited intellect the depths of the experiences described.) Today, however, many techniques are available that enable anyone to directly experience pure consciousness and to grow in such experiences until higher stages of human development are reached. As argued before, the means of histrionic representation detailed in the *Natyashastra* can serve as one such set of techniques, meditation may be another.

Utopian Performatives

Jill Dolan understands utopian performatives as leading to fleeting glimpses, or an 'ephemeral feeling of what a better world might be like' (2003). Dolan's essay on multiple character solo performers and utopian performatives (2002) shows, though, that she shares the predominant understanding of utopia as a concept to describe a socio-political context considered in some ways better than the one we find ourselves living in at the time of developing such utopian ideas. Plato's *The State* and Thomas More's *Utopia* have been groundbreaking treatises on which that understanding is based. In this section, I want to discuss the relevance of utopian performatives against the background of current consciousness studies. By adopting this approach I hope to demonstrate that utopia as an array of ideas of possible socio-political alternatives to the status quo represents only the second stage in the development of utopia from the first stage: higher stages of human development on an individual level as the building blocks of society. I then proceed to discuss the role utopian performatives can play to help achieve individual utopia.

Throughout this book, I have repeatedly referred to higher states of consciousness as defined by Vedic Science. What are the experience and benefits of higher states of consciousness like? Its experience is based on a body that is free from stress, strain, and any symptom of acute or even emerging or latent illness. It is a body that enjoys a state of perfect health: it is able to repel any viruses or bacteria before they can take adverse effect on the body. Individuals living in a higher state of consciousness will not (be able to) make mistakes. They function, permanently, from the level of pure consciousness, which in turn is the level from which the laws of nature operate. Thus all their actions will be in tune with natural law: they will be unable to act against natural law, and that means they will not be able to act in such as way as to harm either themselves, other people, other creatures, or their environment. To such people, an enemy will not even arise, and therefore there will be no need for them to fight an enemy. They will have developed their individual characteristics, abilities, strengths, talents, each to their full potential, thus achieving true unity in diversity (the very opposite of all becoming the same, equal). They will experience bliss, one of the characteristics of pure consciousness, throughout their daily activity and will not lose it even while asleep or dreaming.

For the majority of people reading this, such a higher state of consciousness must indeed come across as a genuine example of individual utopia. Empirical studies of meditation, claiming to enhance the development of higher states of consciousness, suggest that the majority of people practising such meditation experience the first stages of such a development towards higher states of consciousness: tests results, often statistically significant, show that their health improves, as does their mental potential and parameters of social life. There is at least an indication that higher states of consciousness, and their characteristics and implications for human life, are not issues of utopia (in the sense of something realistically unachievable), but are within the scope of what we can achieve, *if only we make the decision to make use, personally, of the means that are available to enhance development of consciousness.*

In chapter two, I showed that glimpses of higher states of consciousness, which have been known throughout history (see the descriptions of mystics, for example), also feature in drama (text) and theatre (performance). I expect further research to yield more instances of utopian performatives understood as descriptions of glimpses of higher states of consciousness in drama and theatre. I now want to turn to the utopian performatives understood as the potential impacts various processes involved in theatre practice can have on actors and spectators with regard to the development of higher states of consciousness.

Aspects, or features of theatre that enable transformation, in Schechner's definition of the concept, of actors and spectators in the sense of constituting development of consciousness are utopian performatives. I want to locate such utopian performatives first in a general Western, and then in an Indian aesthetics, context.

Orme-Johnson has claimed that contents and structure of a work of prose fiction or poetry may serve the function of leading the reader's mind to subtler levels of their mind, in the direction of pure consciousness (1987). Malekin and Yarrow provide a detailed account of processes through which 'spirituality is made available to the receiver' in the context of theatre. (1997: 129). They identify three constitutive elements of theatre: performer, character and audience, and locate processes involving neutrality (pure consciousness in terms of Vedic Science), witnessing and play (characteristic of higher states of consciousness) for each of the elements, giving references to numerous relevant plays. To illustrate their argument with one example: neutrality for the character in theatre is a liminal state. Malekin and Yarrow explain:

> Deaths, displacements, demands to do the 'impossible' or resolve the unresolvable all present the character with the paradigm of the familiar and known, and of hesitation before a threshold of new forms of knowledge and being. (1997: 137)

Such liminality is represented by Vladimir and Estragon in Beckett's *Waiting for Godot*, two characters who are 'cut off from any obvious criteria of personality, geographical situation or function' (1997: 137). Exposing the performers and spectators to those processes serves the function of heightened spirituality, of development of consciousness in terms of the Vedanta model of consciousness. Malekin and Yarrow have opened up a rich area of enquiry, which should particularly suit those who advocate looking within our own traditions for a revitalisation of today's theatre.

Since the main focus of Indian philosophy has been human consciousness and practical techniques for its development, it is worth looking at theatre aesthetics provided within the framework of Indian philosophy, in particular the *Natyashastra*. Towards the beginning of the text we find a passage describing how theatre was created: the golden age, in which all human beings enjoyed a state of enlightenment, complete health and fulfilment, had come to an end. The silver age had begun, and humans were afflicted by first symptoms of suffering. The gods, with Indra as their leader, were concerned and approached Brahma, the creator, asking him to devise a means allowing humans to regain their enlightenment, to restore the golden age. Indra specified that that means should be a fifth Vedic text, an addition to the four main texts of Indian (Vedic) philosophy (*Rig Veda*, *Sama Veda*, *Yajur Veda* and *Atharva Veda*). The fifth Veda should be both pleasing/entertaining and instructive, and should be accessible to the *shudras*, the lowest caste, because they were not allowed to read or listen to recitations of the other Vedas. Brahma listened to Indra's request, immersed himself in meditation, and came up with *Natya*, *drama*, which he asked Indra and the gods to implement. Indra assured Brahma that the gods would be no good at this task, and so Brahma passed on his knowledge about *Natya* to the human sage Bharata, who in turn taught it to his 100 sons, who were thus the first actors. The knowledge imparted to Bharata by Brahma is contained in the text of the *Natyashastra* (*shastra* is a holy text). Following the instructions for acting contained in this text can be conducive to:

> duty (*dharma*), wealth (*artha*) as well as fame, will contain good counsel and collection [of other materials for human well-being], will give guidance to people of the future as well in all their actions, will be enriched by the teaching of all scriptures (*shastra*) and will give a review of all arts and crafts (*silpa*). (Ghosh, 3-4)

Theatre in this context thus has the direct and explicit function to restore the golden age, an age of utopia, for humankind, implying restoration of the state of perfection, liberation (*moksha*), enlightenment, higher states of consciousness for all people on earth.

Exposure of actors and spectators to the experience of *rasa* implies an experience of pure consciousness, and some of this experience remains (*transformation*), and is not lost. Dip the cloth into the dye, and it soaks up the dye. Place it into the sunlight, and most of it fades out again. Repeat the process until the dye is firm and lasting. Expose people to theatre that induces higher states of consciousness, and they will soak that experience up. Then the experience fades, but a little bit of its effect remains. This is transformation (as opposed to transportation) in Schechner's sense.

If we take higher states of consciousness as characteristics of individual utopia, and as such as the basis of social utopia, then theatre has the potential of developing utopia for the individual, and through the individual for society. The utopian performatives are various techniques, which can be located both in Western and, in my examples, Indian traditions of theatre texts and aesthetics. As I suggested, further research should lead to more details for each of those two traditions, and probably to comparable consciousness-related utopian performatives in other cultural traditions, based in Africa, Japan or China.

Summary
In this chapter, I have thrown new light on a number of concepts in theatre (studies): I explained Artaud's concept of *language of nature* as his intuition of the level of *para*, or pure consciousness. I argued that on the level of pure consciousness, life, and that includes theatre, is universal. I proposed to regard theatre (at least if it follows the guidelines of the *Natyashastra*, as a form of Vedic ritual, *yagya*, thus supporting further the *Natyashastra's* claim that theatre is a means for gaining higher states of consciousness. I demonstrated that a major trend of apparently postmodern theatre, the search for *translumination, language of nature, presence* and *total theatre*, understood as a search for the experience of higher states of consciousness, is nothing other than the search for a new overarching hierarchy. Finally, I explored the implications of considering higher states of consciousness achieved through theatre in the context of *utopian performatives*.

7: Vedic Science and Materialism: Comments on Demastes' *Staging Consciousness*

In the final chapter of the book, I discuss in depth William W. Demastes' *Staging Consciousness: Theater and the Materialization of Mind* (Ann Arbor: The University of Michigan Press, 2002). His predominant aim in discussing the relationship between theatre and consciousness is to unearth, describe and make accessible and available for further theatre practice the insight that theatre has unfathomed and to a large extent unused potential in enabling, in theatre artists and audiences, a holistic experience which is non-ordinary, non-day-to-day, what Brook calls *holy theatre*. His aim is thus very close to my own. Yet Demastes' approach is clearly and intentionally materialist, bottom-up, rather than what he would call top-down, mysterious. I summarise the main stages of Demastes' argument, and comment on them from the perspective of Vedic Science.

It was exciting to see the publication of what is probably, after my own book of 1996, the second full-scale book devoted exclusively to the relationship between theatre and consciousness, William W. Demastes' *Staging Consciousness: Theater and the Materialization of Mind*. Reading the book, it came as a surprise that Demastes does not refer to any of the work relating literature or theatre to consciousness, by Haney, Malekin, Yarrow or myself. Demastes responded to my query into the reasons for this omission that he had completed work on his manuscript in 1998. This explains some of the issue, but not the lack of reference to, and discussion of, the highly relevant material available before that time. Having raised this serious point of criticism, I propose to proceed with an assessment of what the book does provide. Demastes' argument is a plea for a new theatre, regarding both new ways of playwrighting, and new ways of directing existing plays. The plea is cogently placed in the context of the rest of consciousness studies except for the omissions noted above. Over the extraordinary four years (!) the book was in press, consciousness studies developed further. In this paper I provide an update on the debate on theatre's relation to consciousness, in the form of a running commentary on Demastes' argument.

Demastes

Demastes begins by describing what he regards as the science-dominated Western world view, which represents an amoral, mechanistic perspective. Within this world view, he points out, over the last decades, quantum mechanics, chaos theory and complexity theory have initiated something like a shift of paradigm away from the mechanistic to 'a more organic vision' (5) that appears to be supportive of some of the vitalist ideas initially replaced by the mechanistic view. As a result of the mechanistic world view, humans have developed science-based abilities which they have used undeniably to their advantage, but also to their disadvantage. To tackle science-caused problems, such as an 'alarming increase in incurable diseases' (5), we need to enter, or re-enter 'the realm once allocated to artists, religious figures, and other non- or anti-empirical dreamers and visionaries' (5). This is clearly a realm of mystery, characteristic of a 'force beyond the domain affected by causality' (123).

Comment

I agree with the need to move away from the mechanistic, materialist mindset responsible for much of today's theatre, deadly theatre in Brook's terminology. From the perspective of such materialism and mechanism, anything outside the area defined by those two isms must, by definition, be mysterious. Thus a different perspective is needed to explain what must remain mysterious to a mechanistic perspective. Applying such a different perspective does not negate or deny the knowledge gained within the boundaries of mechanism and materialism. On the contrary, a different perspective may well enhance our understanding of aspects of knowledge gained within, and valid within, the boundaries of mechanism and materialism. Moreover, applying different perspectives to the same object of enquiry helps to expand the boundaries set, as a matter of course, by any one perspective.

The term *mysterious* implies that the object, or process, thus described is incomprehensible. However, what appears as mysterious, incomprehensible, from within the boundaries of mechanism and materialism appears as quite comprehensible from a different perspective, and while no causality appears to operate in the realm of the mysterious when perceived from the perspective of materialism, it becomes obvious that a different nature of causality is operating in the no-longer mysterious when approached from a different perspective. Demastes argues that a different perspective has been open, traditionally, to artists and religious figures, whom he further characterises as 'non-or anti-empirical dreamers and visionaries' (5). Remember my reference to British poet Kathleen Raine in chapter one. Such an experience can only sound mysterious to a materialist, who regards it within the materialist framework. From a different perspective on consciousness and the experience of consciousness, Raine's experience makes perfect sense. Haney, Malekin and Yarrow have introduced and argued on the basis of such different perspectives of consciousness. Malekin and Yarrow (1997), for example, highlight the parallels of the Vedanta model to the model proposed by Plotinus. Yarrow has independently written repeatedly about neutral consciousness (1985, 1987, 2001). From the perspective of Vedic Science, Raine's experience is that of refined cosmic consciousness.

Demastes

Such a revival of the artist has to take place, however, in conditions that are different from those in the past. The past, on this argument, was characterised by a 'top-down hierarchy', with faith, inspiration or vision, as characteristics of mystery. Today's revival of the arts needs to be 'bottom up', 'material to spiritual' (6), assuming full acknowledgement of 'the reality of the empirical world' (5).

Comment

Demastes' argument is fully accurate and appropriate from within the materialistic perspective. The dichotomy of top-down and bottom-up becomes obsolete, however, once the introduction of the perspective of Vedic Science has explained what used to be mysterious. Achieving 'the spiritual', in Demastes' terms, is the unchallenged and undisputed aim that he argues for. However, the perspective of Vedic Science permits an explanation of faith, inspiration and vision as desirable altered states of consciousness, as regards both their characteristics and why and how they come about. Whereas materialism excludes anything beyond its framework, rejecting it as mystery, Vedic Science grants each level of consciousness its own right: ego, feelings, intellect, mind, desire, and senses. In the following paragraphs, I expand on the outline of states of consciousness according to Vedic Science provided in chapter one.

The ego is the subtlest level of the mind, further defined in Vedic Psychology as the inner value of the experiencer, the most immediate expression of the field of pure consciousness. Maharishi Mahesh Yogi explains:

> The ego is that value of life which is most refined. The ego ... is the experiencer in the individual life ... Ego understands, ego feels, ego thinks. That faculty of the ego which thinks is called mind. That faculty of the ego which understands, discriminates, and decides is called intellect; That faculty which feels-feeling, emotion-is called the heart (1972, lesson 19).

Alexander et al. describe the ego from the perspective of Vedic Psychology as interface between pure consciousness and 'the current process of knowing' (1990: 306). In the function of the ego, pure consciousness has become 'localized and qualified by functioning through the levels of mind and corresponding structures of the nervous system'. At the level of the ego, all impressions or memories of an individual are stored: the ego provides the internal 'reference point' and 'organizing power' necessary to synthesise the information derived from all the levels of mind through which the ego experiences the world (emotions and feeling, mind, intellect, desire, and senses). For each ego, the impressions stored will be different, as will be the organs of perception, thus accounting for the fact that the ego differs from person to person, making each one unique.

The growth of the ego in the direction of higher states of consciousness is characterised by an 'enhanced synthesizing capacity. On this basis, information provided through all other levels of mind could be more objectively appreciated and integrated' (307). However, the ego still remains an expressed level of consciousness, and without the simultaneous experience of pure consciousness, the ego will remain 'localized and constrained' by the limits imposed by the information provided by the other levels of mind, which will also be limited if devoid of the experience of pure consciousness.

According to Vedic Psychology, feelings 'operate at and interconnect all levels of mind' (304). However, they are especially important as interfaces between mind and senses, and between ego and intellect. At an early stage of development, called early representational period, feelings function 'primarily as extrinsically motivated desires' (304), they are dominated by linguistic expression and sequential formal reasoning. At a more mature stage of development, however, feelings help connect the intellect back to the ego and pure consciousness. More self-validating, feelings at this stage become less dependent on intellectual analysis, and function in a more subtle, rapid, holistic and intuitive mode. 'Mature feelings and intuition provide an internal ground for guiding the reflective intellect' (305).

The function of the intellect is to 'discriminate, logically evaluate, and decide' (303). Intellectual activity provides the basis for abstract reasoning and formal operations as defined by Piaget: thinking goes beyond the 'concrete actual' to the 'abstract hypothetical'. Alexander comments:

> This property derives from the intellect's emerging capacity to reflect consciously upon the contents of the mind, rendering thoughts as possibilities rather than actualities in which the knower is immersed. (303)

The intellect without simultaneous experience of pure consciousness is limited in so far as it can only develop concepts about the self, but does not enable direct awareness of the self, i.e. pure consciousness.

The limits of the intellect are further reflected in the methods of conventional science, which, while making enormous progress in gaining objective knowledge of the laws of nature, has as yet made little progress in gaining equal understanding and mastery over subjective existence (304).

The level of the mind is still more active and expressed than that of the intellect. According to Vedic Science, it is characterised by language-based thinking, 'responsible for apprehending, remembering, comparing, and conceptually organizing the multiplicity of perceptions to plan speech and action to fulfill desires' (302). Maharishi Mahesh Yogi comments on the relationship of mind and intellect:

> The intellect filters the information which comes to it through the mind. Useful things are accepted, useless things are rejected. The mind is like an open camera: it receives all the impulses from everywhere. The mind takes in everything that comes in through the senses. We see so many things. The vision gets drawn to one thing which seems to be more enjoyable, more useful, and then the intellect evaluates: it decides whether it is good or bad, and then accepts the

good and rejects the bad. On the basis of that, we act for greater fulfillment and achievement. (Dillbeck, 1988: 264)

Desire is located between the mind and the senses: it may be understood 'as motivating the flow of attention and thus, in daily experience, connecting the mind with the environment through the senses' (Dillbeck, 1988: 264—5). Maharishi Mahesh Yogi explains the relation of desire to the subtler levels of the mind thus:

Experience results when the senses come into contact with their objects and an impression is left on the mind. The impulse of this new impression resonates with the impression of a similar past experience in the mind and associates with that impression. The coming together of the two gives rise to an impulse at the deepest level of consciousness, where the impressions of all experiences are stored. This impulse develops and, rising to the conscious level of the mind, becomes appreciated as a thought. The thought, gaining the sympathy of the senses, creates a desire and stimulates the senses to action (1969: 284).

The senses, finally, serve as the link between the individual mind and the environment.

Demastes

Demastes' argument is clearly a further development of his earlier work relating theatre to chaos theory, which is, as he puts it, 'a creative, interactive fusion of naturalism/determinism and absurdism/randomness, the two dramatic extremes that have held sway in the twentieth century' (7). The emerging paradigm in science reemphasises the existence of patterns. Similarly, theatre has begun to abandon character (representing the urge to understand individual motivation) in favour of abstract pattern, a phenomenon discussed in depth by Elinor Fuchs (1996). Neither science nor theatre dealing with such patterns, however, go beyond description and tackle the question from where those patterns derive. Are they merely an expression of the postmodern fascination with anything on a meta-level, in this case metatheatre, theatricality of life, performativity? 'Or can this new idea of theatre (...) be a way to engage these emergent fundamental patterns and get them to get us closer, in some way, to the emergent essence of life itself' (8).

Comment

According to Vedic Science, the essence of life is its very basis, pure consciousness, an experience (more than merely a concept) increasingly researched in contemporary consciousness studies. Forman describes that the current 'received view' groups pure consciousness with all kinds of mystical experiences, quite true to its tradition. Regarding the Pure Consciousness Events (PCE), materialist 'constructivism' argues that

mystical experience is significantly shaped and formed by the subject's beliefs, concepts and expectations. This view, in turn, emerged as a response to the so-called perennial philosophy school. Perennialists- notably William James, Evelyn Underhill, Joseph Maréchal, William Johnston, James Pratt, Mircea Eliade, and W. T. Stace-maintained that mystical experience represented an immediate, direct contact with a (variously defined) absolute principle. Only after that immediate contact with the 'something more' according to this school, is such a direct contact *interpreted* according to the tradition's language and beliefs. (1990, 3)

Shear very succinctly summarises the relativist argument of hermeneutic critic Stephen Katz:

All mystical experience, like all other experience, is contextual. Consequently no such experiences can be understood outside their appropriate social, linguistic, epistemological etc. contexts. We know in general, therefore, that there can be no universal, culture-independent mystical experience. Thus, in particular, the IME [Introvertive Mystical Experience] cannot be such an experience. In short, despite appearances to the contrary, there is in fact no single, culture-independent IME experience at all. (Shear, 1990, 393)

Shear argues against Katz that the IME experience (which is equivalent to the experience of pure consciousness), is universally described as

absolutely devoid of all empirical content. There are no colors, shapes, sounds, or other sensory content to it. Nor are thoughts or conceptual processes experienced in it. Indeed, not only is the experience described as devoid of spatio-temporal content, but by all accounts even spatiality and temporality themselves are not present in it. (392)

Thus, Shear argues, the kinds of 'culture-dependent factors' Katz is concerned with, 'neither do nor even can play any "shaping", much less any "defining" role' in the experience of pure consciousness (394). Shear also points to empirical evidence from research 'on people of different races, religions, cultures and nationalities throughout the world' which strongly suggests that there is 'a single "core" experience which underlies the descriptions in question and reflects a specific central nervous system state, independent of all external matters or beliefs and other culture-dependent factors' (397-8). Shear is keen to point out that culturally dependent factors '*do* influence the content of our experiences', as hermeneutic philosophers such as Katz insist. 'But this should not be taken to imply that our experiences do not in general also have components which are independent of such cultural factors' (400).

Pure consciousness as proposed by Vedic Science has been linked, mainly by Hagelin (1987) to relevant insights in quantum physics. According to Vedic Science, pure consciousness is self-referral, or self-reflexive. This level of consciousness is 'fully awake to itself. (...) there is nothing else to be aware of but awareness itself. (...) All the forms and phenomena in the universe arise from the self-referral manifestations of the field of pure consciousness' (Orme-Johnson, 1988: 168-9). Self-referral is also the principle at the basis of many of the latest insights in quantum mechanics. At the beginning of the seventies, quantum field theories had their difficulties in explaining the phenomena they could observe in particle accelerators. The problem was based in the assumption that the respective basic fields (electro-magnetic, strong and weak interactions, gravity) had so many and so complex interactions that it was difficult to clearly describe the relationships of those interactions. The discovery of the spontaneous symmetry breaking, which shows deeply hidden symmetries of nature on fundamental space-time scales, made it possible to unify electro-magnetic and weak interaction forces to an electroweak field. This unification is possible by regarding both fields as parts of the same mathematical symmetry group. Thus the interactions of the two become self-referral. Theories of 'grand unification' unify-according to the same principle-weak, strong and electromagnetic forces and particles. A further principle of symmetry, called supersymmetry, allows the unification of fields with opposed spin. By incorporating all other forces into gravity, a unified field theory is now expressed. Today, quantum field theorists work on the most elegant formulation of this unified field theory. All these developments, which took place during the last fifteen years, are based on regarding the different basic forces more and more as self-referral phenomena of a unified field (Hagelin, 1987). Vedic Science identifies this field within the human being as the field of pure consciousness.

Hagelin has explored 'striking parallels between unified field theories of physics and the field of pure consciousness' as described by Vedic Science :

> One of his arguments for asserting that the unified field is the source of conscious-ness as well as of physics involves demonstrating that at the scale of super-unifica-tion, nature displays attributes characteristic of pure consciousness: self-referral, self- sufficiency, and infinite dynamism. (Orme-Johnson, 1988: 175)

In proposing pure consciousness to be at the basis of all creation, expressed consciousness as well as expressed matter, Vedic Science is also in accord with Bohm's implication that 'in some sense a rudimentary mind-like quality is present even at the level of particle physics' (Bohm, 1990: 283). Vedic Science provides a theory of the processes of manifestation from within the field of pure consciousness to expressed consciousness and matter (Dillbeck, 1988). Within the scope of this study, it will suffice to indicate that the process suggested is very close to Bohm's view that 'that which we experience as mind, in its movement through various levels of subtlety, will, in a natural way ultimately move the body by reaching the level of the quantum potential and of the "dance" of the particles' (Bohm, 1990: 283). A final interesting parallel between Vedic Science and Bohm's theory is Bohm's statement that even far distant particles can affect each other on the quantum mechanical level through the quantum potential (Bohm, 1990: 287).

Hagelin maintains that there 'is a precise correspondence between the descriptions of the detailed structure of Natural Law, as described by the Lagrangian of the Unified Field, and the structure of Natural Law as found in Rk Veda Samhita' (Dillbeck and Dillbeck, 1997: 14). It is possible to derive forty qualities as emerging from the Unified Field as described in the Lagrangian, which correspond to the forty qualities involved in structuring Rig Veda, which in turn are commented upon and expanded in the 40 bodies of text comprising Vedic Literature. All those qualities and the mechanisms of their functioning are open to direct experience of the human mind on the level of pure consciousness.

Demastes

Demastes' argument is very accurate within its chosen framework. The need for theatre to overcome the dangers of becoming 'deadly', in Brook's terms, suggests the need to get away from reductive materialism characteristic of much current theatre, and re-emphasise 'mystery', which need not be intangible or immaterial. It may (and should) find physical manifestations and explanations. Taking a look at theatre history of the late nineteenth and twentieth centuries, Demastes argues that realism moves from the material reality of the world 'up' to consciousness, whereas expressionism 'moves from the top down, sojourning through consciousness and affecting the "reality" of the material world beneath it' (15). Stronger dramatists, defined as more complex, are increasingly able to combine and integrate both approaches, in an attempt to overcome the dualism of mind and body inherited from Descartes. The same attempt of finding an alternative to Descartes's dualism is characteristic of current approaches to consciousness in consciousness studies. Demastes refers to Dennett and, in particular, Chalmers, although they are predominantly philosophers and not scientists. He also refers to theatre academics Stanton B. Garner and Bert O. States, who have studied theatre from a phenomenological perspective and 'convincingly argue for increased understanding via concentrating on the physicality of theatre' (25), a perspective backed by applying the philosophy of Merleau-Ponty. In a way that is close to phenomena discussed in complexity theory, the various physical elements of theatre 'somehow' combine to form a phenomenon of higher complexity. This higher level is what Brook refers to as *holy theatre*, it is the theatre that is searching for, and finding, new beliefs, rather than following the pattern of most of twentieth-century theatre in representing a 'theatre of revolt' against held beliefs rather than for new ones.

Comment

Demastes' 'somehow' is reminiscent of Artaud's as yet undiscovered grammar of the language of nature which Artaud seeks to develop for theatre to revive its magic and to immediately and strongly affect the spectator. Artaud calls the language beyond speech, which he intuits, the language of nature. Earlier in this chapter, I pointed out how reference to Vedic linguistics can help us understand this otherwise vague idea more clearly.

Demastes

Demastes discusses further points of contact between consciousness studies and theatre. Descartes, the founder of dualism, suggests that a homunculus (little human) is located in the brain, and, guided by the mind, causes the brain to function in accordance with what the 'I', that is, the mind, wants to be done. This has been called the Cartesian theatre. Current thinking in consciousness studies tends to discredit this analogy, just as current developments in theatre attempt to do away with the homunculus of the director, or with the passive spectator who, homunculus-like, 'merely observes materialized events placed before it' (28).

Having settled for the need of a model of consciousness that is materialist so as to avoid being mysterious, Demastes is at pains to emphasise that although materialist, the required model must not be reductionist. He thus discards Crick's 'astonishing hypothesis' that all conscious experience is 'no more than behavior of nerve cells and their associated molecules' (30, Crick 3). Instead, Demastes favours Dennett's approach, which is in line with Armstrong's ideas about the function of theatre in the context of human evolution.

Were theatre a reflection of the struggle, in consciousness studies, with Cartesian dualism of matter and consciousness, with realism/naturalism equated with materiality and impressionism/expressionism with consciousness, the demarcations of what are realism/naturalism, and impressionism/expressionism, should be distinct. However, Demastes finds that they are not. He concludes that '*Either* consciousness *or* materiality is not really a choice. Inevitably, theatre uses a both/and proposition of confronting consciousness integrally through materialism rather than discretely through mystical or spiritual channels'. (41). Demastes uses parts of the prologue to Shakespeare's *Henry V* to support his argument: whereas at first the muse is invoked, apparently suggesting a top-down approach, Shakespeare immediately turns to a material approach, asking the spectators to engage their 'imaginations with the material, splicing the imagined into the physical' (41). Because whatever we see on stage is material, theatre necessarily 'forces us to think *materially* about everything before us, even the apparently immaterial' (42).

Comment

Demastes argues that whatever we see on stage is material, theatre necessarily 'forces us to think *materially* about everything before us, even the apparently immaterial' (42). This is correct if we consider *thinking*. The immaterial cannot be *thought* about immaterially, because thinking is a function of the intellect, and the intellect, on the model of mind in Vedic literature, cannot grasp any more refined levels than itself, and thus cannot grasp the level of the immaterial, which is the level of pure consciousness. However, while the immaterial cannot be *thought* other than materially, the immaterial, pure consciousness is nevertheless open to direct *experience*. Such experience can be enjoyable (by nature, blissful) for its own sake; it is ideally simultaneous with a sensory impression also created in the theatre.

Demastes

Academic endeavour has conventionally focused on 'serious' analysis of meaning in theatre, revealed in both text and production. Such plays are didactic, 'we are asked to *think* about the world differently' (44) as a result of having seen a production of such a didactic play. Some plays defy such analysis, for example, Wilde's *The Importance of Being Earnest*, as does 'alternative, nondidactic theatre, where the boundaries to performance art begin to disappear. Watching a performance that does not expect us to think about the world differently does still have an effect, though, Demastes argues. Rather, by undermining not what, but how we think, such performances have the potential of changing patterns of thought that are established in our minds on the basis of neurones. Theatre is thus argued to have, potentially, a direct influence on the neuronal functioning in the brain, at a paradigmatic level, which may then influence thought processes on higher levels of consciousness-here defined as levels of serialized processing. Demastes provides an example for this with reference to Ibsen's *A Doll's House*: an antifeminist spectator watches a performance of the play. Although he is not convinced by the play's message (on the level of serial processing), some rewiring of the more paradigmatic level of consciousness might have occurred, which may 'someday result in a transformation of this antifeminist's serial thought' (45).

Comment
In chapter five, I pointed to the possibility of mirror neurones being involved in the reception processes in the theatre.

Demastes
For Demastes, theatre is a 'grounding mechanism'. In realism, he argues, mind and environment are interlocked, with environment foregrounded. Expressionism is characterised by the same components, mind and environment; however, in contrast to realism, mind is foregrounded (51). The dividing lines need not be strict: in later Ibsen, for example, such as *When We Dead Awaken*, realism and non-realism merge. Such merging leads to theatre that is no longer driven by plot and character, but becomes a 'theater of direct experience' (52). In that sense, Demastes regards theatre as 'that place where "mind-stuff" and "physical stuff" intermingle in a manner precisely parallel to our growing sense of material consciousness. In the theatre matters are just more focused than in the diffusion of daily existence' (53).

Philosophers of consciousness Daniel Dennett and Owen Flanagan argue that the human mind succeeds in absorbing a multitude of potentially contradictory, and certainly isolated impressions (through the senses), and constructing a fiction of unity from those numerous impressions. This fiction of unity is at the basis of what we think we see, hear, touch, smell, and taste, and it is equally at the basis of our selfhood. Demastes discusses the nature of the Characters in Pirandello's *Six Characters in Search of an Author* in this context. Turning to Beckett, he notes that Winnie in *Happy Days* is literally grounded, and is revealed through her responses to the world. Similarly, 'we see that mind can only reveal itself as consciousness of *something* (59).

Noting that conventional Western science, grounded in Aristotle, has, until recently adhered to an either / or approach, Demastes argues that some current representatives of science, as well as some cutting edge theatre artists (Robert Wilson and Sam Shepard, among others) attempt to disrupt this tendency towards clear distinctions in favour of multivalence characteristic of Confucian philosophy and 'fuzzy logic'. 'The more we accept multiple values', instead of a binary either/or, 'the more accurately we begin to depict reality' (69). Such an approach leads from binary (either/or) to parallel processing referred to earlier. The danger inherent in multivalence is information overload, which is likely to result in creative paralysis. What is required is thus a balance between binary and parallel processing procedures.

Comment

In chapter five I pointed to the relevance of simultaneity and time in relation to theatre and consciousness.

Demastes

Against this background, Demastes analyses the concept of (artistic) creativity. He concludes that chaos theory is not a likely model to explain creativity, since it suggests that 'nothing is new except in the way it is arranged' (72), and since even chaos theory is ultimately a computational model, and, following Penrose, no computational model can ever duplicate human thought. Following his materialist approach, Demastes rejects a top-down input by the muses in the creative process, re-emphasising his credo that there is no need for mystery. He describes Penrose's quantum theory based model, which suggests that non-computational, microcosmic processes at the quantum level integrate with the macrocosmic events, 'marking those events with their own noncomputational processes' (73). The result of such marking could be the noncomputational, creative spark. An alternative model, which Demastes terms 'organic', is based on Bohm and Peat and refers to the soliton, 'self-organised, self-generated entities that force their ways through otherwise random material bodies' (76). Satellites have been able to follow soliton single waves 'rippling for thousands of miles in the ocean' (76). Bohm also favours the hologram as an illustration to explain the connections between mind and universe: taking a part of the hologram reveals the whole picture, albeit in a less sharp focus and with less possible viewpoints. Demastes proceeds to Dawkins' concept of memes, units of information, which struggle for survival in our minds: strong ideas remain and are multiplied by communication, weak ones die out. The faith meme contains the meme for a disembodied soul. The soul is another object that material scientists are searching for, and which they can rescue from mystery: Demastes suggests that soul is 'a sort of meta-awareness, an accumulation that floods into an awareness of the discrepancy between our mind's linearized awareness of the explicate world around us and our brain's data that houses an implicate reality of underlying forms and patterns' (80). Taking this one step further still, Demastes asks whether in discovering 'patterns of reality' science could, almost inadvertently, have discovered God. Thus there is a major paradigm shift, initiated by science, suggesting that soul and God exist, but that we have been looking for them in all the wrong places.

Comment

In view of my own argument on artistic creativity in chapter one it would be interesting to discuss in more detail whether the various different models of artistic creativity that Demastes rejects or explains and develops further, actually refer to one and the same process, from their different perspectives.

Demastes

In this broad and major paradigm shift, theatre has its major function. It can contribute in furthering the shift 'by capturing these new visions and triggering an explosion in the cultural imagination. What could be the goal of this new theatre is to reflect a sense not only of what science is telling us but also of what we need to relearn in order to live in this increasingly complex world. The new theatre could assist in demonstrating how memically to be infected by this necessary, new paradigm shift. And it can do so in ways that satisfy and even transcend the discursive celebration of science. Theatre could help to promote the shift by giving us a place to experience the possibilities' (83).

The remainder of the book represents an analysis of elements of this new theatre. Demastes is looking both for a new art form, and, equally important and valid, a reemphasis, in terms of criticism and direction, on 'the stage's language of *rhythms* of consciousness'. Physicist David Bohm posits the existence of an implicate order which is 'neither mind nor body but rather a yet higher-dimensional actuality which is their [mind's and body's] common ground and which is of a nature beyond both' (87-88). Bohm proposes the development of a new language to capture 'the essence of this new level of reality' (88). In that proposed new language, emphasis is on movement, on flow, on the verb, rather than on the noun.

Comment

'Cultures of Performativity' is the title of an impressive and far-ranging research project under way at the Free University of Berlin, Germany. Its major point of departure is the insight that '[c]ultural studies - the humanities as well as the social sciences - are currently undergoing a shift of paradigm: from text based models of culture to models based on the notion of performance' (see website http://www.sfb-performativ.de/seiten/frame_gesa.html). The time of the paradigm shift is located in the late 1980s.

Text	Performance
Production of an artefact	Performative character prevails
Artwork	Event
Formal interpretation	Experience
A set of discursive formations	A set of dynamic practices
Structuralist, static view of culture	Exchange, negotiations or transformations
Looking at products of cultural construction	Looking at the processes of cultural construction
Represent cultural events or social identities	Constitute cultural events or social identities
Culture defined by objects, monuments or works of art	Culture defined by the dynamic relations and processes that determine, produce and validate these objects
Central importance of the artist	The relation between the artist and her/his audience
Audience as passive recipient	Audience as active participant in cultural production
Established scholarly positions	Need for review of positions on identity formation, representation, the body, self-fashioning, notions of space and time, or cultural norms and values
Systematic analysis based on verifiability, repeatability and constancy	Requires modification of aims and methods of cultural critique

The shift towards the performative, as defined above, is 'new' and relatively recent in the context of cultural studies.

Demastes

Demastes shows that while much of Aristotle's philosophy is clearly binary, as far as theatre is concerned, in the *Poetics* he 'fundamentally acknowledges that nonlinear data processing is central to the stage, and he concedes that a multivalent perception of reality results' (89). Flow is the ultimate aim of Stanislavski as well as of Method Acting. Those experiences of the actor, just as equivalent experiences of the audience (as Brook sees it, once they are attuned with each other and with the impulses coming from the stage) are more than the sum of the parts. Western culture's preference for taking phenomena apart in order to understand them, without putting them together again, has led, so far, to ultimate failure in comprehending experience ('*explaining* a play never does justice to the *experience* of a play' (90). Demastes acknowledges that much can be learned from Eastern traditions, but prefers to look closely at the Western tradition itself to see whether we are not overlooking relevant material there.

Demastes explains that Artaud's endeavour of converting the ineffable into the concrete has been interpreted, conventionally, as a process of alchemy, 'of rarefying and mystifying mundane reality' (95), characteristic of a top-down approach. Taking recourse to the new materialism, Demastes argues in favour of a bottom-up reassessment, according to which Artaud's alchemy becomes 'a process of materializing a heightened reality' (95). Linear language is to change into non-linear language, a clear parallel to Bohm. Artaud sensed the implications of the new science, without having access to them-in his days they had not been developed. Thus he sought explanations for his intuitions in immateriality, alchemy and Gnosticism. However, reassessing Artaud against the background of the kind of new materialism suggested by Demastes helps to understand Artaud better, and ultimately might lead to a theatre of the kind Artaud envisioned. In an earlier comment, I have already proposed to enhance our understanding of Artaud with recourse to Indian linguistics.

Grotowski's approach of *via negativa* is subjected to a similar reassessment. Here, Demastes concludes that whereas some of the ideas and concepts discussed by Grotowski suggest placing him on a level with Artaud as mystical, much of what he has to say actually makes much sense from the new materialist perspective. Grotowski's agenda, on that reading, is to allow the actors, and through them the spectators, to free themselves from the restriction of linear thought, allowing non-linear patterns to be discovered and experienced. The relationship of mind and body is important for Grotowski. The assumption that the purified body can serve as an antenna for signals from God is reassessed to reveal, applying new materialism, that higher levels (not clearly defined, though), are the cause of neural phenomena. The ultimate aim, an experience beyond the mind-brain barrier and, more rarely, the now-then, or spatio-temporal barrier, is given credibility. Grotowski realises that such experiences are non-linear and cannot be achieved following linear modes. His theatre employs a range of approaches intended to break linearity, including the audience's recognition of the actor behind the character, 'of the man behind the part, of the nature of man which compels him to mask, play roles, and act at the same time that he most wants to break down the defences, narrow distances, and unmask' (Wiles 156, D 103).

Comment

In chapter three, I discussed Grotowski's concept of translumination in the context of the Vedic Science model of consciousness as an experience of pure consciousness. For the duration of the experience of cosmic consciousness or unity consciousness, all action, performative or other, is fully spontaneous, there is no longer a time lapse between inner impulse and outer action. At the same time, all activity in those states of consciousness will be fully disciplined in the sense that there will be no entropy, no waste of energy, actions will lead to the intended result following the principle of least action.

Demastes

Neither Artaud nor Grotowski managed to achieve their aims of reaching what they called the ineffable, at least not beyond fleeting glimpses. Demastes explains that they failed because they were stuck in the dualist world-view characteristic of their time, ironically the world view they unknowingly tried to overcome by rejecting linear processes and striving for non-linear, multivalent ones. They looked for something, i.e. the 'beyond', the ineffable, the invisible, seeking to make it visible through theatre, 'where that something was not. The something they sought was entwined with the physical reality they sought to liberate' (105).

Comment

Precisely because physical reality and the invisible something are entwined, each aspect can influence the other. Theatre that follows the guidelines set out in the *Natyashastra* may serve as one means among others for the actor of using the body in such a way that development of higher states of consciousness results from such use. Alternatively, it is equally possible, and should be equally effective, to train the mind, through meditation, for example, to become able to guide the body in such a way that it expresses experiences of consciousness. Both Artaud and Grotowski, and later Barba and Brook, among others, describe experiences in and through theatre that, in terms of Vedic Science, are experiences of higher states of consciousness. Based on such experience they try to find ways of recreating those experiences in a systematic way. Neither Artaud nor Grotowski had the depth of Vedic knowledge at their disposal. This is why they failed to find systematic methods of expressing the invisible which they had encountered coincidentally. In particular, I discussed how Grotowski's problems with intercultural theatre practice are rooted in the way he understands and uses Indian material.

Demastes

Robert Wilson's 'theatre' is a prime example of 'theatre of consciousness', since it works on a level of parallel processing which is prior to serial processing. 'Wilson's theatre is, to remind ourselves of Brook's charge, a Holy Theatre created from the physical that supplants the mystical via an idiom digestible by a postmodern consciousness' (112). Alternative theatre must avoid being, or becoming solipsistic. Instead, it must be open, accessible and available to a wide range of audience. At the same time, 'through that apparent solipsism we arrive at a larger conception of humanity's means of contacting at least the trace of some cosmic essence. … Awareness of existence unadulterated is impossible, but awareness of its existence via parallelly absorbed traces is not' (116). Further discussions of Foreman and Spalding Gray support this view. In the context of Gray comes a further pointer to Demastes' understanding of *mystery*, when he writes about a 'mystical force beyond the domain affected by causality' (123). In his discussion of

Tony Kushner's *Angels in America*, another basic assumption about the world view he argues against becomes clear when he ascribes to Kushner an 'assault on the notion of discrete individuality/ consciousness hovering above inferior nature awaiting manipulation by that discrete and superior consciousness' (124). Demastes' analysis of Shaffer's *Equus* points to the multivalence in both Alan Strang and Dysart's characters. This view is in opposition to the more conventional critical view that Stang and Dysart represent, bivalently, the Dionysian and the Apollonian. Rather, both represent different forms of an inability of creatively fusing those two forces which are at work in both of them. 'If Dysart could fully engage a multivalent logic, if he could *see* nature and his place in it more fully, completely, and roundedly, then perhaps his consciousness could engage a nature with postmodern sophistication, minus primitive mystery but with a contemporary material reenchantment replacing that mystery. The difference between saying this and actually offering a parallel experience of this parallel potentiality is what separates discursivity from the theatre experience' (141). It is the actors playing the horses/gods with their status as actors never in question that allow this experience of god as bottom-up, non-mysterious, comprehensible, the material reenchantment.

Following an assessment of Sam Shepard's work, Demastes comes back to Shaffer, and his *The Gift of the Gorgon*. Its central character, dramatist Edward Damson, reveals his 'fundamental materialist urge to manifest the mysteries of existence physically' (150). Theatre's role, Demastes concludes from this play, is that of 'distilling reality by making it material on stage and offering it to the audiences to see...' (151). 'The theatre re-minds our consciousness, literally, and in a material way, to that in us that can attune to the patterns inherent in that reality' (152). Ultimately, Demastes concludes that 'united-or reunited-the sciences and arts could effect the changes envisioned by cutting-edge artists and scientists alike' (170).

Comment

Malekin and Yarrow provide a detailed account of processes through which 'spirituality is made available to the receiver' (1997: 129). They identify three constitutive elements of theatre: performer, character and audience, and locate processes involving neutrality (pure consciousness in terms of Vedic Science), witnessing (a characteristic of cosmic consciousness) and play (characteristic of refined cosmic consciousness and unity consciousness for each of the elements), giving references to numerous relevant plays. Neutrality for the character in theatre, for example, is a liminal state. Malekin and Yarrow explain:

> Deaths, displacements, demands to do the 'impossible' or resolve the unresolvable all present the character with the paradigm of the familiar and known, and of hesitation before a threshold of new forms of knowledge and being. (1997: 137)

Such liminality is represented, for example, by Vladimir and Estragon in Beckett's *Waiting for Godot*, two characters who are 'cut off from any obvious criteria of personality, geographical situation or function' (1997: 137). Exposing the performers and spectators to those processes serves the function of heightened spirituality, of development of consciousness in terms of Vedic Science.

Summary: Demastes Reassessed

The following points in Demastes' argument remain unchanged and unchallenged within the context he limits himself to:

1. Theatre has unfathomed and to a large extent unused potential in enabling, in theatre artists and audiences, a holistic experience which is non-ordinary, non-day-to-day, what Brook calls *holy theatre*.
2. Hitherto, this extra-ordinary experience could be described only in vague terms, suggesting something mysterious, coming from outside, from above (God). Such an explanation is characteristic of Cartesian dualism.
3. Today's postmodern view tends to be more materialistic, reluctant to accept anything mysterious.
4. Reductive materialism is unable to explain or account for the extra-ordinary experiences in relation to theatre hitherto described in terms of mysticism, and can provide no conceptual or practical tools to enable further development of such *holy theatre*.
5. Non-reductive, emergent materialism, as found in complexity, chaos and quantum theories, offers a model to explain or account for the extra-ordinary experiences in relation to theatre hitherto described in terms of mysticism, and can provide conceptual and practical tools to enable further development of such *holy theatre*.

In the twelve commentaries I have offered on Demastes' argument, I have suggested that if we apply the model of consciousness proposed by Vedic Science,

1. what the mechanistic framework adopted by Demastes qualifies as mysterious is fully explained and thus demystified;
2. the top-down versus bottom-up dichotomy becomes obsolete;
3. the argument for a shift in paradigm initiated through chaos theory and quantum theory is supported by the argument that pure consciousness is the unifield field described in quantum physics;
4. we are able to understand the principles at work when elements combine into a higher complexity: Artaud's as yet undiscovered grammar of the language of nature;
5. we are able to give a new meaning to theatre's search for new beliefs;
6. the important difference between thinking about something, and directly experiencing it becomes clear;
7. the recent discovery of mirror neuones further supports Demastes' argument for neuronal changes through theatre;

8. further thought about time and simultaneity in theatre further supports Demastes' call for increased multivalence in theatre;

9. artistic creativity should prove a rich field for further research;

10. Demastes' argument for a new language of theatre, with its emphasis on the verb rather than the noun, is further supported by the insight of a major shift in paradigm in cultural studies from the textual to the performative;

11. we can understand better what Grotowski may have had in mind when he wrote about *translumination*;

12. we gain a better understanding of what it means for theatre to make the invisible visible, and why earlier attempts were not always completely successful.

The aim, for Demastes and myself, to argue for a wider application and use of theatre, a theatre for fundamental change of consciousness, is the same. The perspective from which we argue is different. Demastes' book shows the strength of the bottom-up, non-reductive materialistic and mechanistic approach. He explores that approach in its application to theatre to its limits. The limits become apparent when the perspective is broadened; the broadening element, in my argument, is provided by various aspects and concepts proposed by Vedic Science. The Vedic Science-based argument encompasses the arguments proposed by Demastes, and expands them, towards an even fuller understanding of the theatre. Note that I do not claim to have exhausted the potential of the Vedic Science perspective in the twelve comments I offered on Demastes views. Much remains to be investigated; most important of all, Vedic Science-based theatre needs to meet a major challenge: the theory which Haney, Malekin, Yarrow and I have begun to develop (see bibliography) needs to be tested, explored and refined further in theatre practice.

Conclusion

In the course of this book, I wanted to discuss the relation of theatre to consciousness for two main reasons: to see whether we can better understand theatre as a result of such an analysis, and to think through the implications of the *Natyashastra's* claim that theatre may serve as a tool to the development of *moksha*, enlightenment, higher states of consciousness. I have demonstrated the explanatory potential of relating theatre phenomena to insights of consciousness studies as follows:

1. It is possible to explain artistic creative inspiration as a temporary contact of the artist's mind with the state of pure consciousness. Pure consciousness, as conceptualised by Vedic Science, is the field from which all creation emerges. The processes of artistic creation and the moment of inspiration that leads to it mirror general patterns of creation. Artists' experiences that the moment of inspiration, and the creative process resulting from it, are so powerful as to cause physical and/or mental suffering can be explained as well: if an the experience of pure consciousness 'hits' an unprepared nervous system, the 'current' can be too strong.

2. While conventional approaches suffice to explain the depictions of sleep, dream and conventional waking states of consciousness in drama and theatre, Vedic Science is of use in explaining desirable, beneficial altered states of consciousness, such as visionary experiences. Vedic Science can also assist in understanding /interpreting character development.

3. The model of consciousness proposed by Vedic Science serves to explain dual consciousness, advocated, from different perspectives, by theatre artists and critics as diverse as Diderot, Stanislavsky, Meyerhold, Brecht and Strasberg in relation to the issue of whether actors should be emotionally involved with the emotions of the characters they have to portray. Dual consciousness is the coexistence of pure consciousness with waking consciousness, an experience characteristic of the higher state of consciousness termed cosmic consciousness in Vedic Science. Pure consciousness is also found to be the essential ingredient in achieving an actor's *presence* (Barba), *state* (Mnouchkine) and *translumination* (Grotowski). Vedic Science helps to overcome Artaud's paradox of an actor's simultaneous physical presence and neutrality. Finally, in pointing to future developments, Vedic Science allows to take Kleist's ideas about the marionette more literally than was hitherto possible.

4. A reassessment of Indian aesthetics as contained in the *Natyashastra* shows that the predominant aesthetics experience, *rasa*, is an experience that combines pure consciousness with the specific contents of a given performance in which *rasa* is created by the actors in conjunction with music and various aspects of scenography.

5. A reassessment from the perspective of Vedic Science of issues relating to audiences and reception processes in the theatre demonstrates the range of possibilities of affecting the spectator's consciousness through the senses. In

relation to sight, I explained the implications of scenography that follows the guidelines of *Sthapatyaveda*, and gave an example for the application of simultaneity in performance. In relation to hearing, I briefly referred to the Vedic model of language. In relation to smell, Martin Mittwede and I explained the potential of using appropriate fragrances for their consciousness-enhancing properties. With reference to recent developments of cutting-edge research into new forms of matter, in relation to consciousness studies, I suggested that phenomena such as atmosphere, charisma, or other instances of unconventional transfer of information are close to explanation.

6. Various concepts of theatre (studies), many based, initially, on direct experience, can be understood more thoroughly following reassessment from the perspective of the model of consciousness proposed by Vedic Science:

a. Language of nature (Artaud) may well refer to Artaud's intuition of the field of *para* in Vedic linguistics, or the field of pure consciousness;

b. A universal language of the theatre does exist, and can be expressed by recourse to pure consciousness;

c. Vedic Science suggests that theatre that follows the aesthetics of the *Natyashastra* is a form of Vedic ritual, *yagya*;

d. The search for what is ultimately, in different terms, the experience of higher states of consciousness, is nothing else than the search for a new overarching totality, so vehemently opposed by postmodernism. However, the search takes place not in the expressed fields of science, art, morality, or law, as the eighteenth-century philosophers of the Enlightenment, but in a field beyond expression, in the field of consciousness;

e. Theatre that attempts to achieve transformation of consciousness is closely related to *utopian performatives*, making an unobtainable goal achievable;

7. Finally, I explore the relation between emergent materialism (Demastes) and Vedic Science as models of consciousness in relation to their explanatory potential.

On an ongoing basis, I have also dealt with the second issue I set out to tackle in this book: the implications of the *Natyashastra's* claim that theatre may serve as a means of developing higher states of consciousness. I argued that theatre can have a transformative impact on the actors' and spectators' consciousness on all the levels of the mind conceptualised in Vedic Science:

1. on the level of the *senses*, predominantly through sight and sound, but potentially also through smell;
2. on the levels of *mind* and *intellect* by providing 'food for thought', new insights and understanding of the subject matter dealt with in the plays;
3. on the level of the *emotions*, which represent the most important expressed level in the theatre aesthetics of the *Natyashastra*;
4. on the level of *intuition*. In the first chapter, I argued that the more, or better, dramatists are able to work with their inspiration or intuition, the more suffused their work will be with the level of pure consciousness at the basis of

inspiration or intuition, and the more powerful will be its transformative impact on actors and spectators.

Theatre can affect those expressed levels of consciousness in a twofold way: on the one hand, theatre stimuli operate within the context of each level: smell, for example, affects the brain in specific ways characteristic to the how smell functions. Simultaneously, though, the expressed levels can be affected in such a way that the theatre stimuli also facilitate the experience of pure consciousness through their impact within the context of their particular level.

Theatre can affect the actors' and spectators' consciousness not only indirectly, through the expressed levels of consciousness, but also directly on the level of pure consciousness. If the means of acting thus allow the actor to perform while maintaining the experience of pure consciousness, the resulting mode of acting will directly impact on the level of pure consciousness of the spectators.

In the introduction I emphasised that while I claim to present alternative, new thoughts in relation to theatre theory and practice, I do not claim exclusivity. Other approaches to consciousness exist, and I have described and commented on the emergent materialist approach adopted by Demastes in relation to theatre. Gordon Scott Armstrong approaches the relation of theatre and consciousness from the perspective of 'bio-evolutionary complexity in the arts' (2003). What I have done is tease out some of the implications of applying the model of consciousness proposed by Vedic Science to further understanding theatre.

In the introduction, I also pointed out that the material contained in this book is not all that can be said about the relation between theatre and consciousness. Here are just some ideas for further research:

1. In this book, I used the model of consciousness proposed by Vedic Science, based in India as the body of reference. How do my insights compare with theatre aesthetics and underlying bodies of knowledge in other cultures?
2. What are the ethical/moral implications of the insights I presented in this book? If theatre can indeed lead to an increase in well-being (to put it in very general terms), what would be the justification for any theatre that does not have that effect? What are the implications for this question in the light of the political correctness debate and for the literary / dramatic / theatrical canon?
3. More research is needed to work out in more detail some of the suggestions I proposed in this book:
   a. The functioning of mirror neurones in relation to reception;
   b. The role of cold, soft, dark matter in relation to *atmosphere*, *charisma*, *presence*, and non-conventional transfer of information;
   c. The impact on consciousness of scenography that follows the rules of Sthapatyaveda.
4. The two examples of textual interpretation, Prospero's enlightenment and Hamlet's procrastination, in terms of Vedic Science suggest that it should be possible to provide further interpretations of works of literature and theatre in

terms of consciousness studies, of course not limited to the model of consciousness proposed by Vedic Science. The continuing success of the Web-journal *Consciousness, Literature and the Arts*, which provides an outlet for this kind of work, supports my argument, as do, indeed, the launch of this book series with Intellect, or publications of the Web-based Institute for Psychological Study of the Arts at http://www.clas.ufl.edu/ipsa/intro.htm.

5. A brief discussion of the key concept of the *Natyashastra*, *rasa*, with Sri Sri Ravi Shankar led to a fundamental reassessment of this concept (and experience) in terms of consciousness. On that basis I would argue that an in-depth discussion of the *Natyashastra* with Sri Sri Ravi Shankar, in the process of arriving at a new translation and commentary, would yield results we cannot possibly predict.

6. Much work is needed to find ways of systematically applying the range of insights I proposed in the course of this book in theatre training and practice.

Research into consciousness worldwide has grown exponentially over the last ten years. Yet the scientists at the centre of the debate agree that they have not yet established a new *science* of consciousness. The Tucson conferences have all been entitled 'Towards a Science of Consciousness'. None of the scientists, and other academics involved in the study of consciousness, however, would disagree that a new discipline is emerging. My book is a contribution to this emerging discipline in the field of theatre studies, as are the three further books in this series with Intellect.

LIBRARY, UNIVERSITY COLLEGE CHESTER

Bibliography

Aeschylus, *The Persians*, Transl. by Robert Potter. Available online at http://classics.mit.edu/Aeschylus/persians.html

Aiyar, H. N., ed. and transl., *Thirty Minor Upanishads,* Delhi, Arcade Book Company, 1914.

Alexander, C. N. and E. J. Langer (eds.), *Higher Stages of Human Development. Perspectives on Human Growth*, New York, Oxford, Oxford University Press, 1990.

Alexander, C. N. and R. W. Boyer, 'Seven States of Consciousness, Unfolding the Full Potential of the Cosmic Psyche in Individual Life through Maharishi's Vedic Psychology', *Modern Science and Vedic Science* 2:4 (1989), pp. 324-71.

Alexander, C. N. et al., 'Growth of Higher Stages of Consciousness: Maharishi's Vedic Psychology of Human Development', in Alexander, C. N. and E. J. Langer (eds.), *Higher Stages of Human Development. Perspectives on Human Growth*, New York, Oxford, Oxford University Press, 1990, pp. 286-341.

Ambardekar, R. R., *Rasa Structure of the Meghaduta*, Bombay, Andreesh Prakashan, 1979.

Armstrong, G. S., *Theatre and Consciousness. The Nature of Bio-evolutionary Complexity in the Arts*. New York: Peter Lang, 2003.

Artaud, A., *The Theatre and its Double*, (Collected Works Vol. 4, translated by Victor Corti), London, Calder and Boyars, 1974.

Auslander, P., '*Holy Theatre* and Catharsis', *TRI* 9:1 (1984), pp. 16-29.

Banes, S., 'Olfactory Performance', *TDR* 45: 1 (2001), pp. 68-76.

Barba, E., *The Floating Islands, Reflections with Odin Teatret*, ed. Ferdinando Taviani, Holstebro, 1979.

—— 'Interview with Gautam Dasgupta', *Performing Arts Journal* January 1985.

—— 'The Way of Refusal: the Theatre's Body-in-Life', *NTQ* 4:16 (1988), pp. 291-299.

—— 'Eurasian Theatre', *TDR* 32:2 (1988), pp. 126-130.

—— 'The Fiction of Duality', *NTQ* 5: 20 (1989), pp. 311-314.

—— and Nicola Savarese, *The Secret Art of the Performer: A Dictionary of Theatre Anthropology*, London and New York, Routledge, 1991.

Bates, B., *The Way of the Actor: A New Path to Personal Knowledge and Power*, London, Century, 1986.

Bharucha, R., 'A View from India', in Williams, D. (ed.), *Peter Brook and the Mahabharata: Critical Perspectives*, London, Routledge, 1991, pp. 228-52.

Bharucha, R., *Theatre and the World. Essays on Performance and Politics of Culture*, London and New York, Routledge, 1993.

Bhat, G. K., *Sanskrit Dramatic Theory*, (Bhandarkar Oriental Institute Post-Graduate and Research Series No. 13) Poona, Bhandarkar Oriental Research Institute, 1981.

—— *Rasa Theory and Allied Problems*, Baroda, The MS University of Baroda, 1984.

Bennett, S., *Theatre Audiences: A Theory of Production and Reception*, London and New York, Routledge, 1990.

Bice, B., and R. Kennedy, *The Work of Jaques Lacan*, London, Free Association Books, 1986.

Birringer, J., *Theatre, Theory, Postmodernism*, Bloomington and Indianapolis, Indiana University Press, 1991.

Bleich, D., *Subjective Criticism*, Baltimore, Johns Hopkins University Press, 1978.

Bloch, S., 'ALBA EMOTING: A Psychophysiological Technique to Help Actors Create and Control Real Emotions', *Theatre Topics* 3:2 (1993), pp. 121-138.

Bly, R., 'A wrong turning in American poetry', in Hall, D. (ed.), *Claims for Poetry*. Ann Arbor, University of Michigan Press, 1982. [Original work published in 1963).

Bohm, D., 'A new theory of the relationship between mind and matter', *Philosophical Psychology* 3:2 (1990), pp. 271-286.

Bonshek, A., *Mirror of Consciousness: Art, Creativity and Veda*, Delhi, Motilal Banarsidass, 2001.

Bowers, F., 'Hamlet as minister and scourge', *PMLA* LXX (1955), pp. 740-49.

—— 'Hamlet's Fifth Soliloquy, III. 2. 406-417', in: Hosley, R. (ed.), *Essays on Shakespeare and Elizabethan Drama*', Columbia, 1962, pp. 213-22.

—— 'Dramatic Structure and Criticism: Plot in Hamlet', *Shakespeare Quarterly* 15 (1964), pp. 207-218.

Bradby, D. and D. Williams, *Directors' Theatre* (Macmillan Modern Dramatists), London, Macmillan, 1988.

Brandon, J. R (ed.), *The Cambridge Guide to Asian Theatre*, Cambridge, Cambridge University Press, 1993.

Braun, E., *Meyerhold on Theatre*, London, Methuen, 1969.

—— *The Director and the Stage: From Naturalism to Grotowski*, London, Methuen, 1982.

Brent, P. L., *The Indian Guru and his Disciple*, Tunbridge Wells, Institute for Cultural Research, 1971.

Broich, U. und M. Pfister (eds.), *Intertextualität: Formen, Funktionen, anglistische Fallbeispiele*, Tübingen, Narr, 1985.

Brook, P., *The Empty Space*, Harmondsworth, Penguin, 1972 [1968].

—— *The Shifting Point: Forty Years of Theatrical Exploration 1946-1987*, London, Methuen, 1987.

—— 'The Presence of India. An Introduction', in Williams, D. (ed.), *Peter Brook and the Mahabharata: Critical Perspectives*. London, Routledge, 1991, pp. 41-44.

—— 'Theatre, Popular and Special, and the Perils of Cultural Piracy', in Williams, D. (ed.), *Peter Brook and the Mahabharata: Critical Perspectives*. London, Routledge, 1991.

Brown, G. R., 'Postmodernism and Creativity', in Runco, M. A. and S. Pritzker (eds), *Encyclopedia of Creativity*, Vol. 2, London, Academic Press, 1999, pp. 423-8.

Buckley, T., 'Write me, said the Play to Peter Shaffer', *New York Times Magazine* 13 Apr. 1975, pp. 20-40.

Byrski, M. K., *'Grotowski og indisk tradi tion'*, in: *Teatrets teori og teknikk* 18 (1972), pp. 35-8.

Calhoun, C. and R. C. Solomon, *What is an Emotion: Classical Readings in Philosophical Psychology*, New York, Oxford, Oxford University Press, 1984.

Carlson, M., *Theories of the Theatre: A Historical and Critical Survey, from the Greeks to the Present,* Ithaca and London, Cornell University Press, 1984.

—— 'Brook and Mnouchkine: Passages to India?' in Patrice Pavis, (ed.) *The Intercultural Performance Reader*, London, Routledge.

Carrière, J.-C., 'What is not in *The Mahabharata* is nowhere', in Williams, D. (ed.), *Peter Brook and the Mahabharata*: *Critical Perspectives*, London, Routledge, 1991, pp. 59-64.

Chaim, D. B., *Distance in the Theatre: The Aesthetics of Audience Response* (Theatre and Dramatic Studies, No. 17), Ann Arbor, London, UMI Research Press 1984.

Chalmers, D., 'First-Person Methods in the Science of Consciousness', *Consciousness Bulletin*

(fall 1999). n. pag. Online. Internet. 24.07.2001. Available: URL
http://www.u.arizona.edu/~chalmers/papers/firstperson.html

Chambers, C. (ed.), *The Continuum Companion to Twentieth Century Theatre*, London, New York, Continuum, 2002.

Chandler, K., 'Modern Science and Vedic Science: An Introduction', *Modern Science and Vedic Science* 1:1 (1987), pp. 5-26.

Chopra, D., *Perfect Health: The Complete Mind/Body Guide*, London, Bantam Books, 1990.

Clark, J. H., *A Map of Mental States*, London, Routledge and Kegan Paul, 1983.

Clark, T., *The Theory of Inspiration: Composition as a crisis of subjectivity in Romantic and post-Romantic writing*, Manchester, New York, Manchester University Press, 1997.

Colvin, C., *Plays and Players*. April 1986, p. 21.

Conti, R. and T. Amabile., 'Motivation / Drive', in Runco, M. A. and S. Pritzker (eds), *Encyclopedia of Creativity*, Vol. 2, London, Academic Press, 1999, pp. 251-9.

Coward, H. G., *The Sphota Theory of Language: A Philosophical Analysis,* Delhi, Motilal Banarsidass, 1980.

—- *Jung and Eastern Thought*, Albany, State University of New York Press, 1985.

—- *Derrida and Indian Philosophy*, New York, State University of New York Press, 1990.

Crohn-Schmitt, N., *Actors and Onlookers: Theatre and Twentieth-Century Scientific Views of Nature*, Evanston, Northwestern University Press, 1990.

Dacey, J. 'Concepts of Creativity: A History', in Runco, M. A. and S. Pritzker (eds), *Encyclopedia of Creativity*, Vol. 1, London, Academic Press, 1999, pp. 309-22.

Dalal, M., *Conflict in Sanskrit Drama*. Bombay, Delhi, Somaija Publications Pvt. Ltd., 1973.

Dasgupta, G. 'Peter Brook's *Orientalism*', in Williams, D. (ed.), *Peter Brook and the Mahabharata*: *Critical Perspectives*, London, Routledge, 1991, pp. 262-7.

Davy, D. 'Grotowski's Laboratory: A Speculatove Look Back at the Poor Theatre', *Essays in Theatre* 7:2 (1989), pp, 127-138.

Dhayagude, Suresh. *Western and Indian Poetics. A Comparative Study* (Bhandarkar Oriental Research Series No. 18), Poona, Bhandarkar Oriental Research Institute, 1981.

Diderot, D., *The Paradox of Acting*, New York, Hill and Wang, 1955.

DiGaetani, J. L. *A search for a postmodern theater: interviews with contemporary playwrights*, New York, Greenwood, 1991.

Dillbeck, M. C., 'The Self-Interacting Dynamics of Consciousness as the Source of the Creative Process in Nature and in Human Life', *Modern Science and Vedic Science* 2:3 (1988), pp. 245-278.

Dillbeck, S. L., and M. C. Dillbeck, 'Introduction: Twenty-Five Years of Unfolding Knowledge of Pure Consciousness through Maharishi Vedic Science', *Modern Science and Vedic Science* 7: 1 (1997), pp. 1-38.

Doniger, W., with B. K. Smith (transl.), *The Laws of Manu*, Harmondsworth, Penguin, 1991.

Drucker, V., Unpublished letter to Daniel Meyer-Dinkgräfe, 31.8.1985.

Durrenberger, S. D. 'Mad Genius Controversy', in Runco, M. A. and S. Pritzker (eds), *Encyclopedia of Creativity*, Vol. 2, London, Academic Press, 1999, pp. 169-177.

Emst, C. van, 'Smell the show as the story unfolds', *The Croydon Guardian*, *http://www.croydonguardian.co.uk/leisure/reviews/display.var.637618.index.0.html*. Accessed 2.1.2003.

Enkemann, J., 'Politisches Alternativtheater in Großbritannien', *EASt* 2 (1980).

Fischer, R., 'A Cartography of the Ecstatic and Meditative States', *Science* (174: 4012), 26.11.1971, pp. 897-904.

Fischer-Lichte, E. 'Das Theater auf der Suche nach einer Universalsprache', *Forum Modernes Theater* 4:2 (1989), pp. 115-121.

Fish, S. E., 'Literature in the Reader: Affective Stylistics', *NLH* 2 (1970), pp. 123-162.

Flatow, C., *Der Mann, der sich nicht traut...* (*Happy Wedding*). Unpublished script, translation by Daniel Meyer-Dinkgräfe. Performance rights with Jussenhoven und Fischer, Köln, 1973.

Forman, R. (ed.), *The Problem of Pure Consciousness: Mysticism and Philosophy*, Oxford, Oxford University Press, 1990.

Frijda, N. H. *The Emotions*, Cambridge, Cambridge University Press, 1986.

Fugard, A. *The Road to Mecca,* London, Faber and Faber, 1985.

Fuller, C. J., *The Camphor Flame*, Princeton, Princeton University Press, 1992.

Gallese, V., The 'Shared Manifold' Hypothesis: from mirror neurons to empathy, *Journal of Consciousness Studies* 8: 5-7 (2001), pp. 33-50.

Gelderloos, P., and Z. H. A. D. Beto, 'The TM and TM-Sidhi Program and Reported Experiences of Transcendental Consciousness', *Psychologia* 32: 2 (1989), pp. 91-103.

Gems, P., Unpublished letter to Daniel Meyer-Dinkgräfe, May 1985.

George, D., 'On Ambiguity: Towards a post-modern performance theory', *TRI* 14:1 (1989), pp. 71-85.

—— 'Quantum Theatre-Potential Theatre: A New Paradigm?', *NTQ* 5:18 (1989), pp. 171-179.

Ghiselin, B., *The Creative Process: A Symposium,* Berkeley, University of California Press, 1952.

Ghosh, M., (transl.), *The Natyashastra: A Treatise on Hindu Dramaturgy and Histrionics*, Ascribed to Bharata Muni, Calcutta, The Royal Asiatic Society of Bengal, 1950.

Gilman, R., 'Jerzy Grotowski'. *New American Review* 9 (April 1970), pp. 206, 216.

Glaap, A.-R., 'Gespräch mit Tom über Kempinski', Programme Notes to *Duet for One*, Düsseldorf, Kammerspiele, 1985.

Gossman, L., and E. MacArthur, 'Diderot's Displaced Paradox', in Undank, J. and H. Josephs (eds.), *Diderot Disgression and Dispersion.A Bicentennial Tribute*, Lexington, Kentucky, French Forum Publishers, 1984, pp. 106-119.

Goyandka, J., *Shrimad Bhagavadgita As It Is: With English Translation*, Gorakhpur, Gita Press, 1984.

Grear, A., 'A Background to Diderot's *Paradoxe sur le Comédien*: The Role of Imagination in Spoken Expression of Emotion', *Forum for Modern Language Studies* 21:3 (1985), pp. 225-238.

Grotowski, J., *Towards a Poor Theatre*, ed. Barba, E., with a preface by P. Brook, London, Methuen, 1969.

Gupte, R. B., *Hindu Holidays and Ceremonials*, New Delhi / Madras, Asian Educational Services, 1994.

Hagelin, J., 'Is Consciousness the Unified Field? A Field Theorist's Perspective', *Modern Science and Vedic Science* 1 (1987), pp. 29-88.

Haich, E., *Tarot. Die Zweiundzwanzig Bewußtseinsstufen des Menschen*, Engelberg/ Schweiz, München, 1971.

Hamlyn, D. W., *The Penguin History of Western Philosophy*, London, Penguin, 1990.

Haney, W., II, 'Unity in Vedic aesthetics: the self-interacting dynamics of the knower, the known, and the process of knowing', *Analecta Husserliana* 233 (1991), pp. 295-319.

Hansen-Löve, A. H. *Der Russische Formalismus. Methodologische Rekonstruktion seiner Entwicklung aus dem Prinzip der Verfremdung* (Österreichische Akademie der Wissenschaften, Philosophisch-historische Klasse. Sitzungsberichte, 336. Band. Veröffentlichungen der Kommission für Literaturwissenschaft Nr. 5.), Wien, Verlag der Österreichischen Akademie der Wissenschaften, 1978.

Harding, R., *An Anatomy of Inspiration*, Cambridge, W. Heffer& Sons, 1940.

Hartmann, G., *Maharishi-Gandharva-Ved: Die Klassische Musik der Vedischen Hochkultur: Eine Einführung in die musiktheoretischen Grundlagen*, Vlodrop, MVU Press, 1992.

Harung, H. S., Heaton, D. P., Graff, W. W., & Alexander, C. N., 'Peak performance and higher states of consciousness: A study of world-class performers', *Journal of Managerial Psychology* 11: 4 (1996), pp. 3-23.

Harwood, R., *The Dresser*, Ambergate, Amber Lane Press, 1980.

— *British Theatre Since 1955: A Reassessment*, Oxford, Oxford University Press, 1979.

Hilton, J., *Performance. New Directions in Theatre*, MacMillan, London, 1987.

Hirschberger, J. *Geschichte der Philosophie. Neuzeit und Gegenwart*, Freiburg, Herder, 1981.

Hogan, P. C., 'What are Literary Universals?', *Literary Universals Project*, 22 December 2003 http://litup.unipa.it/docs/whatr.htm

Holland, N. N., *The Dynamics of Literary Response*, New York, Oxford University Press, 1968.

Honderich, T., *The Oxford Companion to Philosophy*. (Oxford, OUP, 1995). Online: Internet: 04 January 2003.

Hughes, G., 'The tragedy of a revenger's loss of conscience: a study of Hamlet', *English Studies* 57 (1976), pp. 395-409.

Innes, C., *Holy Theatre: Ritual and the Avant-Garde*, Cambridge, Cambridge University Press, 1981.

Iser, W. *The Act of reading: A Theory of Aesthetic Response*, Baltimore, London, 1978.

— *The Sensuous in Art: Reflections on Indian Aesthetics* (Indian Institute of Advanced Studies), Delhi, Shimla in association with Motilal Barnasidass, 1989.

Jaynes, J. *The origin of consciousness in the breakdown of the bicameral mind*, Boston, Houghton Mifflin, 1977.

Jones, K., 'Jungian Theory', in Runco, M. A. and S. Pritzker (eds), *Encyclopedia of Creativity*, Vol. 2, London, Academic Press, 1999, pp. 109-118.

Johnson, S. F. 'The Regeneration of Hamlet', *Shakespeare Quarterly* 3 (1952), pp. 190-6.

Kafka, F., 'Aus einem Zettelkonvolut'. in: *Individualität*. Europäische Vierteljahresschrift. 7.jg., Nr. 17, März 1988.

Kakar, S., *The Inner World: A Psycho-Analytic Study of Childhood and Society in India*, Delhi, Oxford University Press, 1981.

Kale, P. *The Theatrical Universe: A Study of the Natyashastra*, Bombay, Popular Prakashan, 1974.

Karambelkar, P. V., *Patanjali's Yoga Sutras: With Devanagari Text, Transliteration, Word Meanings and Translation*, Bombay, Kaivalyadhama, 1986.

Karnath, H.-O., Ferber, S. and M. Himmelbach, 'Spatial Awareness is a function of the temporal not the posterior parietal lobe', *Nature* 411 (2001), pp. 950-953.

Kesting, M., 'Stanislavsky-Meyerhold-Brecht', *Forum Modernes Theater* 4:2 (1989), pp. 122-138.

King, B. J. and K. Chapin, *Billie Jean*, New York, Harper & Row, 1974.

Klein, D. A. 'A Note on the Use of Dreams in Shaffer's Major Plays', *Journal of Evolutionary Psychology* 9: 1,2 (1989).

Kleist, H. von, *Das Käthchen von Heilbronn*. Online at Projekt Gutenberg-DE (http://gutenberg.spiegel.de/kleist/heilbron/heilbron.htm).

Knopf, J., *Brecht-Handbuch. Theater. Eine Ästhetik der Widersprüche*, Stuttgart, J.B.Metzlersche Verlagsbuchhandlung, 1980.

Kott, J. 'Grotowski or the limit'. *NTQ* 6:23 (1990), pp. 203-206.

Kouyate, S., 'Energy and the Ensemble: Actors' Perspectives', in Williams, D. (ed.), *Peter Brook and the Mahabharata: Critical Perspectives*, London, Routledge, 1991, pp. 104-107.

Kramer, Richard E. "The Natyasastra and Stanislavsky: Points of Contact". *Theatre Studies* (1991).

Krasner, D., 'The symbolic function of sleep and awakening in Chekhov's *Uncle Vanya*', *Theatre Studies* 39 (1994), pp. 5-18.

Kolin, P. C. and C. H. Kullman, *Speaking on stage: interviews with contemporary American playwrights*, London, University of Alabama Press, 1996.

Kumiega, J., *The Theatre of Grotowski*, London, New York, Methuen, 1987.

Kuppuswami, B., *Dharma and Society: A Study in Social Values*, Columbia, South Asia Books, 1977.

Lawlor, J. J., 'The Tragic Conflict in Hamlet', *The Review of English Studies* 1 (1950), pp. 97-113.

Lee, D., 'Prospero's Magic Power and Its Limitations in *The Tempest*', online at http://www.drama21c.net/shakespeare/articles/prospero.htm

Leiter, S., *From Stanislavsky to Barrault: Repre sentative Directors of the European Stage* (Contributions to Drama and Theatre Studies No. 34), London, Greenwood, 1991.

Lemaire, A., *Jacques Lacan*, London, Routledge & Kegan Paul, 1977.

Levenson, R., P. Ekman, W. V. Friesen, 'Voluntary Facial Action Generates Emotion-Specific Autonomous Nervous System Activity', *Psychophysiology* 27:4 (1990), pp. 363-384.

Lingorska, M. 'Der Zirkel des Verstehens am Beispiel einer klassischen indischen Dichtungslehre',http://www.unibamberg.de/split/dot/kurz/Indologie/Lingorska. htm

Ludwig, Arnold M., 'Altered States of Consciousness', in Tart, Charles T. (ed.), *Altered States of Consciousness: A Book of Readings*, London, John Wiley and Sons, 1969, pp. 9-22.

MacDonald, S., Unpublished letter to Daniel Meyer-Dinkgräfe, 27.3.1985.

McLaren, Robert B. 'Dark Side of Creativity', in Runco, M. A. and S. Pritzker (eds), *Encyclopedia of Creativity*, Vol. 1, London, Academic Press, 1999, pp.483-491.

Maharishi Mahesh Yogi, *On the Bhagavad-Gita. A New Translation and Commentary*, *Chapters 1-6*, Harmondsworth, Penguin, 1969.

—— *The Science of Creative Intelligence*, 33 videotaped lessons, Seelisberg, 1972.

—— *Life Supported by Natural Law*, Washington, Age of Enlightenment Press, 1986.

—— *Perfection in Education*, Jabalpur, Maharishi Vedic University Press, 1997.

Mahon, J. W., 'Providential Visitations in Hamlet', *Hamlet Studies* 8 (1986), pp. 40- 51.

Malekin, P. 'Mysticism and Scholarship', *SMLit* 1, no. 4 (1981), pp. 283-298.

—— 'Wordsworth and the Mind of Man', in Watson, J. R. (ed. & introd.)--Fisher, W. B. (pref.), *An Infinite Complexity: Essays in Romanticism*, Edinburgh: Edinburgh UP for the Univ. of Durham, 1983, pp. 1-25.

—— 'The Perilous Edge: Strindberg, Madness, and Other Worlds', in Murphy, Patrick D. (ed.). *Staging the Impossible: The Fantastic Mode in Modern Drama*, Westport, CT: Greenwood, 1992, pp. 44-55.

—— 'Knowing about Knowing: Paradigms of Knowledge in the Postmodern Fantastic', in:

Ruddick, Nicholas (ed.) *State of the Fantastic: Studies in the Theory and Practice of Fantastic Literature and Film*, Westport, CT: Greenwood, 1992, pp. 41-48.

––– 'The Self, the Referent, and the Real in Science Fiction and the Fantastic: Lem, Pynchon, Kubin, and Delany'. in Langford, Michele K. *Contours of the Fantastic: Selected Essays from the Eighth International Conference on the Fantastic in the Arts*, New York: Greenwood, 1994, pp. 29-36.

Malekin, P. and R. Yarrow, 'Pashyanti Theatre', *Consciousness, Literature and the Arts* 1:2 (2000), n. pag. Online. Available: http://www.aber.ac.uk/tfts/journal/ archive/pash.html

Maslow, A. H., *Towards a Psychology of Being*, New York, Van Nostrand, 1962.

Marasinghe, E. W., *The Sanskrit Theatre and Stagecraft* (Sri Garib Dass Oriental Series No. 78), Delhi, Sri Satguru Publications, 1989.

Mason, P., *The Maharishi. The Biography of the Man who gave Transcendental Meditation to the West,* Shaftesbury, Element, 1994.

Masson, J. L. and M. V. Patwardhan, *Santarasa and Abhinavagupta's Philosophy on Aesthetics* (Bhandarkar Oriental Series No. 9), Poona, Bhandarkar Oriental Research Institute, 1969.

Marshall, J. and G. R. Fink, 'Spatial Cognition: Where We Were and Where We Are', *Neuroimage* 14 (2001), pp. S2-S7. Available online at http://www.idealibray.com

Martin, J., *Voice in Modern Theatre*, London and New York, Routledge, 1991.

Meyer-Dinkgräfe, D., Unpublished interview with David Pownall, 4.3.1985a.

––– Unpublished interview with Tom Wilkinson, 29 March 1985b.

––– 'Hamlet at the Crossroads', *Hamlet Studies* 8 (1986), pp. 77-82.

––– *Consciousness and the actor: a reassessment of western and Indian approaches to the actor's emotional involvement from the perepective of Vedic psychology*, Frankfurt am Main, Peter Lang, 1996a.

––– `The Function of Theatre in Society', in Brian Carr (ed.), *Morals and Society in Asian Philosophy*, London: Curzon, 1996b, pp. 119-124.

––– 'The role of consciousness in Indian theatre aesthetics', *The Philosopher* LXXXV: 1 (1997a), pp. 2-5.

––– 'Barba's concepts of the pre-expressive and the third organ of the body of the theatre and theories of consciousness', *Contemporary Theatre Review* 7/1 (1997b), pp. 35-47.

––– 'Higher States of Consciousness in the Theatre', *Philosophical Writings* 8:2 (1998a), pp. 37-

44.

—– 'Welsh Folk-Tale in performance: *The Sea Maiden', Studies in Theatre Production* 17 (1998b), pp. 50-58.

—– 'Altered States of Consciousness in the Theatre: The Indian/Vedic Perspective of Maharishi Mahesh Yogi', *Studies in Spirituality* 8 (1998c), pp. 305--314.

—– 'Writing about Artists: Self-referral in Drama and Society', *Critical Survey* 10:2 (1998d), pp. 52-60.

—– 'Hamlet's Procrastination: A Parallel to the *Bhagavad-Gita*', in Marta Gibinska and Jerzy Limon (eds.), *Hamlet East West*, Gdansk: Theatrum Gedanese Foundation, 1998e, pp. 187-195.

—– 'Consciousness and Theatre: Euro-Indian Conceptions', in Frank Brinkhuis & Sascha Talmor (eds). *Memory, History & Critique. European Identity at the Millennium. Proceedings of the Fifth Conference of the International Society for the Study of European Ideas (ISSEI)*, 19-24 August 1996, Utrecht, The Netherlands' // Eds. // Publ. by University for Humanist Studies/ISSEI, Utrecht, The Netherlands // ISBN 90-73022-11-8. - Publication date: June 1998.

—– 'The Quest for a Universal Language of the Theatre', *Language, Society and Culture* (http://www.educ.utas.edu.au/~Thao.Le/JOURNAL/NJournal.html) 3:1998g. Journal ISSN 1327-774X.

—– 'Consciousness and the Concept of *Rasa*', *Performing Arts International* 1:4 (1999), pp. 103-115.

—– 'Suggestion in Peter Brook's *Mahabharata*', *Studies in the Literary Imagination* 34:2 (2001), 117-127.

—– 'Peter Brook and The Freedom of Intercultural Theatre', *The Paris Jigsaw*. Ed. David Bradby and Maria M. Delgado, Manchester, Manchester UP, 2002, 71-82.

—– 'Performance Art', in Chambers, C. (ed.), *The Continuum Companion to Twentieth Century Theatre,* London, Continuum, 2002, pp. 590-1.

—–, E. Valentine and C. Haimerl, 'Transportation and Transformation as a Result of Theatre Training: An Exploratory Study', *Transpersonal Psychology Review* 6:2 (2002), 29-42.

Mishra, H. R., *The Theory of Rasa in Sanskrit Drama: With a Comparative Study of General Dramatic Literature*, Bhopal, Sayar, Chhatapur, Vindhyachal Prakashan, 1964.

Mishra, V., 'The Great Indian Epic and Peter Brook', in Williams, D. (ed.), *Peter Brook and the Mahabharata: Critical Perspectives*, London, Routledge, 1991.

Mishra, S. K., 'Ulysses. An Indian Perspective', online, Internet, 07.24.2001, available URL *http://institutocamoes.org/pnldocs/05mishra01.htm*

Nader, T., *Human Physiology: Expression of Veda and Vedic Literature*, Vlodrop, Maharishi Vedic University, 1995.

Orme-Johnson, R., 'A Unified Field Theory of Literature', *Modern Science and Vedic Science* 1:3 (1987), pp. 323-373.

Orme-Johnson, D. W. 'The Cosmic Psyche as the Unified Source of Creation'. *Modern Science and Vedic Science* 2:2 (1988), pp. 168-169.

Pandey, K. C., *Comparative Aesthetics Vol. 1: Indian Aesthetics*, Banaras, The Chpwkhamba Sanskrit Series Office, 1950.

Pandit, L., 'Dhvani and the 'Full Word': Suggestion and Signification from Abhinavagupta to Jacques Lacan', *College Literature* 23:1 (1996), pp. 142-63.

Perry, J. O., 'World Literature in Review: Hindi', *World Literature Today*, summer 1999, online, Internet. 07.24.2001, available at URL: http://www.britannica.com/ magazine/article?content_id=73095&query=brahman

Pfister, M., *Das Drama: Theorie und Analyse*, München, Wilhelm Fink, 1977.

Phillips, J., 'Why does Hamlet delay? Hamlet's subtle revenge', *Anglia* 89 (1980), pp. 34-50.

Plato, *Ion* Translated by Benjamin Jowett, Provided by The Internet Classics Archive, available online at http://classics.mit.edu//Plato/ion.html

Policastro, E. 'Intuition', in Runco, M. A. and S. Pritzker (eds), *Encyclopedia of Creativity*, Vol. 2, London, Academic Press, 1999, pp. 89-93.

Pribram, K., 'Brain and the Creative Act', in Runco, M. A. and S. Pritzker (eds), *Encyclopedia of Creativity*, Vol. 2, London, Academic Press, 1999, pp. 213-217.

Prince, G., 'Introduction à l'étitude du narrataire', *Poetique* 14 (1973), pp. 178-196.

Pronko, L. C. 'L.A. Festival: Peter Brook's *The Mahabharata*', *Asian Theatre Journal* 5:2 (1988), pp. 220-224.

Prosser, E., *Hamlet and Revenge*. Stanford, Stanford University Press, 1967.

Raine, K., *The Land Unknown,* New York, George Braziller, 1975.

Ramachandran, V.S., 'Mirror Neurons and imitation learning as the driving force behind 'the great leap forward' in human evolution'. Accessed on 27.03.2003 at http://www.edge.org/3rd_culture/ramachandran/ramachandran_index.html

Rhagavan, V., *The Concept of the Beautiful in Sanskrit Literature*, Madras, The Kuppuswami Sastri Research Institute, 1988.

Richards, G. 'The world a stage: A conversation with Ray Reinhardt', *San Francisco Theater Magazine* winter 1977, p, 46.

Rix, R., 'ALBA EMOTING: A Preliminary Experiment with Emotional Effector Patterns', *Theatre Topics* 3:2 (1993), pp. 139-146.

Roach, J. R., Jr. 'Diderot and the Actor's Machine', *Theatre Survey* 22:1 (1981), pp. 51-68.

—- *The Player's Passion: Studies in the Science of Acting*, Newark, University of Delaware Press, 1985.

Roose-Evans, J., *Experimental Theatre: From Stanislavsky to Peter Brook*, London, Routledge, 1989.

Runco, M. A. and S. Pritzker, *Encyclopedia of Creativity,* London, Academic Press, 1999.

Ryckman, R. M., *Theories of Personality*, Monterey, Brooks/Cole Publishers, 31985.

Sarabhai, M., 'Energy and the Ensemble: Actors' Perspectives', in Williams, D. (ed.), *Peter Brook and the Mahabharata*: *Critical Perspectives*, London, Routledge, 1991, pp. 99-103.

Sarup, M., *An Introductory Guide to Post-Struc turalism and Postmodernism*, London, Harvester Wheatsheaf, 1988.

Saunders, G., *'Love me or kill me': Sarah Kane and the theatre of extremities,* Manchester, Manchester University Press, 2002.

Sauter, W. (ed.), *New Directions in Audience Research*: *Advances in Reception and Audience Research 2*. Utrecht, 1988.

Schechner, R., *Between Theatre and Anthropology*, Philadelphia, University of Pennsylvania Press, 1985.

—- *Performance Theory*, New York and London, Routledge, 1988.

—-, and W. Appel (eds.), *By Means of Performance: Intercultural Studies of Theatre and Ritual*, Cambridge, Cambridge University Press, 1990.

—- *The Future of Ritual*: *Writings on Performance and Culture*, London, Routledge, 1993.

Schiller, F., *Die Braut von Messina*, online at Projekt Gutenberg-DE. http://gutenberg.spiegel.de/schiller/messina/messina.htm

Schoenmakers, H. (ed.), *Performance Theory: Advances in Reception and Audience Research 1*, Utrecht, 1986.

—— (ed.), *Performance Theory, Reception and Audience Research*: *Advances in Reception and Audience Research 3*, Amsterdam, 1992.

Schwartz, E. 'The possibilities of a Christian Tragedy', *College English* 21 (1960), pp. 208-13.

Schuldberg, D., 'Chaos Theory and Creativity', in Runco, M. A. and S. Pritzker (eds), *Encyclopedia of Creativity*, Vol. 1, London, Academic Press, 1999, pp. 259-272.

Schumacher, C., *Artaud on Theatre*, London, Heinemann, 1989.

Shaffer, P., *Amadeus*, Burnt Mill, Longman, 1984.

Shakespeare, W., *Hamlet*. Edited by Harold Jenkins, London, New York, 1982.

Shear, J., 'Mystical experience, hermeneutics, and rationality', *International Philosophical Quarterly* 30:4 (1990), pp. 391-401.

——, and R. Jevning, 'Pure Consciousness: Scientific exploration of meditation techniques', in Varela, F. and J. Shear (eds.), *The View from Within: First-person approaches to the study of consciousness*, Thorverton, Imprint Academic, 1999, pp. 189-210.

Shevtsova, M., 'Interaction- Interpretation. *The Mahabharata* from a social-cultural perspective', in Williams, D. (ed.), *Peter Brook and the Mahabharata*: *Critical Perspectives*, London, Routledge, 1991, pp. 206-27.

Shrady, M., *Moments of Insight*: *The Emergence of Creative Ideas in the Lives of Great Men*, New York, Harper and Row, 1972.

Sierz, A., *In-Yer-Face Theatre: British Drama Today*, London, Faber and Faber, 2001.

Sinfield, A., 'Hamlet's special Providence', *Shakespeare Survey* 33 (1980), pp. 89-97.

Sinha, N. (transl.), *The Samkhya Philosophy*, New Delhi, Oriental Books Reprint Company, 1971.

Skulsky, H., 'Revenge, Honour and Conscience in Hamlet', *PMLA* 85 (1970), pp. 78-87.

Smith, J., Unpublished working notebook. AHRB funded workshop into Transformation and Transportation through theatre, August 2000, Aberystwyth.

Srigley, M., *Images of Regeneration: A Study of Shakespeare's* The Tempest *and Its Cultural Background*, Acta Universitatis Upsaleiensis, Studia Anglistica Upsaliensia 58, Uppsala, 1985.

Srinivasan, S. A., *On the Composition of the Natyasastra* (Studien zur Indologie und Iranistik Monographie 1), Reinbek, Dr. Inge Wezler Verlag für Orientalische Fachpublikationen, 1980.

Stace, W.T., *Mysticism and Philosophy*, London, MacMillan, 1960.

Stamenov, M., and V. Gallese (eds.), *Mirror Neurons and the Evolution of Brain and Language*, Amsterdam, John Benjamins, 2002.

Stanislavsky, C., *Building a Character*, Translated by E. R. Hapgood, New York, Theatre Arts Books, 1949.

—- *Creating a Role*, Translated by E. R. Hapgood, edited by H. I. Popper, New York, Theatre Arts Books, 1961.

—- *An Actor Prepares*, Translated by E. R. Hapgood, London, Methuen, 1986.

Stern, S. L. 'Drama in Second Language Learning from a Psycholinguistic Perspective', *Leanguage Learning* 3:1 (1980), pp. 77-100.

Sternberg, R. J. and J. E. Davidson, 'Insight', in Runco, M. A. and S. Pritzker (eds), *Encyclopedia of Creativity*, Vol. 2, London, Academic Press, 1999, pp. 57-69.

Stewart, G., *Reading Voices: Literature and the Phonotext*, Berkeley, University of California Press, 1990.

Strasberg, L. 'Working with Live Material', in Munk, E. (ed.), *Stanislavsky and America: The 'Method' and its Influence on the American Actor,* New York, Hill and Wang, 1966.

—- *A Dream of Passion: The Development of the Method*, Morphos, E., (ed.), London, Bloomsbury, 1988.

Suleiman, S. S. and I. Crosman, *The Reader in the Text: Essays on Audience and Interpretation*, Princeton, N.J., 1980.

Tart, C.T., *Transpersonal Psychologies*, London, Routledge and Kegan Paul, 1975.

Taylor, M., 'Tragic Justice and the House of Polonius', *Studies in English Literature* 8 (1968), pp. 273-81.

Thomas, N. J. T. 'Mental Imagery', in Zalta, E.N. (ed.), *The Stanford Encyclopedia of Philosophy*. [http://plato.stanford.edu/entries/mental-imagery/]

Thoreau, H. D., *Walden*. New York, NAL, 1960 (Original Work published 1854).

Travis, F. and D. W. Orme-Johnson, 'A Field Model of Consciousness: EEG Coherence Changes as Indicators of Field Effects', *International Journal of Neuroscience* 49:3, 4 (1989), pp. 203-211.

Ure, P. 'Character and Rhole from Richard III to Hamlet', *Stratford-upon-Avon Studies* 5(1964), pp. 9-28.

Varela, F. and J. Shear (eds.), *The View from Within: First-person approaches to the study of consciousness*, Thorverton, Imprint Acedemic, 1999.

Venkatesananda, Swami, *The Concise Yoga Vasishta*, Albany, State University of New York Press, 1984.

Vireswarananda, Swami, *Brahmasutras* Calcutta, Advaita Ashrama, 1970.

Volkamer, K. *Agnim, oder: Evolution, das Wechselspiel von Ordnung und Entropie*, Husum, Hannemann, 1983.

—, C. Streicher and K. G. Walton, *Intuition, Kreativität und ganzheitliches Denken: Neue Wege zum bewußten Handeln,* Frankfurt/Main, Suhrkamp, 1996.

— and C. Streicher, 'Experimental Evience of a New Type of Quantized Matter with Quanta as Integer Multiples of the Planck Mass', *Apeiron* 6:2 (1999), pp. 63-82.

Wagenknecht, E., 'The Perfect Revenge - Hamlet's Delay - A Reconsideration', *College English* 10 (1949), pp. 188-95.

Wallace, R. K., *The Physiology of Consciousness*, Fairfield, Maharishi International University Press, 1993.

Wardle, I., 'Wordy Verdi in the stalls', *The Times*, 20 March 1986.

Warhaft, S., 'The Mystery of Hamlet' *ELH* 30 (1963), pp. 193-208.

Watson, I., *Towards a Third Theatre: Eugenio Barba and the Odin Teatret*, London and New York, Routledge, 1993.

Welsch, W., 'Postmoderne: Genealogie und Bedeutung eines umstrittenen Begriffs'. in: Kemper, P. (ed.), *Postmoderne, oder: Der Kampf um die Zukunft. Die Kontroverse in Wissenschaft, Kunst und Gesellschaft*, Frankfurt/ Main, Fischer, 1988, pp. 9-36.

Willett, J. (ed. and transl.), *Brecht on Theatre: The Development of an Aesthetic*, New York, Hill and Wang, 1978.

Williams, D. (ed.), *Peter Brook: A Theatrical Casebook,* London, Methuen, 1991.

—- (ed.), *Peter Brook and the Mahabharata: Critical Perspectives*, London and New York, Routledge, 1991.

—- 'Theatre of Innocence and of Experience: Peter Brook's International Centre. An Introduction', in Williams, D. (ed.), *Peter Brook and the Mahabharata: Critical Perspectives*, London, Routledge, 1991, pp. 3-28.

—- 'Transculturalism and myth in the theatre of Peter Brook', in Pavis, P. (ed.), *The Intercultural Performance Reader*, London, Routledge and New York, Routledge, pp. 67-78.

—— (ed.), *Collaborative Theatre: The Théâtre du Soleil sourcebook,* London and New York, Routledge, 1999.

Wordsworth, W., *Poetical Works,* Hutchinson, T. (ed), revised by Ernest de Selincourt, Oxford, Oxford University Press, 1969.

Yarrow, R. 'Neutral' consciousness in the experience of theatre', *Mosaic* 19:3 (1987), pp. 1- 20.

—— 'The potential of consciousness: towards a new approach towards states of consciousness in litera-ture', *Journal of European Studies,* 15 (1985), pp. 1-20.

—— 'He was never entirely himself: theatre and forms of consciousness', *New Comparison* 9 (Spring 1990), pp. 28-40.

—— 'Grotowski, Holiness and the Pre-Expressive', *Contemporary Theatre Review*, Vol. 7/1 (1997), pp. 25-34.

—— 'Identity and Consciousness East and West: the case of Russell Hoban', *Journal of Literature & Aesthetics*, Vol. 5, No. 2 (July-Dec. 1997), pp. 19-26.

Zarrilli, P. B., 'What does it mean to 'become the character': power, presence, and transcendence in Asian in-body disciplines of practice' in Schechner, R. and W. Appel (eds), *By Means of Performance. Intercultural Studies of Theatre and Ritual*, Cambridge, Cambridge University Press, 1990, pp. 131-148.

—— 'On the Edge of a Breath, Looking. Disciplining the actor's bodymind through the Martial Arts in the Asian/Experimental Theatre Program', in Zarrilli, P. (ed.), *Acting (Re)Considered: Theories and practices*, London and New York, Routledge, 1995, pp. 177-196.

—— *Kathakali Dance Drama: Where Gods and Demons come to Play*, London, Routledge, 2000.

Appendix 1

Maharishi Mahesh Yogi and Vedic Science

This appendix provides further information about Maharishi Mahesh Yogi and his conceptualisation of Indian Vedanta philosophy in terms of *Vedic Science.*

Maharishi Mahesh Yogi was born as Mahesh Prasad Varma on Friday 12 January 1917 (other sources suggest 18 October 1911, 12 January 1918, or 18 October 1918). His parents were comfortably well off, and his father "is believed to have been a minor official in the Department of Forestry" (Mason, 1994, 10). Mahesh learnt English and studied Physics and Mathematics at Allahabad University. Interested in yoga, one day he had a chance to see Swami Brahmananda Saraswati, who held the position of Shankaracharya of Jyotir Math, the head of one of the four monasteries (*Math*) founded by the sage Shankara to safeguard his *Advaita Vedanta* philosophy. Maharishi Mahesh Yogi became the Shankaracharya's disciple and spent thirteen years with him, serving as his private secretary, and receiving instruction in the Vedic scriptures and techniques of meditation for spiritual development. After the death of Swami Brahmananda on 20 May 1953, Maharishi Mahesh Yogi spent a year and a half in meditative seclusion in a cave in Uttar Kashi (The Northern Place of Shiva, also known as the valley of the saints) in the Himalayas. Then he travelled to southern India, where he was invited to give lectures on the knowledge he had gained while with Swami Brahmananda, culminating in a three-day conference in 1955. During further years of successful lecture tours, Maharishi instructed numerous people in meditation as he had learnt it from Swami Brahmananda. Towards the end of 1957, he organised a Seminar of Luminaries which attracted more than 10,000 participants. On January 1, 1958, Maharishi founded the Spiritual Regeneration Movement:

> The one aim of the Spiritual Regeneration Movement is to provide simple and easy method of meditation and infuse this system of meditation in the daily life of every-body everywhere on earth. To meet this end, this movement had been started to work for the construction of meditation centres everywhere in every part of human habitation (Maharishi Mahesh Yogi, 1986, 208)

Subsequently, he toured the world several times over, establishing meditation centres and teaching what by now had become known as Transcendental Meditation (TM). At his lectures, Maharishi would present TM in Indian philosophical discourse as a method for gaining enlightenment, for development of higher states of consciousness. The media, however, were alerted by comparatively superficial effects such as an improvement of insomnia, ignoring or expressing doubt about Indian philosophy. In consequence, Maharishi Mahesh Yogi changed the marketing strategies towards scientific research on the TM technique, with the first publication by Wallace in *Science* in 1970, based on his PhD thesis. Since then, more than 500 studies have been conducted, most of them also published. In 1980, while continuing the scientific marketing strategy, Maharishi Mahesh Yogi started to turn his attention to the Indian tradition, from which the TM technique originates in the first place.

During the eighties, scientists at Maharishi International University (renamed Maharishi University of Management in 1995), USA, discussed with Maharishi Mahesh Yogi parallels between their disciplines and concepts and knowledge found in Vedic literature. Findings of this major research project have been published in the journal *Modern Science and Vedic Science* since 1987, with articles on psychology, physics, literature, literary theory, physiology, sociology, computer science, education, art, mathematics, biology, agriculture, and economics. In addition to a study of parallels between Western and Vedic concepts of knowledge, Maharishi Mahesh Yogi places substantial emphasis on elucidating Vedic concepts in their own right, as in his reassessment of *Ayurveda*, *Jyotish* or *Sthapatyaveda* (Vedic medicine, astrology and architecture respectively).

Maharishi Mahesh Yogi has termed the reassessment of Vedic literature in comparison with Western traditions of knowledge *Vedic Science*, a term which "indicates both the ancient traditional origins of this body of knowledge and the modern commitment to experience, system, testability, and the demand that knowledge be useful in improving the quality of human life" (Chandler, 1987, 8). Vedic Science describes in detail the processes of creation of all existence, including human beings, and theatre as one of the numerous activities human beings can engage in. In order to experience understand the very roots of theatre, it is necessary to first of all understand the process of creation as proposed by Vedic Science.

Appendix 2

Vedic Science and Creation

In chapter one of this book, I argue that the process of artistic creation follows the same principles as the process of creation as a whole, and I briefly introduce the basic principles of creation as proposed in *Vedic Science*. In this appendix, I provide a much more detailed account of those principles and processes of creation in general.

The first word of the *Rig-Veda* is *Agnim*. The sound of *A* represents the fullness of the absolute, *Brahman*, of unmanifest wholeness. The next sound, *G*, represents the collapse of fullness in a point value. There is a gap between *A* and *G*, and between this first syllable and the next one, etc. The mechanics of the gap is as follows:

5. The sound value collapses into the point value of the gap. This process is called *Pradhvamsa Abhava*.
6. The silent point of all possibilities within the gap, called *Atyanta Abhava*.
7. The structuring dynamics of what happens in the gap, called *Anyonya Abhava*.
8. The mechanics by which a sound emerges from the point value of the gap, i.e. the emergence of the following syllable. This is called *Prag Abhava* (adapted from Nader, 1995, 34).

It becomes clear that the mechanism inherent in the first two letters of *Rig Veda*, *A* and *G*, are reflected in the mechanism of the gap: in both cases, fullness collapses to point value. In both cases, eight successive stages are involved. *Atyanta Abhava* is a state of absolute abstraction. As such, it is also called *Purusha*. Paradoxically, it would seem, *Atyanta Abhava* has got qualities within it which make up its nature, *Prakriti*. The aspect of diversity within *Atyanta Abhava* is called *Ayonya Abhava*.

Originally, that diversity within *Atyantabhava* takes the form of an interaction of three elements in unity (*samhita*). The elements are *rishi*, *devata*, and *chhandas*. *Rishi* here is not the individual human seer of Vedic literature, but an abstract principle of consciousness: the knower, experiencer, observer, or subject. *Devata* corresponds to process of knowing, experiencing, observing, or subject-object relationship. *Chhandas* corresponds to the known, the experienced, the observed, or the object. The three components of unity (*Samhita*), subject, subject-object relationship and object (*rishi*, *devata* and *chhandas*) interact with the unity and among each other. The interaction of *rishi, devata* and *chhandas* among each other and with *samhita*, takes either an emerging mode, leading out of the gap (the process of *Prag Abhava*), or submerging mode, leading into the gap (the process of *Pradhvamsa Abhava*). Together, the interaction can thus take on eight values, which are called *Apara Prakriti*. At the basis of the changing *Apara Prakriti* is the unchanging *Para Prakriti*. Both *Apara Prakriti* and *Para Prakriti* are witnessed, as it were, from the unity aspect of uninvolved wakefulness, *Purusha*. These ten values or qualities, eight active *Apara Prakriti*, the ninth non-active *Para Prakriti* and *Purusha*, "constitute the structure of *Atyanta-Abhava* and the self-interacting dynamics of its functioning intelligence' - *Anyonya-Abhava* (Maharishi Mahesh Yogi, 1997, 168).

Following the first syllable of *Rig Veda*, AG, sound collapses into the gap, just as fullness (*A*) had collapsed into point value (*G*). The gap thus also represents a point value in the sequential development of *Rig Veda*: it is characterised by non-fullness, absolute emptiness. The fullness of *A* or the previous sound/syllable is still latent, but no longer expressed (Volkamer, 1983, 179). This is the latent potential of fullness in *Atyanta Abhava*, taking unmanifest shape in the ten qualities or values of *Anyonya Bhava*. The eight stages of collapse of *A* to *G* are elaborated in the eight syllables of the first phrase (*Pada*) of *Rig Veda*. Those eight syllables correspond, in turn, to the eight *Apara Prakriti*: AG - Ahamkara; NI - Buddhi; MI - Manas; LE - Akasha; PU - Vayu; RO - Agni; HI - Jala; TAM - Prithivi.

In this structure, there are eight gaps: The first within the first syllable, between *A* and *G*, and thereafter between the syllables, i.e. between AG and NI, between NI and MI, between MI and LE, and so on.

Three such *Padas* (phrases) of eight syllables each make up the first verse (*Richa*) of *Rig Veda*. The first *Pada* expresses the eight *Prakritis* with respect to the *rishi* aspect of the absolute. The second *Pada* with respect to *Devata*, the third *Pada* with respect to *Chhandas*. Together, this first verse (*Richa*), constituted of three phrases (*Pada*) of eight syllables (*Akshara*) each, shows 24 gaps (*Sandhis*). Out of those gaps, 24 further *Padas* emerge, constituting *Richas* 2 - 9.

Richas 2-9 together have 192 gaps and 192 syllables. They give rise to the 192 hymns (*Suktas*) that make up the first *Mandala*. In turn, the 192 gaps between the 192 *Suktas* of the first *Mandala* give rise to the 192 *Suktas* of the 10th *Mandala*. Finally, all the gaps between the nine *richas* of the first *sukta* are elaborated in *Mandalas* 2 - 9, thus completing the entire *Rig Veda*.

From Veda to Vedic Literature

Rig-Veda serves as a basis for the emergence of all other sets of texts that make up Vedic literature, including *Gandharva-Veda*, which deals specifically with dance, music and theatre. This emergence can be understood on two levels: first, with reference to the predominant qualities of Vedic literature. Those qualities, to be more specific, are the qualities involved in structuring *Rig Veda*, and thus provide a commentary on *Rig Veda*.

Rig Veda	holistic
Sama Veda	flowing wakefulness
Yajur Veda	offering and creating
Atharva Veda	reverberating wholeness
Sthapatya Veda	establishing

Dhanurveda	invincible, progressive
Gandharvaveda	**integrating, harmonising**
Shiksha	expressing
Kalpa	transforming
Vyakarana	expanding
Nirukta	self-referral
Chhandas	measuring, quantifying
Jyotish	all-knowing
Nyaya	distinguishing and deciding
Vaisheshika	specifying
Samkhya	enumerating
Yoga	unifying
Karma Mimamsa	analysing
Vedanta	I-ness (the Transcendent)
Ayur-Veda	balancing
Smriti	memory
Purana	ancient, eternal
Itihasa	blossoming
Brahmana	structuring
Aranyaka	stirring
Upanishad	transcending

Each one of these texts of Vedic literature functions on two levels: it comments on the identified quality of *Rig Veda*, and it provides detailed knowledge about specific areas of human life (Ayurveda, for example, is the discipline of medicine). This latter aspect will be discussed in detail when the development of human life out of the field of *Brahman* has been established further.

The second way of understanding the relationship between *Rig Veda* and Vedic literature is with reference to the interaction between *samhita, rishi, devata* and *chhandas*. The nature of that interaction is self-referral. The interaction of *samhita* and *rishi, devata* and *chhandas* begins on the absolute, unmanifest level. The interaction, even though unmanifest, creates a vibration. The varieties in vibration resulting from the different interactions (*samhita-rishi, samhita-devata, samhita-chhandas, rishi-samhita, devata-samhita, chhandas-samhita, rishi-devata, devata-chhandas, chhandas-rishi,* etc.) bring forth the different sets of Vedic literature. The interactions have a direction. The following table shows the interactions and the resulting parts of Vedic literature.

Aspect	**Directed Towards**	**Resulting Vedic Literature**
Rishi	Samhita	Samaveda
Devata	Samhita	Yajurveda
Chhandas	Samhita	Atharvaveda
Samhita	Rishi	Upanishads
Samhita	Chhandas	Brahmanas

The six Vedangas

Rishi	Chhandas	Shiksha (phonetics)
Chhandas	Devata	Kalpa (rituals)
Devata	Rishi	Nirukta (semantics)
Rishi	Devata	Vyakaran (grammar)
Devata	Chhandas	Chhandas (metrics)
Chhandas	Rishi	Jyotish (astrology)

The six Upangas

Shiksha	Samhita	Nyaya
Kalpa	Samhita	Vaisheshika
Nirukta	Samhita	Samkhya
Vyakaran	Samhita	Yoga
Chhandas	Samhita	Karma Mimansa
Jyotish	Samhita	Vedanta

All transformations of the *rishi* aspect of the *samhita* are shown in the *Itihasa*, the epics of *Ramayana* and *Mahabharata*. All transformations of the *devata* aspect are portrayed in the *Puranas*, and all aspects of the *chhandas* aspect in the *Smritis*.

From Veda and Vedic Literature to Matter

Rig Veda and resulting Vedic literature initially exist on the level of *Brahman* only, as "laws of nature" structuring the process of creation. The intricate pattern of interactions on the level of *Brahman* ultimately gives rise to manifest creation. A third perspective, related to, but different from the two offered above to understand the process of how Vedic literature develops from *Rig Veda*, is helpful to understand how matter arises from consciousness. From this perspective, *Brahman* is called *Purusha*, as already discussed in relation to the structure of the gaps in *Rig Veda*. The primal substance of creation, undifferentiated but with latent full potential of creation, is *Prakriti*, nature. Its governing principles are the three *gunas*, *sattva*, *rajas* and *tamas*. According to Vedic Science,

the entire creation consists of the interplay of the three gunas (...) born of prakriti or Nature. The process of evolution is carried on by these three gunas. Evolution means creation and its progressive development, and at its basis lies activity. Activity needs rajo-guna to create a spur, and it needs sato- guna and tamo-guna to uphold the direction of the movement. The nature of tamo-guna is to check or retard, but it should not be thought that when the movement is upwards, tamo-guna is absent. For any process to continue, there have to be steps in that process, and each stage, however small in time and space, needs a force to maintain it and another force to develop it into a new shape. The force that develops it into a new shape is sato-guna, while tamo-guna is that which checks or retards the process in order to maintain the state already produced so that it may form the basis for the next stage. (Maharishi Mahesh Yogi, 1969, 128)

The first state of evolution, indicating that *prakriti* moves towards manifestation, is called *mahat*. Its emergence is caused by a disturbance of the state of perfect equilibrium between the three gunas. *Mahat* proceeds towards individuation, and the individuation principle is called *ahamkara*. The result of the individuation process is *manas*, the cosmic mind. "In the state of manas, the urge of prakriti towards manifestation becomes clearly defined" (482).

The cosmic mind (*manas*) is connected with the manifest world of objects by the ten senses (*indriyas*), five senses of perception (*gyanendriya*), i.e. hearing, touch, seeing, taste, and smell, and five organs of action (*karmendriya*), i.e. language, ability to take hold of, ability to walk, discharge, and procreation. Subtle matter arises in the next stage of development: the *tanmatras* constitute the five basic realities, or essences, of the objects of the five senses of perception. They express themselves in the five elements which go to make up the objects of the senses, and which provide the material basis of the entire objective universe. Thus the essence of sound (*shabda tanmatra*) expresses itself in space, the essence of touch (*sparsha tanmatra*) in air, the essence of form (*rupa tanmatra*) in fire, the essence of taste (*rasa tanmatra*) in water, and the essence of smell (*gandha tanmatra*) in earth. (482-3)

The elements that constitute material creation are called *mahabhutas*, and they are space (*akasha*), air (*vayu*), fire (*tejas*), water (*apas*) and earth (*prithivi*).

From the five elements, all matter is formed. *Ayurveda* describes how this manifestation continues in the human body. There are three places "sandwiched between mind and body, where thought turns into matter; it is occupied by three operating principles called *doshas*". The three *doshas* are *vata*, in control of movement; *pitta*, in control of metabolism; and *kapha*, in control of structure. *Vata* arises from the combination of space (*akasha*) and air (*vayu*). *Pitta* is associated with fire (*tejas*) and water (*apas*), and *kapha* has its origin in water (*apas*) and earth (*prithivi*). Each main *dosha* consists of five sub-*doshas*, each located in different parts of the body. The following table gives a survey.

Dosha	Subdosha	Location of Subdosha
Vata	Prana	brain, head, chest
	Udana	throat and lungs
	Samana	stomach and intestines
	Apana	colon, lower abdomen
	Vyana	throughout the body via the nervous system, skin, and circulatory system
Pitta	Pachaka	stomach and small intestine
	Ranjaka	red blood cells, liver, spleen
	Sadhaka	heart
	Alochaka	eyes
	Bhrajaka	skin
Kapha	Kledaka	stomach

Avalambaka	chest, lungs, lower back
Bhodaka	tongue
Tarpaka	sinus cavities, head, spinal fluid
Shleshaka	joints

The next level of concreteness is cell metabolism, dominated by the thirteen forms of digestive fire, *agni*. Their activity leads to tissues, or *dhatus, rasa, rakta, mamasa, meda, ashthi, majja*, and *shukra*. Some sources place *ojas* as the first of these, as the most expressed, or as the last, the most subtle. Vedic Science holds that *ojas* pervades all *dhatus*. From the tissues (*dhatus*), all further levels of the body naturally follow, anatomy, functional systems, etc.

The human physiology taken together is thus an expression of *Brahman*. Just as *Rig Veda* and Vedic Literature are an expression of *Brahman* within the realm of the Absolute, human physiology and all other objects within and beyond the range of human perception are manifestations of *Brahman*. Recent research has indicated that *Rig Veda* and Vedic literature have their distinctive parallels in human physiology. Such correspondence has been derived in two ways:

The first is by showing the *functional* correspondence between the quality of a specific area of the Vedic Literature and an area of the physiology, and the second is a *structural* analysis of the number of components of the corresponding areas of physiology and the Vedic Literature (Dillbeck and Dillbeck, 1997, 15).

Index